REVIVAL

SKETCHES AND MANUAL.

IN TWO PARTS.

BY REV. HEMAN HUMPHREY, D. D.,
PITTSFIELD, MASS.

PUBLISHED BY THE
AMERICAN TRACT SOCIETY,
150 NASSAU-STREET, NEW YORK.

CONTENTS.

CHAPTER VII.

THE REVIVAL EPOCH ABOUT 1800—CONTINUED.

PART II.

REVIVAL MANUAL.

CHAPTER VIII.

"PREPARE YE THE WAY OF THE LORD."

CHAPTER IX.

BRIEF APPEALS.

REVIVAL CONVERSATIONS

BETWEEN A PASTOR AND INQUIRERS.

INTRODUCTION.

It is now more than thirty years since it struck me that a concise history of revivals from about the beginning of the nineteenth century might be acceptable to the churches, as a sort of Christian manual to help the cause of pure and undefiled religion in the present and in "the generations following." Having come upon the stage just at the commencement of that memorable epoch, and witnessed many revivals, I was moved to inquire whether the duty of attempting to gather and arrange the materials for such a history to the praise of sovereign redeeming mercy devolved upon me. I consulted Dr. Griffin on the subject, than whom few men had larger experience in revivals. He encouraged me to go on, and I made some collection of the narratives which were within my reach. But I soon became convinced that to do any thing like justice to the glorious theme, within reasonable limits, was a task beyond my powers, and for which I then could not command the time. As professional and public duties soon became more exacting and arduous, I dismissed the subject, and there the matter rested for more than twenty years.

After I had withdrawn from the cares and labors of a public seminary, and of course had more leisure for miscellaneous duties, I was requested to take up the question anew, of preparing a volume of revival narratives and reminiscences, reaching back to about the beginning of the present century. The request was from time to time renewed, by persons in whose judgment I had much confidence. My answer was, I am too old for such an undertaking: I could not satisfy myself, much less hope to do justice to the subject.

Moreover, as I reflected upon it, although the materials at hand were ample, the field appeared to me quite too narrow. If I said any thing, I wished to go farther back and take a wider range. It seemed to me that I ought to inquire how far back the history of revivals could be traced; and if they were found to be of very ancient date, to inquire whether their essential features had been everywhere the same; and whether or not the work of redemption had been carried on by the Holy Spirit chiefly by these "times of refreshing from the presence of the Lord." I suspected it would be found that religion has never flourished and rapidly extended its saving influence, but in connection with special reformations, or revivals as we now call them, interrupted by longer or shorter seasons of declension.

As this opened so wide and so interesting a field of inquiry, I at length consented to the attempt, though with many misgivings as to my being able to go over so much ground, gather the materials scattered along the ages, and bring out a book worthy of being received by the churches as a small contribution to confirm their confidence in the desirableness of more frequent and powerful revivals than have yet been enjoyed. The result of these inquiries has more than answered my anticipations, and will be found embodied in these sketches. Going back to the time of Joshua, and tracing this branch of the history of redemption down through the Old and New Testaments to the close of the apostolic age; then onward, groping my way through the dark ages, to the Protestant Reformation; and advancing still, from stage to stage, down to "the Great Awakening" about the middle of the last century, and the perhaps still more glorious work commencing almost simultaneously with the present century, I have brought down the history, or rather the brief sketches embraced in the first part of this volume, to the present time.

In the second part, which I have ventured to call a *Revival Manual,* I have first given my view of the way in which revivals should be sought for and promoted, then inserted brief practical addresses such as I have been accustomed to make in seasons of the outpouring of the Spirit, and closed the volume with some Pastoral Conversations, out of many which I have been permitted to hold with inquirers.

I have fallen far short of reaching my own ideal of what such a book should be, but have "done what I could:" gratefully acknowledging special obligations to the several pastors and others whose communications, written chiefly in the memorable era of the outpouring of the Spirit about the year 1831, were requested from them by the Rev. Dr. Sprague, and embodied as an appendix to his Lectures on Revivals. And now nothing remains but, lifting up my heart in fervent thanksgivings to the Infinite Source and Author of all true revivals, and imploring his blessing on this feeble "essay to do good," to commit it to Him who is able to make the weakest instrumentality subservient to the building up of his kingdom in the world, and the accomplishing of his glorious purposes in the awakening, conversion, and salvation of sinners. H. H.

PITTSFIELD, April 16, 1859.

PART FIRST.

REVIVAL SKETCHES.

CHAPTER I.

SUMMARY VIEW—TO THE DAY OF PENTECOST AND THE APOSTOLIC AGE.

THE history of the church, including all the times of refreshing and drought that have marked its progress, is identical with the history of Redemption. It is a living stream, as it were, springing just outside of the garden of Eden, scarcely discernible at first, but flowing down from age to age; sometimes sparkling in the sunlight; sometimes all but swallowed up in the sands of the desert; breaking out again in the promised land; at one period a wide river, then a contracted rivulet almost hidden for long reaches, and widening again to keep the promise alive, when it seemed to have disappeared for ever in the stagnant marshes of Babylon. To drop the figure: the history of the church, broken off by the seventy years' captivity, was renewed again when the remnant returned to their own land, under Ezra and Nehemiah.

After that, scarcely any thing is said of her till we come down to the New Testament, to that remarkable awakening which took place in the days of John the Baptist, when a new and more spiritual dispensation was close at hand, to be introduced and carried forward by the Lord Jesus Christ, as "Head over all things to the church."

The first glorious era of her triumphs was that which marked the apostolic age, and to which, in spite of all opposition, so many chapters, full of the first promise, have since been added, which promise will reach its high and glorious culmination when those great voices shall be heard in heaven, saying, "Tho kingdoms of this world are become the kingdoms of our Lord and his Christ, and he shall reign for ever and ever."

How, then, has this work of Redemption been mainly carried on hitherto; and how have we reason to expect it will be hereafter? In looking back, we shall find that seasons of special absorbing religious interest, which by common consent are now called the Revival of Religion, have a history. When did this history begin? How far back does it date? These are important questions; but before answering them there is a preliminary one.

WHAT IS A REVIVAL OF RELIGION? What are some of its phases and true characteristics? When may it be said there is a true Revival of Religion in any age or part of the world?

We answer, a temporary religious excitement, however high it may rise, which does not go down into the hidden man of the heart, and stir up the depths of the soul to the earnest inquiry, "What must we do to be saved?" is not a true revival of religion. There may be a whirlwind, and the Lord not be in it. There may be great mental and physical excitement where there are few or no conversions. Nor where only a very few persons are about the same time awakened and truly converted by the Spirit of God, is there what we understand by a revival, though it is the self-same Spirit that worketh so mightily when hundreds are born again and seen flying as a cloud and as doves to their windows. As it is not here and there a ripening cluster that makes a vintage, nor a few sheaves that make a harvest, nor a few drops that make a shower, so a few drops of mercy, falling on individual souls here and there, do not constitute what is usually termed a revival of religion.

What is it, then? A genuine revival is the fruit or effect of a supernatural Divine influence, which restores the joy of God's salvation to backsliding Christians, startles the dead in trespasses and sins, convinces them of their lost and perishing condition, and makes them willing in the day of God's power. In the church there is a genuine revival when she rises and shakes herself from the dust and puts on her beautiful garments, which have been laid aside to her great discomfort and reproach. In a congregation there is a true revival when impenitent sinners in considerable numbers are awakened and converted within a few days or weeks, and "many are added to the Lord of such as shall be saved."

In their essential nature and effects, all genuine

revivals are alike. Since true religion is everywhere the same in essence, so must genuine revivals be in every age and in every part of the world. But there may be great diversities in many respects. They may be frequent, or far between. They may be isolated, here and there one springing up while the wise and foolish virgins all around are slumbering together; or they may simultaneously occur over wide regions that had long been parched by spiritual drought. In like manner, a revival of religion may be more or less powerful, and may continue for a longer or shorter time. It may show the sovereignty of God in having mercy upon whom he will have mercy, in a more or less striking manner. He may send the blessing by whom he will send, and may bring scores or hundreds or thousands into the church, or only a smaller number. One revival originates in a Sabbath-school, and spreads over a whole congregation; another breaks out suddenly in an academy, a factory, in a sailor's Bethel, or in a penitentiary. One revival takes in persons of all classes, and another reaches one or two classes, leaving the rest as it found them. One pervades the whole town, while another is confined mainly to the centre, or the out districts. One begins among the higher classes, and another among the lower; one with the young men, another with the young women, and another with one or both sexes in middle life. But wherever and however, it is the same Holy Spirit "turning men from darkness to light, and from the power of Satan unto God."

So, again, while all genuine revivals agree in the essential things, the subjects of them are variously wrought upon in the progress of the work. In some cases, God makes a short work, drawing sinners at once to the foot of the cross; in others, convictions of sin and wrath long continue before Christ is revealed to them. In one revival the thunderings of the law as it were constrain sinners to "flee from the wrath to come" to the only Refuge; in another, the sweet voice of mercy sounding out from Calvary by the same divine power draws them as with cords of love.

Revivals may and actually do exhibit all these and other different phases, modified by such agencies as God is pleased to employ for his own glory in building up his spiritual kingdom.

Bearing in mind these leading characteristics, and divers operations by the same Spirit, the way is now prepared to inquire where and how long ago did these special operations of the Spirit begin, and briefly to trace them down through the ages to the present time.

Whether any thing like a revival took place when, in the days of Enos, men began to call upon the name of the Lord, we are not informed; but when the flood came, the whole earth was filled with violence.

And so after Noah, when Abraham was called, it seemed as if the apostasy had again become nearly or quite universal. Certain it is that he went out alone as a true worshipper, "not knowing whither he went." There was no organized church in the world, nothing like it, till through his faith in the divine promise one was established in his family; and then Isaac and Jacob and Joseph, and others of like precious faith, became heirs of the promise.

But among their posterity there was rapidly a great falling away from the worship of the true God. All along there was doubtless a remnant, according to the election of grace; but we do not find recorded a general reformation till we come to the last chapter of Joshua. Of those who were twenty years old and upward when they left Egypt, all, save Joshua and Caleb, had perished in the wilderness. But now the time had come when there was to be a great national reformation. Joshua, knowing that he must soon lay down his high commission and die, gathered all the tribes together at Shechem, that he might meet them for the last time, and give them his dying charge.

It was a solemn and imposing national convocation. All the people hastened with alacrity to meet their aged and beloved chief, and to hear his parting words. As the chosen captain of the Lord's hosts, he had led them on from victory to victory, had divided the promised land among them according to their tribes, and nothing now remained but his final charge and benediction. When the hour had come, we seem to see him rising in the midst of the vast assembly, every whisper hushed, and every eye fastened upon him, as he waved his hand and commenced his address by glancing at the origin of their nation, the remarkable history of God's dealings with them, from the calling of Abraham down through their sore Egyptian bondage, their miraculous deliverances, their wanderings in the wilderness, and their now quiet settlement in the land of promise. This done, he proceeded to pronounce the final charge for which he had called them together. And what a charge!

"Now therefore fear the Lord, and serve him in sincerity and truth, and put away the gods which your fathers served on the other side of the flood and in Egypt, and serve ye the Lord." The appeal was overwhelming. It melted down the whole of that vast assembly, and they answered as one man, "God forbid that we should forsake the Lord, to serve other gods." Joshua, following up the appeal, held them to their promise. "Ye are witnesses against yourselves that ye have chosen the Lord, to serve him. And they said, We are witnesses. The Lord our God will we serve, and his voice we will obey. So Joshua made a covenant with the people that day, and set them a statute and an ordinance in Shechem."

Had the record closed here, we could not know that the tribes were sincere in these solemn reiterated promises, or that if they were sincere, it was not a mere burst of sympathetic emotion, which soon subsided. But the event proved that it was a great and abiding national reformation, by whatever name it might be called; the most remarkable in this respect on sacred record, for it is added, "When Joshua had let the people go, the children of Israel went every man unto his own inheritance, to possess the land. And the people served the Lord all the days of Joshua, and all the days of the elders that outlived Joshua, who had seen all the great works of the Lord that he did for Israel." This was indeed a glorious revival of true religion.

After that generation passed off from the stage,

there was a great falling away under the *Judges*, down to the time of Samuel, a period of about three hundred years. Towards the close of his life there seems to have been something like what we should call a general awakening. The people were brought under great alarm, and confessed their sin in rejecting the Lord and asking for a king. But the prophet had not been long in the grave when the great body of the people relapsed into their former state, or rather, for the most part waxed worse and worse.

The succeeding centuries under the *Kings*, many of whom, especially those of the ten tribes, God "gave in his anger" to a people who "would not have HIM to reign over them," were marked by shameless idolatry, high-handed, heaven-daring sins, by awful prophetic warnings and denunciations, and by marvellous divine interpositions, both in judgment and in mercy. Under David and Solomon, God fulfilled all the good things which he had spoken; and in the Psalms of David then sung, perpetuated his exalted praises through all periods of time. But though the pious Asa and Jehoshaphat reigned in Judah, and Elijah seemed to have exterminated the worship of Baal in Israel; though Hezekiah, strengthened by the prophecies of Isaiah, wrought a glorious and wide-spread reformation; and though, "weary with forbearing," God had driven the ten tribes into captivity, yet Manasseh sinned beyond all who had gone before him, and hope almost expired.

I do not mean to say that at any period there were no true conversions; there certainly were a great many. The church was kept alive from age to age, notwithstanding the general apostasy. In the darkest time, when Elijah himself gave up all for lost, and fled, he was assured that there were seven thousand men in Israel who had not bowed the knee to the image of Baal.

We now come to that most remarkable, though temporary reformation, which took place in the reign of Josiah. It commenced on this wise: In looking over some ancient records, Hilkiah the high-priest found the book of the law in the house of the Lord, which had been for a very long time out of sight and out of mind. He brought it out, and when it was read in the ears of the king, he rent his clothes, and trembled under its terrible denunciations. He felt that something must be done at once to turn away the great wrath of the Lord, which hung like a storm of fire over the nation. He saw that it admitted of no delay, and issued his proclamation for a general gathering of the people. When the time came, he went up into the house of the Lord, and all the men of Judah, and all the men of Jerusalem with him, and the priests and the prophets, and all the people, both small and great, and he read in their ears all the words of the book of the covenant which was found in the house of the Lord. It was an august assembly, and a most solemn occasion. It was the first step in the reformation. Josiah next made a tour through the kingdom, destroying all the places of idolatrous worship as he went, and commanding all the people to keep the passover, as enjoined in the book of the law. They hastened to obey; and the sacred historian adds, "There was not held such a passover in the days of the judges that judged Israel, nor in all the days of the kings of Israel." Externally it certainly was a wonderful reformation; and we have no reason to doubt that many truly repented and turned unto the Lord. But again there was an alarming decline, which continued to increase for a hundred years, till the captivity of Judah in Babylon, and was not arrested till the days of Ezra and Nehemiah.

Soon after the return of the people from their long captivity, there was a great reformation. The people gathered themselves together in Jerusalem as one man, and called upon Ezra to bring out the book of the law of Moses, which the Lord had commanded to Israel; and he read therein from morning till midday, "and the ears of all the people were attentive unto the book of the law." And when he opened the book in the sight of all the people, they all stood up. And when he blessed the Lord, the great God, "all the people answered, Amen, amen, lifting up their hands; and they bowed their heads, and worshipped the Lord with their faces on the ground." And they proved their sincerity by hastening to do works meet for repentance. They at once restored the worship of God which had fallen into disuse, and separated themselves from the heathen family alliances which they had formed during the captivity. This was the severest test of all.

After that we hear no more of their idolatries. Malachi, who lived a little later, was the last of the Old Testament prophets; and for what more we know of the religious state of the Jews during the four subsequent centuries, at the close of which Shiloh came, we are indebted to uninspired writers.

My object, in these rapid historical sketches from the Old Testament history, has been to show that God preserved the church from utter apostasy by special seasons of reformation, after long intervals of decline. This was the divine economy under the Old Testament.

JOHN THE BAPTIST.

Passing to the New Testament, we are naturally led to inquire, what evidence there is, if any, that the same divine economy was still to prevail.

And first, how was it in the day of JOHN THE BAPTIST? Was there any thing under his preaching like what are now called revivals? There was. "The word of the Lord came unto John in the wilderness, and he came into all the country about Jordan, preaching the baptism of repentance for the remission of sins," and under his fearless and rousing appeals, there was a great and general excitement among all classes of the people. The publicans, the soldiers, and even the Pharisees and Sadducees, came to him to be baptized, asking, "What shall we do?" It was more like a national religious awakening than we have found since the days of Joshua; for as Matthew testifies, "Jerusalem, and all Judea, and all the region round about Jordan, went out and were baptized in Jordan, confessing their sins;" and though we have reason to fear that in many cases it fell short of true repentance, we can scarcely doubt, I think, that many who came for baptism, were "born of water and of the

Spirit," and brought forth good fruits. Such a general religious excitement could never have taken place without a supernatural influence upon the hearts of men. The instrument was John, "crying in the wilderness, Repent ye, for the kingdom of heaven is at hand;" but the excellency of the power was of God. It was what would now be called a general revival, though by no means so pure as those afterwards in the apostolic age.

THE APOSTOLIC AGE.

We pass to the glorious "ministration of the Spirit," given to "abide" with the church as the characteristic of the Christian dispensation—a gift which the Saviour promised to his disciples as better than his own personal presence. The riches of this gift were marvellously displayed on the DAY OF PENTECOST, when thousands were converted and baptized. This wonderful scene was an earnest of what might be expected under the faithful preaching of the gospel, not of course in its visible miraculous features, but in its awakening and saving power upon the hearts of sinners.

This we know was followed by a remarkable series of revivals during the apostolic age. Thus, in the fourth chapter of Acts, we read that when Peter and John preached Jesus and the resurrection from the dead, many who heard the word believed, and the number of men was about five thousand. Again, in the sixth chapter, in connection with the solemn service of choosing and setting apart deacons, "the word of the Lord increased; and the number of the disciples multiplied in Jerusalem greatly; and a great company of the priests were obedient to the faith." In the eighth chapter, the disciples, scattered by persecution throughout the regions of Judea and Samaria, "went everywhere preaching the word." Again, chapter ninth, "As Peter passed throughout all quarters, he came down to the saints at Lydda," and after the healing of Eneas, all that saw him in Lydda and Saron, "turned to the Lord." Again, chapter eleventh, "They which were scattered abroad upon the persecutions that arose about Stephen, travelled as far as Phenice, and Cyprus, and Antioch, and spake unto the Grecians, preaching the Lord Jesus. The hand of the Lord was with them; and a great number believed, and turned unto the Lord." These were all so many glorious revivals in the midst of the years of the right hand of the Most High. And so we may be sure it was in all the cities where the gospel was planted in the primitive age. Indeed, it is hardly conceivable how the gospel could otherwise have so mightily prevailed in so short a time. That was preëminently the revival epoch of the church.

Thus far we trace the divine economy by the unerring guide of sacred history. It was not mainly by isolated conversions that the churches were built up, but under the outpouring of the Spirit, turning many at once from darkness to light, and from the power of Satan unto God.

In tracing the history of the church down through the subsequent ages, we can look for no further guidance of the inspired record; but the most obvious analogies would lead us to expect that we should find the same footsteps of Christ travelling in the greatness of his strength along his triumphant march, till he shall have subdued all things unto himself.

The revival epoch, which began on the day of Pentecost, extended down through the second and into the third century; and though ecclesiastical history throws less light on the subject than we could wish, more than enough is found in the writings of the early fathers to show that the Christian religion rapidly spread throughout the Roman empire, and even beyond its boundaries, in spite of all the rage of earth and hell to crush it out.

Pliny the younger, who was some time governor of Bithynia under the bloody emperor Trajan, earnestly dissuaded him from persisting in his persecuting edicts against the Christians in that province, not only by assuring him that they were a harmless people, chargeable with no crime, "meeting together to sing hymns and worship Christ as God," but that they were very numerous all over the province, and that the more they were punished the more they increased.

Tertullian, who lived a century later, and died in 216, writing to the Roman government in vindication of the new religion, as it was called, says, "Though we are strangers of no long standing, yet we have filled all places of your dominions, cities, islands, corporations, councils, armies, tribes, the senate, the palace, the courts of judicature. If the Christians had a mind to avenge themselves, their numbers are abundant; for they have a party, not in this or that province, but in all quarters of the world. Nay, if they were to combine and forsake the Roman empire, how vast would be the loss. The world would be amazed at the solitude which would ensue."

In another place he expostulates thus with the persecuting governors of Africa: "If you persevere in your persecution, what will you do with these many thousands, both of men and women of every rank and every age, who will promptly offer themselves? Carthage itself must be decimated."

Once more, after enumerating the nations who had believed in Christ, he declared that the gospel had penetrated into regions which were inaccessible even to the eagles of Rome. "Excellent governors," he exclaims, "you may torment, afflict, and vex us; your wickedness puts our weakness to the test, but your cruelty is of no avail. It is but a stronger invitation to bring others to our persuasion. The more we are mowed down, the more we spring up again. THE BLOOD OF THE CHRISTIANS IS SEED."

Here we have undeniable evidence of the rapid and wide spread of the church by the mighty power of God in what would now be looked upon as a marvellous series of revivals over many countries. The main difference, compared with any thing that has been witnessed in these modern times, lies in their permeating immensely greater populations. Call them great *reformations*, if you will. It is only another name, on a vast scale, of what we mean by the word revivals—turning "multitudes, multitudes," almost simultaneously, from the worship of dumb idols, from the power of Satan unto God.

CHAPTER II.

"THE GREAT REFORMATION."

SIXTEENTH AND SEVENTEENTH CENTURIES.

During the thousand years between the fifth and the fifteenth century, the annals of the true church are so illegible, so interlined and interpolated, so blotted by the grossest superstition, that it is difficult to trace her progress by any light we have. And yet, even in that long midnight of the world, the light glimmered as it were upon the tops of the mountains, and now and then broke out from the gloom, illuminating the promises when it seemed as if "the mercies of God were clean gone for ever." He who was with the church in the wilderness during her forty years' wanderings, did not forsake her, but kept the pillar of cloud and fire over her till she emerged into the glorious morning of the Protestant Reformation.

Thus the gospel was wonderfully preserved among the Waldenses of Italy and the Culdees of Britain. In the thirteenth century there must have been great revivals, for in Bohemia alone, where the gospel had won its way, there were reckoned, in 1315, no less than 80,000 witnesses for the truth. So again in the fourteenth century, John Wyckliff, "the morning-star of the Reformation," heralded the day-spring in our fatherland, and many turned to the Lord. So was it also in the fifteenth century, under the labors of John Huss and Jerome of Prague, and more signally still in the great religious revolution which a hundred years later shook the Papal throne to its foundations, through the instrumentality of Luther, Zwingle, Calvin, and the other illustrious reformers of that remarkable epoch.

This reformation commenced early in the sixteenth century, and so rapidly did the light of the gospel spread over the principalities and kingdoms of Europe, so mightily did the word of God grow and prevail over all opposition, that it has ever since been called THE GREAT REFORMATION; and it was no less than a wide-spread and glorious revival. It was the reappearance of the divine economy in carrying forward the work of redemption.

The night of the middle ages had been so long, that it seemed as if the day would never dawn. But the rising of the sun, glancing from land to land, proved that "God is not slack concerning his promises." The prince of darkness could no longer hold all the nations in bondage. "The man of sin," drunk with the blood of saints and martyrs, and "exalting himself above all that is called God and is worshipped," received a deadly wound, of which he has never been fully healed and never will be.

The Protestant Reformation in the sixteenth century, under Martin Luther as the first and chief instrument, was a religious *revival* on a vast scale. No other word so well expresses it. "Never certainly, since the days of the early Christians," says Rev. Dr. James W. Alexander, "was there so wide-spread a concern about religion. Never were there so many conversions. The published correspondence of the reformers, and particularly of Martin Luther and John Calvin, shows that a large part of their time was employed in giving counsel to inquiring souls. All the good and great men who were the chief instruments in this amazing revival felt and avowed that it was entirely of God, and that nothing but the omnipotent Spirit would have produced the change which they observed and experienced..... So rapid was the progress of it, that in less than *forty* years, in face of the united opposition of the church and the empire, against all proscription, in spite of rack and fagot, the principles of evangelical religion had overspread Germany, France, Switzerland, Holland, and the British isles. It was an outpouring of the Spirit, under which the mountains flowed down at His presence; it was a converting power that was acknowledged by tribes and nations.

"The remarkable condition of religious things among our *Puritan and Scottish ancestors*, was the simple consequence of this reformation revival prosperously carried out and made permanent. The work of grace was upon the hearts of multitudes..... North America was planted by Protestants, and largely by a race of men whose activity owned evangelical religion as its animating principle. They came out from the midst of great awakenings, and every arrival from the old country brought them news of the revivals which took place under the Bunyans and Baxters of England.

"In Scotland, religion made its progress in a kind of triumphal march..... The subjugation of a whole people within a brief period to the principles of the gospel, is proof that the church was increased with rapidity, and by large accessions; in other words, that there was a great revival throughout the kingdom, in the modern sense of the term."

Thus, in looking back three hundred years from our present stand-point upon that mighty upheaving of the moral world, "known and read of all men" as THE GREAT REFORMATION, and making every abatement for its not having accomplished all that could have been desired, it is past controversy that it was the most remarkable Christian epoch since the days of the apostles. One of its main features was the resurrection, as it were, of the cardinal doctrine of *Justification by Faith alone*, which being once disinterred from the Popish rubbish under which it had been buried for more than eight centuries, the combined efforts of earth and hell have not been able to force back into the old charnel-house of penances and purgatory.

SCOTLAND—KIRK OF SHOTTS, 1625-8.

The influence of the Great Reformation most distinctly appeared, the next century, in England, Scotland, and Ireland. In the reign of Charles I., there was a great persecution of the saints in SCOTLAND who adhered to the faith of their pious fathers. The king and his counsellors were determined at all hazards to enforce Conformity there, as well as in England, to the national establishment. They doubtless would have prevailed, had not the Lord raised up witnesses for the truth, in the spirit of John Knox in the preceding century, and with much of his power. To all human appearance, that cruel usurpation would have been fastened upon that kingdom, but for remarkable divine interpositions, the most signal of which was the great revival of vital religion which began in *Stewarton*, in 1625, and lasted about five years.

"This," says Fleming in his Fulfilling of Scripture, "was, by the profane rabble of that time, called the *Stewarton sickness*; for in that parish first, but afterwards through much of that country, particularly at Irvine under the ministry of Mr. Dickson, it was remarkable, where it can be said that for a considerable time few Sabbaths did pass without some evidently converted, or some convincing proof of the power of God accompanying his word. And truly this great spring tide, as I may call it, of the gospel, was not of a short time, but of some years' continuance; yea, thus, like a spreading moor-burn, the power of godliness did advance from one place to another, which put a marvellous lustre on those parts of the country, the savor whereof brought many from other parts of the land to see its truth."

"Another token for good to the suffering church of Scotland, occurred in the year 1628. At a meeting of the Synod of Edinburgh, in the spring of that year, it had been agreed upon to apply to his majesty that a general fast might be held all over the kingdom. The ostensible causes adduced for this proposal, were the dangerous state of the Protestant churches abroad, and the prevalence of vice and immorality at home. To these causes the Presbyterians naturally added the consideration of their own suffering state, and of the oppressive innovations imposed upon the people. Much of the searching power of the Holy Spirit seems to have been granted to both ministers and people during their solemn fast, and many felt that in humbling themselves before God and making an earnest confession of sin, both national and individual, they obtained strength not their own, a spiritual strength preparing them for greater sufferings, and giving earnest of final deliverance.

"In no individual instance, probably, was the power of the Spirit more signally displayed than at the *kirk of Shotts*, on Monday, the first of June, 1630. It appears that John Livingstone, a young man about twenty-seven years of age, who was at that time domestic chaplain of the Countess of Wigton, had gone to attend the dispensation of the Lord's supper at the kirk of Shotts. There had been a great confluence of both ministers and people from all the adjacent country, and the sacred services of the communion-sabbath had been marked with much solemnity of manner, and great apparent depth and sincerity of devotional feeling. When the Monday came, the large assembly of pious Christians felt reluctant to part without another day of thanksgiving to that God whose redeeming love they had been commemorating. Livingstone was prevailed upon to preach, though reluctant and with heavy misgivings of mind at the thought of his own unworthiness to address so many experienced Christians. He even endeavored to withdraw himself secretly from the multitude, but a strong constraining impulse within his mind caused him to return and proceed with the duty to which he had been appointed.

"Towards the close of the sermon, the audience, and even the preacher himself, were affected with a deep, unusual awe, melting their hearts and subduing their minds, stripping off inveterate prejudices, awaking the impenitent, producing conviction in the hardened, bowing down the stubborn, and imparting to many an enlightened Christian a large increase of grace and spirituality."

"It was known," says Fleming, "as I can speak on sure ground, that nearly *five hundred* had at that time a discernible change wrought on them, of whom most proved lively Christians afterwards. It was the sowing of a seed through Clydesdale, so that many of the most eminent Christians of that country could date their conversion, or some remarkable confirmation of their case, from that day.

"Mr. Livingstone, the honored instrument by which this great work was wrought, was one against whom the tyranny of the suspicious prelates had been directed. Spottswood drove him away from his beloved charge in Torphichen. But in every case of contest between right and wrong, the most politic measure will prove injurious to those who employ it. When such men as Livingstone were driven from a parish, they were compelled to extend their influence over a wider sphere than would otherwise have been possible.

"Not unfrequently, as in his case, they were received into the families of some of the nobility, where their unassuming manners and deep personal piety produced the most beneficial results, both to their protectors and the cause for which they suffered. In this manner the ejected ministers, by their fervent and widely diffused labors, did much to prepare the great body of the nation for that struggle and revulsion which was erelong to take place."

Thus it was when, after the martyrdom of Stephen, there was a great persecution of the church in Jerusalem, the disciples "went everywhere preaching the word," and many were turned unto the Lord who might otherwise never have been converted.

NORTH OF IRELAND, 1625.

In 1625, there was also a remarkable revival in the NORTH OF IRELAND.* It took place under the labors of a band of faithful ministers, most of whom went over from Scotland—Brice, Glendenning, Ridge, Blair, and others.

The province of *Ulster*, which has ever since been the brightest spot on the map of Ireland, was, when this reformation began, in a deplorable state of ignorance and ungodliness. A great number of those who came over from England with the original proprietors and occupied their lands, were openly profane and immoral, and generally inattentive to the institutions of the gospel. The following description of the character of the population is given by Stewart.

"From Scotland," he says, "and from England not a few, yet all of them generally the scum of both nations, from debt, or breaking, fleeing from justice, or seeking shelter, came hither, hoping to be without fear of man's justice, in a land where there was noth-

* See Dr. James S. Reid's History of the Presbyterian Church in Ireland, vol. I.

ing, or but little as yet of the fear of God. Most of the people were all void of godliness, who seemed rather to flee from God in this enterprise than to follow their own mercy.

"Thus on all hands atheism increased and disregard of God, iniquity abounded, with contention, fighting, murder, adultery, etc.; and as they had nothing within them to overawe them, so their ministers' example was worse than nothing; 'for from the prophets of Israel profaneness went forth into all the land.' Thus it was, that when any man would have expected nothing but God's judgment to have followed this crew of sinners, behold, the Lord visited them in admirable mercy, the like whereof had not been anywhere seen for many generations."

This account is confirmed by Blair, who says, "The mercy (alluded to by Stewart) consisted in the band of faithful ministers who were now encouraged to take their lot in Ulster, and whose labors were remarkably blessed to the converting of many out of so profane and godless a multitude. Seven ministers constituted the first band, who labored with apostolic earnestness to remove the ignorance, formality, and profaneness which characterized the greater part of the early colonists. Possessed of the true missionary spirit, and inspired with a holy zeal to propagate the gospel, they commenced with vigor the work of evangelizing the land; and though few in number and beset with many difficulties, they were favored with an extraordinary, if not unprecedented measure of success.

"It was not long before their labors began to be visibly blessed. A remarkable improvement in the habits and demeanor of the people was speedily effected. The thoughtless were roused to serious inquiry on the subject of religion, and the careless were alarmed; the profane were in a great measure silenced, and the immoral reclaimed; while the obstinate opposers of the gospel were converted into its willing and decided supporters. This spirit of religious inquiry and reformation, which in a short time pervaded a considerable portion of the counties of Down and Antrim, was no doubt the result of that devotedness and fidelity by which the ministers in this part of Ulster were so eminently distinguished; yet it appears to have first manifested itself under the ministry of the weakest of these brethren, whose limited attainments and ill-regulated zeal were providentially overruled for the furtherance of the gospel."

"This," says Mr. Stewart, "was the Lord's choice, to begin with him the admirable work of God, which I mention on purpose that all men may see how the glory is only the Lord's in making a holy nation in this profane land, and that it was 'not by might, nor by power,' nor by man's wisdom, 'but by my Spirit, saith the Lord.'

"At Oldstone, God made use of him to awaken the consciences of a lewd and secure people thereabouts; for, seeing their character, he preached to them nothing but law, wrath, and the terrors of God for sin; and in very deed for this only was he fitted, for hardly could he preach any other thing. But behold the success: for the hearers, finding themselves condemned by the mouth of God speaking in his word, fell into such anxiety and terror of conscience, that they looked on themselves as altogether lost and damned; and this work appeared not in one single person or two, but multitudes were brought to understand their way, and to cry out, 'Men and brethren, what shall we do to be saved?' And of these were some of the boldest spirits, who formerly feared not with their swords to put a whole market-town in affray. I have heard one of them, then a mighty strong man, now a mighty Christian, say that his end in coming to church was to consult with his companions how to work some mischief; and yet at one of those sermons was he so catched, that he was fully subdued. But why do I speak of him? We knew, and yet know, multitudes of such men, who sinned, and still gloried in it, because they feared no man, yet are now patterns of sobriety, fearing sin because they fear God. And this spread through the country to admiration, especially about that river commonly called the Six Mile water, for there this work began at first.

"These religious agitations continued for a considerable time. The ministers were indefatigable in improving the favorable opportunities thus offered for extending the knowledge and influence of the gospel. The people awakened and inquiring, many of them desponding and alarmed, both desired and needed guidance and instruction. The judicious exhibition of evangelical doctrines and promises by these faithful men was in due time productive of those happy and tranquillizing effects which were early predicted as the characteristics of gospel times. Adopting the beautiful imagery of the prophets, the broken-hearted were bound up and comforted, the spirit of bondage and of fear gave way to a spirit of freedom and of love, the oil of joy was poured forth instead of mourning, and the spirit of heaviness exchanged for the garments of praise and thankfulness. As the people emerged from the anxiety and alarm produced by the stern preaching of the law, and gradually experienced the hope of the gospel, they would be naturally led to maintain among themselves a closer religious fellowship than they had done; and this proved to be the case. Hence originated those monthly meetings at Antrim which afterwards attracted so much attention, and which in the mean time tended materially to strengthen and consolidate the good work that had been commenced."

The men whom God employed to carry on that great work were instant in season and out of season, laboring to instruct their people and promote vital religion, with a singleness of purpose and intensity of desire and untiring diligence, which, if ever equalled, has at least been seldom surpassed. Blair thus describes his ministerial labors at Bangor: "My charge was very great, about six miles in length, and containing above twelve hundred persons come to age, besides children who stood greatly in need of instruction. This being the case, I preached twice every week, besides the Lord's day, on all which occasions I found little difficulty either as to matter or method. But finding still that this fell short of reaching the design of the gospel ministry, and that the most part continued vastly ignorant, I saw the necessity of trying the more plain and familiar way of instructing them; and therefore, besides my public preaching, I spent as much time every week as my bodily strength could hold out with in exhorting and catechizing them. The knowledge of God increasing among the people, and the ordinance of prayer being precious in their eyes, the work of the Lord did prosper in the place. And in this we were very much encouraged, both by the assistance of holy Mr. Cunningham and by the good example of his little parish of Holywood; for knowing that diversity of gifts is entertaining to the hearers, he and I did frequently preach for one another, and we also agreed to celebrate the Lord's supper four times in each of our congregations annually, so that those in both parishes who were thriving in religion did communicate together on all these occasions."

The religious sentiments of all these ministers were those usually called Calvinistic, which at this period were maintained throughout the three national churches of the empire. A delightful harmony also prevailed.

"Among all the ministers," says Livingstone, "there was never any jar or jealousy; yea, nor among the professors, the greater part of them being Scots, and some good number of very gracious English, all whose contention was to prefer others to themselves; and although the gifts of the ministers were much different, yet it was not observed that the people followed any to the undervaluing of others. Many of these religious professors had been both ignorant and profane, and for debt and want, and worse causes, had left Scotland. Yet the Lord was pleased by his word to work such a change, that I do not think there were more lively experienced Christians than were there at this time in Ireland. Being but lately brought in, the lively edge was not yet gone off them, and the perpetual fear that the bishops would take away their ministers made them with great hunger wait on the ordinances."

The singular success which attended the preaching of the word at this period, is also attested by another writer, who says, "I shall here instance that great and solemn work of God which was in the church of Ireland about the year 1628, and some years thereafter, which may with propriety be said to have been one of the largest manifestations of the Spirit, and of the most solemn times of the down-pouring thereof, that almost since the days of the apostles hath been seen. Then it was sweet and easy for Christians to come thirty or forty miles to the solemn communions which they had, and there continue, from the time they came till they returned, without wearying or making use of sleep; yea, with but little either meat or drink, and as some of them professed, they did not feel the need thereof, but went away most fresh and vigorous, their souls so filled with the sense of God."

This remarkable revival in the north of Ireland, of which I do not remember to have met with any account till lately, so strikingly resembles in all its essential features those with which I have been familiar now for more than half a century, that the narrative strikes me as a familiar acquaintance, and I cannot doubt that it was wrought by "one and the selfsame Spirit."

ENGLAND.

At the same time that God was so gloriously reviving his work in Scotland and Ireland, about the middle of the seventeenth century, he was raising up a host of mighty champions for the truth in ENGLAND. The persecution which raged so furiously against the Non-conformists, headed under the crown by such instruments as Archbishop Laud and Jeffries, and especially the "Act of Uniformity," passed in 1662, with the "Five Mile Act," by which two thousand godly pastors were forbidden to labor within five miles of their own churches, was a mighty struggle; but instead of crushing and silencing the witnesses, the pent-up fire broke out even in their sufferings and imprisonments into a flame that was to enlighten and bless all coming generations. The Lord was on their side, and the gates of hell could not prevail to blot out their testimony. Many of them were driven across the ocean to America, here in the wilderness to bear a prominent part in laying the foundations of civil and religious liberty, which have ever since been the bulwark and glory of our land.

It was a great Protestant Reformation, though it had not, I believe, to much extent, those distinctive revival features which marked its progress in Scotland and Ireland.

Among the noble band of confessors we find the names of Bunyan, Baxter, Owen, Bishop Hopkins, Flavel, Alleine, Howe, and others, who have not been surpassed in any age for talents, for theological learning, for deep Christian experience, and for the valiant defence of "the faith once delivered to the saints." We hazard little in saying that for doctrinal, practical, and experimental religious instructions and authorship, it was *the golden age* in the fatherland. What other age has produced so many volumes full of the marrow of the gospel, and indited as it were so close on the verge of heaven? What thousands have been guided in the Way of Life by Bunyan's "Pilgrim's Progress," and his "Grace Abounding to the Chief of Sinners;" and what thousands more have had the fulness of Christ revealed to them in Flavel's "Fountain of Life" and "Method of Grace." What would our own land as well as Great Britain have been but for this revival period in the seventeenth century? Who can tell how much of the seed that was then sown sprung up in that great awakening which is the subject of our next chapter?

Of the labors of these persecuted ministers, we find an illustrious example in Baxter at Kidderminster, where he wrote his "Reformed Pastor," a standard work for those who would witness the fruit of revivals in any age.

Having been separated from his people in the violent political agitations and confusion of the times, and been brought near to death, when he wrote his "Saints' Everlasting Rest," he at length resumed his charge at Kidderminster. In his own account of his labors among them during fourteen years, he says,

"I preached before the wars twice each Lord's day; but after the war, but once, and once every Thursday, besides occasional sermons. Every Thursday evening, my neighbors that were most desirous and had opportunity, met at my house and there one of them repeated the sermon; and afterwards they proposed what doubts any of them had about the sermon, or any other case of conscience, and I resolved their doubts. And last of all, I caused sometimes one and sometimes another of them to pray, sometimes praying with them myself. Once a week also, some of the young, who were not prepared to pray in so great an assembly, met among a few more privately, where they spent three hours in prayer together. Every Saturday night they met at some of their houses to repeat the sermon of the last Lord's day, and to pray and prepare themselves for the following day. Once in a few weeks we had a day of humiliation, on one occasion or other. Two days every week my assistant and myself took fourteen families between us for private catechizing and conference, he going through the parish, and the town coming to me. I first heard them recite the words of the catechism, and then examined them about the sense; and lastly urged them, with all possible engaging reason and vehemence, to answerable affection and practice. If any of them were perplexed through ignorance or bashfulness, I forbore to press them any farther to answers, but made them hearers, and either examined others, or turned all into instruction and exhortation. I spent about an hour with a family, and admitted no others to be present, lest bashfulness should make it burdensome, or any should talk of the weaknesses of others; so that all the afternoon, on Mondays and Tuesdays, I spent in this; and my assistant spent the mornings of the same days in the same way."

"I have mentioned my sweet and acceptable employment; let me, to the praise of my gracious Lord, acquaint you with some of my *success*. My public preaching met with an attentive, diligent auditory. Having broke over the brunt of the opposition of the rabble before the wars, I found them afterwards tractable and unprejudiced.

"Before I ever entered into the ministry, God blessed my private conference to the conversion of some, who remain firm and eminent in holiness to this day. Then, and in the beginning of my ministry, I was wont to number them as jewels; but since then I could not keep any number of them.

"The congregation was usually full, so that we were led to build five galleries after my coming hither, the church itself being very capacious, and the most commodious and convenient that ever I was in. Our private meetings also were full. On the Lord's day there was no disorder to be seen in the streets, but you might hear a hundred families singing psalms and repeating sermons as you passed through the streets. In a word, when I came thither first, there was about one family in a street that worshipped God and called on his name; and when I came away, there were some streets where there was not more than one family in the side of a street that did not so, and that did not, in professing serious godliness, give us hopes of their sincerity. And of those families which were the worst, being inns and alehouses, usually some persons in each did seem to be religious. Though our administration of the Lord's supper was so orderly as displeased many, and the far greater part kept themselves away, yet we had six hundred that were communicants, of whom there were not twelve that I had not good hopes of as to their sincerity; and those few that came to our communion and yet lived scandalously, were excommunicated afterwards. And I hope there were many who feared God that came not to our communion, some of them being kept off by husbands, by parents, by masters, and some dissuaded by men that differed from us.

"When I commenced personal conference with each family and catechizing them, there were very few families in all the town that refused to come; and those few were beggars at the town's ends, who were so ignorant that they were ashamed it should be manifest. And few families went from me without some tears or seemingly serious promises for a godly life. Yet many ignorant and ungodly persons there were still among us; but most of them were in the parish, and not in the town, and in those parts of the parish which were farthest from the town. Some of the poor men competently understood the body of divinity, and were able to judge in difficult controversies. Some of them were so able in prayer that very few ministers equalled them in order and fulness, apt expressions, holy oratory, and fervency. A great number of them were able to pray very appropriately with their families, or with others. The temper of their minds, and the correctness of their lives, were even more commendable than their talents. The professors of serious godliness were generally of very humble minds and conduct, of meek and quiet behavior towards others, and blameless in their conversation.

"One *advantage* which I had was through the zeal and diligence of the godly people of the place, who thirsted after the salvation of their neighbors, and were in private my assistants; and being dispersed through the town, they were ready in almost all companies, to repress seducing words, and to justify godliness, and convince, reprove, and exhort men according to their needs; and also to teach them how to pray, and to help them to sanctify the Lord's day. Those people that had none in their families who could pray or repeat the sermons, went to the houses of their neighbors who could do it, and joined with them; so that some houses of the ablest men in each street were filled with them that could do nothing or little in their own.

"And the holy, humble, blameless lives of the religious was a great advantage to me. The malicious people could not say, Your professors here are as proud and covetous as any. But the blameless lives of godly people shamed opposers, and put to silence the ignorance of foolish men, and many were won by their good conversation."

Among the Puritan worthies was Blackerby, whose memoirs were blessed in kindling to higher Christian zeal the eminent Andrew Fuller, who was a leading spirit in establishing the monthly concert of prayer for foreign missions, and planting at Serampore the first of modern missions to India.

CHAPTER III.

"THE GREAT AWAKENING."

EIGHTEENTH CENTURY—ABOUT 1740.

PRECIOUS and permanent as were the fruits of the great work of God in the seventeenth century, and though God all along raised up many valiant witnesses for the truth, yet, for some fifty years, beginning towards the close of that century, especially through the disabilities enforced by the "Act of Uniformity," and the ravages of death among the champions of the gospel, there was a falling away in the Protestant churches that became extremely alarming to those who still clung to the ark of the covenant. It was not so much that the Philistines threatened to come and carry it away, as that the priests, who should have borne it on, deserted it one after another, and went over to the enemy.

Dr. Macfarlan, in his History of Revivals in the Eighteenth Century, says in respect to both England and Scotland, "About the end of the seventeenth and the beginning of the eighteenth century most of the churches were in a comparatively low state. The old style of preaching was being fast laid aside, and cold formal addresses, verging towards a kind of Socinianism, were becoming fashionable."

Old Mr. Hutchison, who saw but the beginning of this progress, used to say, "When I compare the times before the Restoration with those since the

Revolution, I must own that young ministers preach accurately and methodically; but far more of the power and efficacy of the Spirit and the grace of God went along with sermons in those days than now."

From the Restoration down to the early part of the seventeenth century, both churchmen and Nonconformists unite in deploring the decayed condition of religion and morals.*

Bishop Burnet says, "I am now in the seventieth year of my age, and as I cannot speak long in the world in any sort, I cannot hope for a more solemn occasion than this for speaking with all due freedom both to the present and to the succeeding ages. I cannot look on without the deepest concern, when I see the imminent ruin hanging over this church, and by consequence, over the whole Reformation. The much greater part of those who come to be ordained are ignorant, to a degree not to be apprehended by those who are not obliged to know it. There are those who have read some few books, yet many seem never to have read the Scriptures."

Dr. Watts declares that there was a general decay of vital religion in the hearts and lives of men, and that it was common among dissenters and churchmen, and a matter of mournful observation among all who laid the cause of God to heart; and he called upon every one to use all possible efforts for the recovery of dying religion in the world. In these sentiments it is well known that his endeared friend Dr. Doddridge fully sympathized.

Another writer says, "The religion of nature

* See Stevens' History of Methodism, vol. I.

makes up the darling topics of our age, and the religion of Jesus is valued only for the sake of that, and only as far as it carries on the light of nature, and is a bare improvement of that kind of light."

Archbishop Secker says, "In this we cannot be mistaken, that an open professed disregard has become the distinguishing character of the present age. Such are the dissoluteness and contempt of principle in the higher part of the world, and the profligacy, intemperance, and fearlessness in committing crimes in the lower, as must, if this torrent of impiety stop not, become absolutely fatal. Christianity is ridiculed and railed at with very little reserve, and the teachers of it without any at all."

Bishop Butler says, "It has come to be taken for granted that Christianity is no longer a subject of inquiry; and accordingly it is treated as if, in the present age, this were an agreed point among all persons of discernment, and nothing remained but to set it up as a principal subject for mirth and ridicule."

Southey says, "The clergy had lost that authority which may always command at least the appearance of respect."

Archbishop Leighton spoke of the church as a fair carcass without a spirit.

Isaac Taylor, in his history of Methodism, says that when Wesley appeared, "the Anglican church was an ecclesiastical system under which the people of England had lapsed into heathenism, or a state hardly to be distinguished from it."

Natural religion was the favorite study of the clergy and of the learned generally, and included most of their theology. Collins and Tindall had denounced Christianity as priestcraft. Whiston pronounced the miracles to be Jewish impositions. Woolston declared them to be allegories. Arianism, Socinianism, taught by such men as Samuel Clarke and Whiston, had become fashionable among the best English thinkers.

Some of the brightest names of the times can be quoted as exceptions to these remarks, but such was the general condition in England. The higher classes laughed at piety, and prided themselves on being above what they called its fanaticism; the lower classes were grossly ignorant, and abandoned to vice; while the church, enervated by a universal decline, was unable longer to give countenance to the downfallen cause of truth.

The night was long and stormy; but at length the day dawned, and the clouds began to break away.

It is a fact worthy of the most profound consideration, and of grateful praise, that God opened the windows of heaven, and poured out a blessing *almost simultaneously* on England, Scotland, and America, about the year 1730.

SCOTLAND.

To begin, as in our notice of the work in the preceding century, with SCOTLAND. The habitations of horrid cruelty abroad, and the abominations of immorality at home, began to engage the public mind. There were here and there encouraging indications that the Sun of righteousness was about to arise upon the mountains and the moors with healing in his wings.

Among other indications, Mr. Robe of Kilsyth speaks of providential events affecting that parish, and preparing the way for what followed, as early as 1733; and the direct means afterwards blessed, began to be used two years before the commencement of the revival.

In 1740, (three years after Whitefield's public ministry commenced in England,) Mr. Robe says, "I began to preach on the doctrine of regeneration. This course of sermons was acceptable to the Lord's people, and there was more than ordinary seriousness in hearing them; yet I could see no further fruit. But the Lord, who is infinitely wise and knoweth the end from the beginning, was preparing us for the uncommon dispensation of the Spirit, which we looked not for."

About the same time there were similar encouraging preparations at *Cambuslang*. Mr. McCulloch the pastor, for nearly a twelvemonth before the work began, had been preaching on those subjects which tend most directly to explain the nature and prove the necessity of regeneration. This was the state of things in the spring and summer of 1741. The revival which followed in Cambuslang, and spread widely over that part of Scotland, was as life from the dead to the churches. It was unmistakably commenced and carried on by the mighty power of God; and many, both old and young, of all classes, were added to the Lord. The narrative before me is so deeply interesting and instructive, that I would gladly enrich my historical sketches with copious extracts, but want of space forbids. I have only room to say that the glorious work in its progress exhibited all the leading scriptural characteristics of revivals before and since, under the faithful preaching of the doctrines of grace set home upon the hearts of men by the Holy Spirit, who worketh all things according to the counsel of his own will.

As every tree is known by its fruits, so is every revival. We naturally and properly inquire, What are its fruits? So in this case. What were the fruits of the great revival just glanced at in Scotland? Mr. Macfarlan's History contains this testimony from Rev. Mr. McCulloch, the faithful pastor at Cambuslang, which I have much condensed:

"First, all the persevering subjects of the work agree in professing faith in Christ as the Mediator, through whom alone we can come to God the Father, through the power and grace of the Holy Spirit; and secondly, there is evidence that in their walk and conversation they adorned their Christian profession. They have from that time till now, or till the time of their death, behaved as became their Christian profession, with such exceptions as must always be made in judging of imperfect creatures. But besides this general statement, the following particulars are submitted, either on my own personal knowledge, or good and credible information.

"They adorn the doctrine of God their Saviour, glorify their heavenly Father, and excite others to do so on their account, by practising justice and charity, relative duties, public spiritedness, humility, meekness, patience, close and diligent attendance on gospel ordinances, heavenly-mindedness, watchfulness against sin, especially against such sin as easily besets them.

"Such as were given to cursing and swearing have laid aside the practice, learning to speak the language of heaven, having upon them a holy awe of God and of things divine. Such as were accustomed to frequent taverns, to drink, and play at cards, etc., till late, or it may be morning hours, have for *nine* years past avoided all occasions of the kind, and kept at home, spending their evenings in Christian conference, in matters profitable to their families, and in secret and family devotion. He who was formerly drunken, accustomed to lie in bed till eight or nine o'clock in the morning, sleeping off his night's intoxication, has for these nine years been in the habit of getting up at three or four o'clock in the morning, of reading his Bible and other good books, of being engaged in prayer or meditation, till seven or eight, when he calls together his household for family devotion, which is again repeated in the evening.

"Those who were formerly covetous and selfish, have acquired much of public spirit and of concern for the kingdom and glory of Christ, especially in the salvation of sinners; and with this view they are not only exemplary in their conduct, but useful to all within their reach. They contribute cheerfully, and some of them beyond their ability, at collections for the interests of religion or the relief of the distressed. They carefully observe seasons fixed for the concert for prayer, and join in earnest supplication for the further spread of the gospel and the outpouring of the Spirit on the churches. 'As new-born babes, they desire the sincere milk of the word, that they may grow thereby;' flocking with eagerness to hear in their different localities. The weekly lecture on Thursday, which was established in this place in 1742, has been continued ever since, summer and winter, even in harvest, when the reapers come running from the fields, where they have been toiling all day. They are careful in their preparations for the Lord's supper, and frequent in the observance. These have been indeed remarkable times of communion with God. This people have seen the goings of their God and King in the sanctuary. They have been made to sit under Christ's shadow with great delight, and his fruit has been sweet to their taste. They have been feasted in the banqueting-house, and his banner over them has been love.

"To conclude, they abound much in prayer, both secret and domestic, and also in the observance of fellowship meetings. In every town or village almost in this country side, where there is any competent number of serious and lively Christians, and where religion is in a thriving state, many private meetings are held. Common tradesmen, who are members and who work for so much a day, allow their employers to deduct so much from the time they are absent. Some of these meetings besides have also special seasons for fasting and prayer on extraordinary occasions, such, for example, as on receiving news of heavy losses, or dangers occurring to any of themselves, or of what threatens the interests of religion; and on these occasions they enjoy much of the divine presence, though less, alas, than in former times.

"Now to Him who is able to keep us from falling, and to present us faultless before the presence of his glory with exceeding joy, to the only wise God our Saviour, be glory and majesty, dominion and power, both now and for ever. Amen."

To this was added the following attestation, signed by the elders of the church:

"We the undersigned, elders and members of the kirk session of Cambuslang, having heard the foregoing read to us by our pastor, and having maturely considered the same, paragraph by paragraph, do hereby make it our own, being persuaded that it contains a just and true account of the extraordinary work here in 1742, and of the comfortable and abiding effects of it on many, probably on more than *four hundred*, mentioned in the foregoing attestation, and particularly as regards those who lived in this parish until 1742, and from that time down, or till their death, who lived, to the best of our knowledge, as becomes their profession."

The foregoing is but a hasty glance at the glorious revival which descended from the opening heavens upon Scotland, which arrested the alarming progress of infidelity and ungodliness, turned back the captivity of scores of churches that might have remained in bondage even until now, and restored to life the doctrines of the Reformation, of which John Knox was the exponent and the powerful advocate. Perhaps no work in Scotland has borne richer fruits than this of the eighteenth century, in which Mr. McCulloch, Whitefield, Robe, Bonar, Hamilton, McKnight, Gillies, Alexander, Anderson, and others of kindred spirit, bore a conspicuous part.

ENGLAND AND WALES.

Returning now to ENGLAND and WALES, we recall the lamentations of such men as Hutchinson and Burnet and Watts and Secker and Butler over the alarming prevalence of infidelity, ignorance, and immorality throughout the United Kingdom in the earlier part of the eighteenth century. To human view, the state of religion was more hopeless in England than in Scotland. The Established church scarcely had a name to live, save in her articles and liturgy, and religion in the dissenting churches was at a very low ebb. It was evident that nothing short of some special interposition by the great Head of the church could restore the fallen interests of Zion.

But man's extremity is God's opportunity, and such an interposition was at hand. God had been raising up three young men in the university of Oxford, the two brothers John and Charles Wesley, and George Whitefield, to commence and carry on the work. He prepared them for it by long and sharp personal convictions of their own lost estate; and that they might endure hardness as good soldiers of Jesus Christ, by subjecting them to the fiery ordeal of scorn and persecution in the university, and as they were almost hopelessly feeling their way into the ministry, after they left it. It was in Oxford that they and the few others who sympathized with them were contemptuously called *Methodists* by their ungodly fellow-students, little thinking that they were giving an honorable name to one of the largest denominations in England and America.

As the university was their Alma Mater, so was the Established church of their native land. They were strongly attached to her ecclesiastical polity, to her liturgy, to her forms and ceremonies, and had not the most distant thought of leaving her communion. They preached in her churches till they were driven out into the open fields as deluded schismatics; and they clung to the Establishment through evil report as long as they could, the Wesleys as long as they lived. They never formally broke off their connection, though they were forced by persecution to avail themselves of that liberty wherewith Christ had made them free, to turn as many as possible to the Lord, whether within or without the pale of the Established church.

As the reformation advanced, God raised up Fletcher and Romaine and Madan and Berridge and Shirley and Benson and Howel Harris and others, to take part with them in their itinerant ministry; and so rapidly did the work spread, that, "or ever they were aware," the converts had so greatly multiplied outside of the Establishment as to demand an organization of some sort. Wesley could not resist the pressure. The thousands were liable to be scattered as sheep without a shepherd. They must be taken care of, or the roaring lion would come and devour them; and though he would not, even in that extremity, form a new denomination, he organized them under what was called the Methodist *Connec-*

tion, "so mightily did the word of God grow and prevail."

The history of this remarkable era of revivals which commenced about 1740, and spread so widely over England, Wales, and Ireland, is so fully recorded in the lives and writings of Whitefield, Wesley, Lady Huntingdon, and others, that it is needless for me to descend to particulars.

That there was intermingled with this work much of animal excitement among the thousands upon thousands who hung upon the lips of Whitefield and the Wesleys in Moorfields, on Kensington common, and other out-door stations, and who sometimes rent the air with their sobs and outcries, and that the preachers looked upon these impassioned demonstrations with too much allowance, there is no room to question; nor, on the other hand, can any but sceptics doubt that "the power of the Highest" was there, by which multitudes were arrested, convicted, and truly converted.

Mysterious and trying as was the opposition these distinguished preachers received from the Established church of that day, I think we can see the wisdom and goodness of God in permitting it. Had it come entirely from without, the leaven could scarcely have been infused into the great lump, where it was so much needed. As the first great revival preachers were churchmen, and labored within the pale of the church wherever they could get an opportunity, the truth found an entrance where the doors would otherwise have remained closed. Some of the clergy were raised from their moral depression, and gained over to "the faith once delivered to the saints," and became zealous preachers in their own parishes. The evangelical element was thus infused into the churches of the Establishment, or if it were already there, was quickened into life, where it had long been petrified by formalism. How much the large class of evangelical churches of the Establishment in the British isles are indebted to the blessed influence of that "great awakening," it were impossible to say; but that there is now much more of the power of godliness, of vital, active piety in the English church than there would otherwise have been, I think all will agree who candidly study the religious history of that eventful period, and trace the growing evangelism of that church down to the present time. The good seed which was then sown has been springing up and bearing fruit, more or less, ever since.

The Independents too, of different sects, who did not fall in with the Methodists, shared in the blessing, and some of their ablest preachers were active in promoting the revival. All in all, it was a glorious ingathering of souls to Christ, though much was lost for want of able stationary pastors to bring the converts into regularly organized churches, and by a pious watch and care build them up in the most holy faith. This Whitefield and the other evangelists could not do, as they went on from place to place, crying, like John in the wilderness, "Prepare ye the way of the Lord."

The chief apostles of that reformation had different gifts, and did not harmonize exactly in all their theological speculations; but the same spirit animated them and dwelt in them. Their grand and all-absorbing aim was to win souls to Christ. The differences between Whitefield and the Wesleys at one time threatened to create a lasting alienation; but mutual forbearance and charity reconciled them. They found they had no time to dispute while sinners whom they might hope to save were perishing. They labored and prayed together as before; their personal friendship was, if possible, more closely cemented, as they went on sowing the good seed over the same fields. Essentially they were of one heart and one mind, till death came and took them up to that brighter world, where it is impossible not to see eye to eye, or to fall into any mistakes. Whitefield preached the offers of a free salvation to all, without distinction or exception, as earnestly as it was possible for Wesley to do. So Wesley, in his prayers, rejoiced to exalt God on the throne, and magnify his grace; and I never heard a Methodist pray in a revival who did not. Indeed, how can any body pray that the unconverted may be born again, without first believing that they are dead in trespasses and sins; and in this view of their lost condition, invoking the Holy Spirit to come down in his sovereign and mighty power to awaken, renew, and sanctify them?

So long as the number of converts was comparatively small, and some of the churches of the Establishment yet opened their doors to the revival preachers, the necessity of outside chapels was not very urgent, especially as there was so much field preaching to the thousands without, whom the Lord stirred up to press eagerly around the stands, inquiring what they must do to be saved. But as the revival spread on every hand, and great numbers of converts needed to be gathered into societies for regular instruction and oversight, the want was severely felt.

But the mass of the converts were poor, and how were the chapels to be built? Who would furnish the means? Anticipating the growing necessity, the great Head of the church had been raising up help in high quarters, from which the necessary aid could hardly have been expected.

And just here I have been forcibly struck with the remarkable coincidence between this state of things and what we read of the first great revival period, in the Acts of the Apostles. God then raised up helpers from the higher classes, without whose aid the thousands of converts, being mostly poor and sorely persecuted, could scarcely have subsisted. Thus, when Paul and Silas passed over from Troas into Macedonia, and came to Philippi, they found there a certain woman named Lydia, a seller of purple from Thyatira, whose heart the Lord opened, that she attended to the things which were spoken of Paul, and she constrained them to come into her house to abide, which they did as long as their mission would allow them to stay. Her traffic had probably made her rich. Still more striking is the record in the next chapter. When Paul and Silas went down to Berea and preached the gospel in that city, many of the Jews received the word with all readiness of mind; also of "honorable women," who were Greeks, and of men not a few. These women are here called honorable, as belonging to the higher classes, who having both the disposition and the means, encouraged and helped the missionaries to go on with their work, when other resources must have failed.

So here, in this great revival, God raised up *honorable women* just when they were most needed to help the preachers, and provide places of worship for those who were too poor to do it themselves. Several of their names are mentioned, as Anne and Frances Hastings, Lady Mary Hamilton, Lady Gertrude Hotham and Countess Delitz, sisters of Lady Chesterfield, Lady Chesterfield herself, Lady Fanny Shirley, and others of the aristocracy, who established the first female prayer-meeting that I remember to have seen noticed anywhere. Though all connected with the Established church, they looked with great favor upon the wonderful reformation that was going on among the hitherto uncared-for masses outside, and cheerfully contributed, more or less, to help build them chapels, in parts where they were most needed.

Thus many daughters did virtuously, but there was one that excelled them all. This was that remarkable "elect lady," the Countess of Huntingdon, who was remotely related to the royal family, and who moved in the highest circles. Amid all the allurements and fascinating worldly prospects of her exalted rank, God arrested her by an alarming sickness, brought her to renounce all for Christ at the foot of his cross, and brought her into fellowship with his despised and persecuted disciples, of whom the world was not worthy. While in her doctrinal belief she sympathized strongly with Whitefield her favorite preacher, she welcomed to her house all the prominent preachers of the other branch of the Connection of whom Wesley was the leader; and deemed it an honor to number Dr. Watts, Dr. Doddridge, and other dissenting ministers of the day, among the warmest of her friends in the household of faith. Time would fail me to reckon up her munificent charities for building chapels, and supporting the brotherhood in their self-denying labors to win souls to Christ; to speak of her boundless hospitality at home; to follow her as she "went about doing good," and in her shining upward progress towards the saints' everlasting rest. Considering her moderate income, her contributions, after the death of her husband, for religious and charitable purposes, were almost incredible. They were estimated to have amounted to at least $500,000.

Thus did that illustrious lady the Countess of Huntingdon go on from strength to strength, serving God and her generation by the will of God, till, ripened for the inheritance of the saints in light, she, at the advanced age of eighty-four, rested from her labors, and her works followed her. For what she was and what she did, the reader is referred to the volume entitled, "Lady Huntington and her Friends," published by the American Tract Society, to Isaac Taylor's History of Methodism, and other religious histories of the times. She was certainly one of the most remarkable women of that or any age. Her name will be had in everlasting remembrance. We can hardly see how Whitefield and Wesley and the other prominent leaders in that religious movement would have carried on the work as they did, without her pecuniary assistance and other efficient aid. Certain it is, that in all subsequent ages her name will be associated with those of the most illustrious reformers of that extraordinary revival epoch. And who can doubt that when she died, she ascended to join those holy women of old, whose memorial stands upon the sacred record, in their eternal services and songs?

THE UNITED STATES.

Leaving the fatherland and crossing the ocean, we proceed to inquire what was the state of religion in the AMERICAN CHURCHES previous to the "Great Awakening," at which we have just glanced in the mother country. Certainly, when that remarkable revival commenced, the churches had not sunk so low here as there. From the beginning of the century, we find there had been isolated revivals here and there. There were verdant inclosures in the vineyard, while also the drought was wide and sore.

The Rev. Mr. Danforth of Taunton, Massachusetts, wrote, in 1704–5, "We are much encouraged by a universal and amazing impression made by the Spirit of God on all sorts among us, especially on the young men and women. It is almost incredible how many visit me with discoveries of extreme distress of mind they are in about their spiritual condition. The young men, instead of their merry meetings, are now forming themselves into regular meetings for prayer, repetition of sermons, and singing. The profanest among us seem startled at the sudden change upon the rising generation. We need much prayer that these strivings of the Spirit may have a saving issue and effect."

Again he writes, "My time is spent in daily discourse with the young people visiting me with their doubts, fears, and agonies. Religion flourishes to amazement and admiration, that so we should be at once touched with soul affliction, and this in all corners of the place. But I hope that the deeper the wound, the more sound may be the cure. I have little time to think of worldly matters, scarce time to study sermons as I used to do; but find God can bless mean preparations whenever he pleases that such shall be most cried up and commended which I have had scarce time to methodize. I sometimes think that the time of the pouring out of the Spirit upon all flesh may be at the door."

President Edwards mentions revivals in Northampton in 1712 and 1718, under the ministry of his predecessor Rev. Mr. Stoddard. In the year 1721, there was a remarkable revival in Windham, Connecticut. In 1730 and the three following years, there was a considerable revival in Freehold, New Jersey, under the ministry of the two Tennents, John and William; and other places might be mentioned.

Nevertheless there had been, in the early part of the century, a great falling away, which we find grievously lamented by pious ministers, who remembered those better days when the candle of the Lord shone upon the churches planted by the Puritan fathers.

Dr. Increase Mather, in a book entitled, "The Glory departing from New England," printed in 1702, says, "We are the posterity of the good old

Puritan Non-conformists in England, who were a strict and holy people. Such were our fathers who followed the Lord into this wilderness. O New England, New England, look to it that the glory be not removed from thee, for it begins to go. O tremble, for it is going; it is gradually departing. You that are aged persons, that can remember what New England was fifty years ago, that saw the churches in their first glory, is there not a sad decay and diminution of that glory? Time was when these churches were 'beautiful as Tirzah, comely as Jerusalem, terrible as an army with banners.' What a glorious presence of Christ was there in all his ordinances. Many were converted, and there were added to the churches daily such as should be saved. But are not sound conversions become rare in this day, and in many congregations? Look into the pulpits, and see if there is such a glory there as once there was. When will Boston see a Cotton and a Norton again? When will New England see a Hooker, a Shepard, a Mitchell, not to mention others?

"Look into our civil state; does Christ reign there as once he did? How many churches, how many towns are there in New England that we may sigh over them and say, the glory is gone! And there is sad cause to fear that greater departures of the glory are hastening upon us; our iniquities testify against us, and our backslidings are many. That there is a general defection from primitive purity and piety in many respects, cannot be denied. The providence of God is threatening to pull down the wall which was a defence to these churches."

Again he writes in 1721, "I am now in the eighty-third year of my age, and having had an opportunity to converse with the first planters of this country, and having been for sixty-five years a preacher of the gospel, I cannot but be in the disposition of those ancient men who had seen the foundation of the first house, and wept with a loud voice to see what a change the work of the temple had upon it. The children of New England are, or once were, for the most part, the children of godly men. What did our fathers come into this wilderness for? Not to gain estates as men do now, but for religion, and that they might leave their children in a hopeful way of being truly religious. There was a famous man that preached before one of the greatest assemblies that ever was preached unto seventy years ago, and he told them, 'I have lived in a country seven years, and all that time I never heard one profane oath, and all that time I never did see a man drunk in that land.' Where was that country? It was New England; but Oh, degenerate New England, what art thou come to at this day! How are those sins become common in thee that once were not so much as heard of in this land!"

In a public lecture printed in 1706, Dr. Cotton Mather says, "It is confessed by all who know any thing of the matter—and Oh, why not with rivers of tears bewailed?—that there is a general and a horrible decay of Christianity among the professors of it. The glorious and precious religion of our heavenly Christ generally appears with quite another face in the lives of Christians of this day, than what it had in the lives of the saints into whose hands it was first of all delivered. The modern Christianity is but too generally but a very shadow of the ancient."

The Rev. Thomas Prince of Boston, in a sermon delivered before the General Assembly of the province of Massachusetts, May 27, 1730, states as his design to "commemorate the righteous and wonderful works of God towards us, both in our own days and in the days of our fathers," and thus proceeds: "Who were our fathers, and what were their distinguishing characters? The generality of them were the near descendants of the first reformers in England. They were born of pious parents, who brought them up in a course of strict religion under the most awakening preachers of those days. Under such means they became inspired with a spirit of piety, and with a growing zeal to reform the worship of God to the most beautiful and perfect model of his own institutions.

"And to the great glory of God be it spoken, there never was perhaps before seen such a body of pious people together on the face of the earth. Their civil and ecclesiastical leaders were exemplary patterns of piety. They encouraged only the virtuous to come with and follow them. They were so strict, both in the church and the state, that the incorrigible could not endure to live in the country, and went back again. Profane swearers and drunkards were not known in the land. And it quickly grew so famous for religion abroad, that scarce any other but those who liked it came over for many years after."

The Rev. Samuel Blair, speaking of the state of religion in Pennsylvania, says, "True religion lay as it were adying and ready to expire its last breath of life, in this part of the visible church, in the spring of 1740, when the God of salvation was pleased to visit us with the blessed effusions of the Holy Spirit. I doubt not that then there were some sincerely religious people up and down. But a very lamentable ignorance of the essentials of true practical religion, and of the doctrines relating thereto, very generally prevailed. The nature and necessity of the new birth were little known, or of the Holy Spirit opening and applying the law to the conscience, in order to saving closure with Christ. The common notion seemed to be, that if people were aiming to be in the way of duty as well as they could, they imagined there was no reason to be much afraid."

These lamentations over the degeneracy of the times must certainly be taken with some abatements from what a comparison between other periods in the history of the American churches would require. The primitive standard of morals and piety in the first and second generations starting from Plymouth rock was so high, that the declension over which the fathers mourned seemed to them to have brought religion to a lower ebb than it would have otherwise appeared. No wonder they were alarmed. No wonder they lifted up their voices like a trumpet. There was "a cause" before their eyes. They had seen those better days, and felt that if God did not soon appear and revive his work, all would be lost.

Among the causes which led to this lax and downward tendency of the churches, was the introduction of the so-called "*Half-way Covenant.*" It crept in gradually at first, but erelong spread widely over New England. It was intended to open the door for parents who were not members of the churches, and who made no pretensions to personal piety, to bring their children for baptism. The substance of it was, a general confession of faith in the truth and inspiration of the Scriptures, and a promise to "*come up to the Lord's supper as soon as they should see their way clear*," which most of them never did. Hence the name, "Half-way Covenant." This system was introduced as early as 1662. The consequence was, that the membership of the churches in full communion rapidly decreased. Having got their children baptized, few of the parents came into full communion, and hardly any of the unmarried were found at the Lord's table.

To keep the churches full, the next departure from the Puritan organization was to hold up *the Lord's supper as a converting ordinance*, and thus to throw the door wide open for the entrance of the unconverted. The Rev. Solomon Stoddard of Northampton, with the best intentions no doubt, in a sermon published in 1707, maintained that "sanctification is not a necessary qualification for partaking of the Lord's supper, and that it is a converting ordinance." Dr. Increase Mather published an able reply to this sermon; but the principles of Mr. Stoddard were adopted by the church in Northampton, and soon in other parts of New England.

I have dwelt the longer on the period preceding the Great Awakening to show what formidable obstacles had accumulated in the way of a revival.

Nothing strange was the opposition which it had to encounter from the pulpit and the press; but strange indeed it would have been, if, in the progress of that remarkable revival, with such hostile antecedents, there had been nothing mixed with it to be regretted by its warmest friends and advocates.

It would be easy to fill more than one large volume with the narratives and records in various forms of that ever memorable revival in the American churches. It was almost as life from the dead, so deep was the spiritual apathy in which it found them. But my notice must be extremely brief, and indeed that is all which seems to be called for, since the progress of the work was so largely and faithfully chronicled at the time in Prince's History, Gillies' Historical Collections, Edwards' Thoughts on the Revival of Religion in New England, published by the American Tract Society, and "The Great Awakening," an octavo volume by the Rev. Joseph Tracy, of which a new edition has just been issued.

The more prominent agents whom the great Head of the church employed in carrying on that glorious work on this side of the Atlantic, were Mr. Edwards, Mr. Whitefield, Dr. Bellamy, the two Tennents, William and Gilbert, President Davies, Mr. Blair, and Mr. Parsons. Scores of other good ministers coöperated with them or labored successfully without them in their respective parishes, though some of the pastors doubted whereunto it would grow, and stood aloof.

Small space as I can spare for this revival, which arrested the deplorable backslidings of the churches,

I feel bound to magnify the grace of God by borrowing some brief extracts from the copious narratives to which I have just alluded.

As the first revival took place under the preaching of Mr. Edwards, and as he stood at the head of the most able defenders of that mighty work of the Spirit, and was one of the most judicious and successful laborers both at home and abroad, I shall first make condensed extracts from his "Narrative of the Revival in Northampton, in 1734," as a fair example of the character of the remarkable series which followed and spread so widely over the land.

"Just after my grandfather's death, it was a time of remarkable dulness in religion. Many of the youth were much addicted to night-walking, frequenting the tavern, and lewd practices. They would often spend the greater part of the night in frolics, without regard to any order in the families they belonged to; and indeed family government did too much fail in the town.

"But in two or three years after Mr. Stoddard's death, there began to be a sensible amendment. The young people by degrees left off their frolicking, and thenceforward there was a remarkable reformation among them. In the month of April, 1734, there happened a very sudden and awful death of a young man in the bloom of youth, and the sermon which was preached on that occasion very much affected many of the young. This was followed by the death of a young married woman. In the beginning of her illness she was greatly distressed about the salvation of her soul, but seemed to obtain satisfactory evidence of God's saving mercy before she died, and in a most earnest and moving manner counselled and warned others. This seemed much to affect many young persons, and increased the religious concern on people's minds.

"It was in the latter part of December that the Spirit of God began extraordinarily to act in and wonderfully to work among us. Very suddenly five or six persons, one after another, were to all appearance savingly converted, some of them in a very remarkable manner. Presently a great and earnest concern became universal in all parts of the town among persons of all ages. The noise among the dry bones waxed louder and louder. All the conversation in all companies was upon spiritual things, except so much as was necessary for ordinary secular business. Men seemed to follow their business more as a part of their duty than from any disposition to it. Religion was with all sorts the great concern. It was then a dreadful thing among us to lie out of Christ, in danger every day of dropping into hell. All would eagerly lay hold of opportunities for their souls, and very often met together in private houses for religious purposes. There was scarcely a person in town, young or old, that was left unconcerned about the great things of the eternal world.

"Those that had been disposed to think and speak lightly of religion, were now generally subject to great awakenings. The work of conversion was carried on in the most astonishing manner. Souls did, as it were, come by flocks to Jesus Christ.

"From day to day for many months might be seen

evident instances of sinners being brought out of darkness into marvellous light. It made such a glorious alteration in the town, that in the following spring and summer, 1735, the town seemed to be full of the presence of God. It was so in almost every house. Our public assemblies were then beautiful. The congregation was alive in God's service, and every hearer eager to drink in the words of the minister. The assembly were in general from time to time in tears, some weeping with sorrow and distress, others with joy and love; others with pity and concern for the souls of their neighbors. Our young people, when they met, were wont to talk of the dying love of Jesus Christ and the glorious way of salvation, the wonderful free and sovereign grace of God, and his glorious work in the conversion of souls. Those among us who had been formerly converted, were greatly enlivened with fresh and extraordinary incomes of the Spirit of God.

"This dispensation has also appeared very extraordinary in the numbers of those on whom we have reason to hope it has had a saving effect. We have about six hundred and twenty communicants, which include almost all our adult persons. I am far from pretending to determine how many have been the subjects of such mercy, but I hope that more than *three hundred* were brought home to Christ in this town in the space of half a year, and about the same number of males as females.* I hope that by far the greater part of persons in this town over sixteen years of age

* The population of the town was then about *eleven hundred.*

are such as have a saving knowledge of Jesus Christ; and so, by what I have heard, I suppose it is in some other places, particularly at Sunderland and South Hadley.

"This has also appeared a very extraordinary dispensation, in that the Spirit of God has so much extended not only his awakening but his regenerating influences, both to elderly persons and also to those that are very young. It has been a thing heretofore scarcely to be heard of, that any were converted past middle age. But now we have as much reason to think that many such have been changed, as that others have been in more early years.

"It has heretofore been looked upon as a strange thing, when any have seemed to be savingly wrought upon and remarkably changed in their childhood; but now I suppose that near *thirty* were, to appearance, between ten and fourteen years of age, two between nine and ten, and one of about four years.

"God has also seemed to have gone out of his usual way in the quickness of his work, and the swift progress his Spirit has made in his operations on the hearts of many. Many have been taken from a loose and careless way of living, and seized with strong convictions of their guilt and misery, and in a very little time 'all things have become new' with them. God's work has also appeared very extraordinary, in the degree of saving light and love and joy that many have experienced, and in the extent of it, being so swiftly propagated from town to town. In former times of the pouring out of the Spirit of God upon this town, though in some of them it was very remarkable, it reached no further.

"The work of God seemed to be at its greatest height here in March and April, at which time God's work in the conversion of souls was carried on in so wonderful a manner, that so far as I can judge, from what I have witnessed in the progress of this work, conversions have been at the rate at least of *four* persons in a day, or near *thirty* in a week, take one week with another, for five or six weeks together. When God so remarkably took the work into his own hands, there was as much done in a day or two as, in ordinary times, with all endeavors that men can use, and with such a blessing as men commonly have, in a year."

Then follow brief notices of the work in many other towns, as South Hadley, Sunderland, Deerfield, Hatfield, West Springfield, Westfield, Hadley, Northfield, and other places, marked by the same unmistakable evidences of the Divine presence, though with "diversities of operations, according to His pleasure who worketh all things according to the counsel of his own will." Among the places specially visited in Connecticut, were East Windsor, Coventry, Lebanon, Stratford, Durham, New Haven, Guilford, Mansfield, Tolland, Hebron, Bolton, Preston, and Woodbury.

And so far was that glorious work, which lasted several years, and was at its height about 1740, from being confined to New England, that it was equally powerful in many parts of New Jersey and Pennsylvania. New York too shared in the blessing, beyond which there was no *West* then, and the same Spirit wrought powerfully in some parts of the southern states, particularly in Delaware, Virginia, and South Carolina. To all human appearance, it was the salvation of the church from an irrecoverable departure from the faith once delivered to the saints. It was as if the Saviour had said to his desponding disciples, "Be not faithless, but believing, and ye shall see greater things than these."

We have already seen that the Rev. George Whitefield was one of the most zealous and successful preachers of that day. I cannot follow him through his marvellous mission, having the everlasting gospel to preach wherever he went. It would require a volume. I am happy that the American Tract Society have published his life, in a volume of five hundred pages. But it has seemed to me I could not do less, in justice to him and to "the grace of God which was in him," than to glance for a moment at what he was and what he did.

It is questionable whether any preacher since the days of the apostles has done so much, in a degenerate age, to rouse the churches, and "turn back their captivity" from dead formalism, latitudinarian indifference, and erroneous proclivities, and to bring them into the old paths in which their Puritan fathers walked, both on this side and beyond the sea. From the commencement of his extraordinary career, like a flaming seraph as it were, he passed from city to city, and from land to land, having the everlasting gospel to preach; attracting the gaze of thousands wherever he went, swaying uncounted multitudes by his fervid and matchless eloquence, and beyond all peradventure, bringing great numbers, on both sides of the ocean, to the foot of the cross.

Of Jonathan Edwards, his compeer, and much more in the depths of theological science, it may be said that, in his great sermon on Justification by Faith alone, he struck the key-note of the songs of new-born souls in that revival.

Restricted as my limits are, I must not omit to add a paragraph or two, from a letter of the Rev. Thomas Prince, Jr., touching that great awakening in Boston.

"Great numbers in this town were so happily concerned about their souls, as we had never seen any thing like it before. Our assemblies, both on lectures and Sabbaths, were surprisingly increased.

"After Mr. Whitefield left, the Rev. Gilbert Tennent came, and he seemed to have as deep an acquaintance with the experimental part of religion, as any I ever conversed with, and his preaching was as rousing and searching as I ever heard. He aimed directly at the hearts and consciences of his hearers. His aim was to lay open the delusions of sinners, and show them their numerous hypocritical shifts, and drive them out of every deceitful refuge. From the terrible convictions he had passed through in his own soul, he had such a lively view of the divine Majesty, and of the strictness, spirituality, extent, and justice of his law, that the terrors of God seemed to rise fresh in his mind, when he displayed and brandished them in the eyes of unreconciled sinners.

"I do not recollect any crying out, or falling down, or fainting, either under Mr. Whitefield's or

Mr. Tennent's preaching; and though terrible preaching may strongly work on the animal passions, and frighten the hearers, rouse the soul, and prepare the way for terrible convictions, yet those mere animal terrors are quite different things from such convictions as were wrought in many hundreds by Mr. Tennent's searching ministry; and such was the case of those many scores, in several of the congregations as well as mine, who came to me and others for direction under them. It was such a time as we never knew. Mr. Cooper was wont to say, that more came to him in one week, in deep concern about their souls, than in the whole twenty-four years of his preceding ministry. He had about *six hundred* different persons visit him in three months' time; and Mr. Webb informs me he has had, in the same space, above a *thousand*. Sometimes rising of sixty bills were put up at once, in public, by the awakened; and their cases represented were, a blind mind, a vile and hard heart; some under great temptations, some in concern for their souls; some in great distress of mind for fear of being unconverted, others for fear they had been all along building on a righteousness of their own; some for a long time, even for several months, under these convictions; some fearing lest the Holy Spirit should withdraw; others having quenched his operations, were in great distress lest he should leave them for ever.

"Within six months, to the end of January, 1741, there were scores joined to our communicants, the greater part of whom gave a particular account of the work of the Spirit of God on their souls and effectual calling, as is described in the Westminster Assembly's Shorter Catechism. Mr. Webb, senior pastor of the New North, informs me that of admissions to full communion of those hopefully wrought upon in this day of grace, about one hundred and sixty joined his church, of which one hundred and two joined from January, 1741, to 1742, and many more give good evidence of grace. In this year, 1741, the very face of the town seemed to be strangely altered. Some who had not been here since the fall before, have told me of their great surprise at the change in the general look and carriage of the people, as soon as they landed. One of our worthy gentlemen informed me that whereas, when he used with others on Saturday evening to visit the taverns in order to clear them of their town inhabitants, they were wont to find many there, and meet with much trouble to get them away, he now found them empty of all but lodgers. Thus successfully did the divine work go on in town, without any lisp, as I remember, of a separation, either in this town or province, for about a year and a half after Mr. Whitefield left us."

I have exceedingly interesting accounts before me of nearly simultaneous revivals in Natick, Wrentham, Bridgewater, Plymouth, Sutton, Taunton, Middleborough, Halifax, Reading, Gloucester, Northampton in 1740, Raynham, Rochester, Cambridge, Plympton, and other places in Massachusetts; Westerley and Charlestown, in Rhode Island; Portsmouth and New Castle, in New Hampshire; Enfield, and other towns already mentioned by Mr. Edwards, in Connecticut; Newark, Elizabethtown, and several other places in

New Jersey; Philadelphia, New Providence, Nottingham, White Clay Creek, and Neshaminy, in Pennsylvania. The revival also extended to Virginia, and was quite powerful in some of the counties of that ancient commonwealth.

The labors of Rev. Mr. Frelinghuysen, who came over from Holland in 1720, were greatly blessed in New Jersey, especially among the Reformed Dutch churches.

The Rev. Jonathan Dickinson of Elizabethtown, New Jersey, speaking of Elizabethtown and Newark, says, August 23, 1743, "In these towns religion was in a low state, and there was but little of the power of godliness among us till some time in August, 1739, when there was a remarkable revival in Newark. It was chiefly among the young people till the following March, when the whole town was brought under a common concern about their eternal interests; and there is good reason to conclude that a considerable number experienced a saving change. The summer following this awakening was sensibly abated, till in February, 1741, they were again visited by the special effusions of the Holy Spirit, when a plain familiar sermon was set home with power. Many were brought to see and feel that till then they had no more than a name to live, and there seemed to be but very few in the whole congregation who were not moved more or less, though mostly among the rising generation. There is good reason to believe that there were now a greater number brought to Christ than in the former gracious visitation."

Mr. Dickinson goes on to say that about the same

time there was a powerful revival in Elizabethtown. "Under the preaching of the word, there was a sudden and deep impression on the congregation. There was no crying out or falling down, as elsewhere happened, but tears and sobbing in almost all parts of the assembly. There appeared such tokens of a solemn and deep concern as I never saw before in any congregation. All our opportunities for public worship were carefully attended. Numbers were almost daily repairing to me for direction and assistance in their eternal concerns."

In another letter written by Mr. Dickinson about that time, he says, "I have still the comfortable news to inform you of, that there is yet a great revival of religion in these parts. I have had more young people address me for direction in their spiritual concerns in three months, than in thirty years before.

"Though so many were brought under conviction at once, we had very little appearance among us of those irregular heats which are so loudly complained of in other parts of the land. This work was substantially the same in all the subjects of it. Though some were more distressed, and for a longer time than others, none obtained satisfying discoveries of safety in Christ till they were first brought to despair of help from themselves or any of their own refuges.

"It is remarkable, that as this work began among us in a time of the greatest health and prosperity, so it began sensibly to wear off in a time of the greatest mortality that had ever been known in the town, which makes it appear more evidently to be the work of God himself. If we may judge the tree by the fruits which we have now had so long a time to observe—three years or more—we have reason to suppose that about sixty have received a saving change in this congregation."

It was estimated that, at that time, the population of all the colonies was about 2,000,000; and it was believed that the number of converts amounted to not less than *fifty thousand*. If so, they bore as great a proportion to the whole number of inhabitants, and would as much change the relative proportion of the religious and irreligious, as the conversion of *six hundred thousand* would now. How many were hopefully born again, during the same revival in England, Scotland, and Wales, I have no means of ascertaining. But it admits not of a doubt, that a great multitude were "turned to the Lord." It was a mighty and glorious work of the Holy Spirit, both here and there, such as had not been witnessed for ages.

In looking back, it is exceedingly interesting to find a revival of the cardinal doctrines of the Reformation, in the preaching of all the distinguished ministers under whom the work was carried on. However they might differ on some points, they "saw eye to eye," and "their testimony agreed together" in every thing that was essential for bringing sinners to repentance, and building up the churches in the most holy faith.

Enemies there were to the truth, opposers there were to the revival, scattered all over the land; ministers there were who stood aloof from it, but the preaching was evangelical. "The subjects chiefly insisted on, were the sin and apostasy of mankind in

Adam; the blindness of the natural man in the things of God; the enmity of the carnal mind; the evil of sin; the desert of it, and the utter inability of the fallen creature to relieve itself; the sovereignty of God; the way of redemption by Christ; justification through his imputed righteousness received by faith; this faith the gift of God, and a living principle that worketh by love; the nature and necessity of regeneration, and sanctification by the Holy Spirit; and that without holiness no man shall see the Lord."

"The principal means of the great revival," says the "Testimony" of a large number of pastors in eastern Massachusetts, printed and sent out to the churches in the summer of 1745, "were the more than ordinary preaching of the more important doctrines of Scripture: as these, namely, The all-seeing eye, purity, justice, truth, power, majesty, and sovereignty of God; the spirituality, holiness, extent, and strictness of his law; our original sin, guilt, depravity, and corruption by the fall, including a miserable ignorance of God and enmity against him; our impotency and aversion to turn to him, the necessity that his law should be fulfilled, his justice satisfied, the honor of his holiness, authority, and truth, maintained in his conduct towards us; our utter impotence to help ourselves, and our continual hazard of being sent into endless misery; the astonishing displays of the absolute wisdom and grace of God, in contriving and providing for our redemption; the divinity, mediation, perfect holiness, obedience, sacrifice, merits, satisfaction, purchase, and grace of Christ; the nature and necessity of regeneration to the holy image of God by the supernatural operation of the divine Spirit, with the various parts of his office in enlightening our minds, awakening our consciences, and wounding, breaking, humbling, subduing, and changing our hearts. Also the nature of gospel obedience and holiness, and their necessity, not as matter of justification, but as the fruit and evidence of justifying faith, and to glorify God and enjoy him, the principal end both of our creation and redemption; and lastly, the sovereignty of the grace of God in this whole transaction, from its original purpose to its consummation in glory."

I am next constrained, in passing, to glance at those "bodily exercises" which profit little, and which in some places disturbed the regular order of worship, both in public and private. It were to be wished, that in a revival there should be no excitement beyond what the truth, faithfully addressed to the understanding, and applied to the heart and the conscience, is calculated to produce. But the time had not then come. There were nervous contortions, fainting, shrieking, and other disturbances, which sometimes quite drowned the voice of the preacher; which were looked upon by many as the genuine operations of the Holy Spirit, and of course encouraged, rather than repressed.

Mr. Whitefield, in the early part of his rousing ministry, undoubtedly rejoiced to witness these surgings and outcries in the vast multitudes under his preaching. Long experience and observation, however, very much modified his early impressions, if they did not convince him that shrieks and convulsions were no certain proofs of genuine conviction. Some other popular preachers evidently encouraged these outbreaks, under the persuasion that they were excited by the mighty power of God. Even Edwards, in his early experience in revivals, seems not very decidedly to have discountenanced them; but observing how little they profited, how soon they passed away, as the morning cloud and the early dew, he "stood more and more in doubt of them," and used his influence to discourage them, as in his searching treatise on the Affections.

The leading ministers in Boston and many others were from the first afraid of them, as calculated rather to mar and bring the revival into discredit, than to promote and extend it; and wherever they were promptly checked, the revival went on quietly, with great solemnity, and produced more genuine and abundant fruit.

On the other hand, while some of the most zealous and successful preachers of the day relied too much upon such outward demonstrations, others went quite into the opposite extreme, and set themselves to discountenance the work and keep it out of their parishes, under the impression that if there was some good in it, it was vastly overbalanced by the fanaticism which it engendered and promoted. This opposition was a great damper upon the revival, and great evils and divisions grew out of the two extremes. As religion had sunk so low when this great awakening broke in upon the deep slumber of the churches, it is not strange that they fell into mistakes and extremes which many of the ministers afterwards saw and lamented. Notwithstanding these agitations upon the surface, the undercurrent was borne on by the Spirit of God, and watering the fields, produced abundant harvests.

But a check was coming in from an unexpected quarter, which, to a lamentable extent, arrested its progress. It was not the opposition of the enemies of the work. In spite of all they could do to arrest it, it might have gone on indefinitely. It was not an enemy but a friend who did it; and of this he deeply repented, when it was too late to repair the mischief.

In looking back upon the progress of the great awakening, up to 1742, it is evident that the excitements which attended it, and were but too much encouraged in many places, prepared the way for that outburst of fanaticism which Edwards and others, who had seen and rejoiced in the salvation of God, so deeply deplored.

From the strong persuasion that those bodily agitations, groans, and outcries which they had witnessed, were essential features and parts of the revival, it was but a step or two more to visions and revelations, when a leader should arise, of unquestioned piety, whose praise was in the churches. Such a leader was the Rev. James Davenport, a lineal descendant of the renowned John Davenport of New Haven and Boston, which circumstance no doubt added to his influence over many predisposed minds. He was settled at Southold, Long Island, and was a favorite of Whitefield. He had stood high in the opinion of the Tennents. Mr. Whitefield said he never knew one keep so "close a walk with God;" and Mr. Parsons of Lyme, another distinguished laborer in the work, said that not one minister whom he had seen was to be compared to Mr. Davenport for living near to God, and having his conversation always in heaven. When he had lost his balance, after performing great and successful labors, he, more than any other man, embodied in himself and promoted in others the extravagances into which the revival was running. In admiring the "spirit of the age," as it appeared in him, men of a fanatical turn admired their own spirit. Going foremost in the wrong direction, he was by many regarded as a model man and preacher, by a comparison with whom all others were to be judged.

It appears from the concurrent testimony of all parties, that his influence, so far as it was felt, brought the revival to a crisis. Commencing with his own church, he called those whom he esteemed regenerate, brother, and the others, neighbor; the latter of whom he soon forbade to come to the Lord's table. He next went from place to place denouncing churches that hesitated to receive him, claiming the right to demand of ministers the grounds of their Christian hope; and when they refused to answer, or their answers were unsatisfactory, he declared them to be unconverted, and warned the people against hearing them. When, on a certain occasion, four ministers called to see him and remonstrate against his career, he broke out and vehemently lectured them as unconverted men, blind guides, wolves in sheep's clothing, and the like; and wound up by offering a prayer, partly for their conversion, and partly against them. Thus he went on from place to place, demanding of ministers an account of their religious experience, and condemning all who refused to give it. In this fanatical mission, to which he nothing doubted God had called him, he became more and more excited in denouncing all who opposed him, encouraging visions and revelations among his deluded followers, dividing and breaking up churches, and bringing great reproach upon the revival by leading many unwarrantably to identify it with these deplorable proceedings.

The epidemic reached its crisis at New London, in the month of March, 1743, where he gave out a catalogue of religious books which must be brought together and burned, as unsafe in the hands of the people. They were accordingly carried to the wharf and burned by his followers, singing round the pile Hallelujah and glory to God, and declaring, that as the smoke of these books ascended up in their presence, so the smoke of the torment of such of their authors as died in the same belief, was now ascending in hell. Strange to tell, among those authors were Berridge, Flavel, Mather, Colman, and Sewall, not even sparing Parsons, one of the most fervid revivalists. This was the last and crowning act of fanaticism, so far at least as Davenport was concerned. From this time he disappears from the stage, till the summer of 1744. Charity believes that this burning zeal, spurning all restraint, then reached the crisis of absolute mental derangement. But, blessed be God, it was not to last; and when he came to himself, he the next year published, July 28, 1744, his humble recantations, from which, in justice to him, I make the following brief extracts :

"Although I do not question at all but there is great reason to bless God for a glorious and wonderful work of his power and grace, in the edification of his children, and the conviction and conversion of numbers in New England, in the neighboring governments, and several other parts, within a few years past, and believe that the Lord hath favored me, though most unworthy, in granting special assistance and success, the glory of all which be given to Jehovah, to whom the glory belongs; yet, after frequent meditation and desires that I might be enabled to apprehend things justly, I am fully convinced and persuaded that several appendages of this glorious work are no essential parts thereof, but of a different and contrary nature and tendency, which I have been instrumental in promoting by a misguided zeal; being, further, much influenced in the affair by the false spirit which prompted me to unjust apprehensions and conduct in several particulars, which have been great blemishes to the work of God, very grievous to some of God's children, no less ensnaring and corrupting to others of them, the sad means of many persons questioning the work of God, concluding and appearing against it, and of the hardening of multitudes in their sins, and an awful occasion of the enemy's blaspheming the right way of the Lord, and very offensive to that God before whom I would lie in the dust prostrate in deep humility and repentance, imploring pardon for the Mediator's sake, and thankfully accepting the token thereof.

"The articles which I specially refer to, and in the most public manner retract and warn others against, are these which follow:

"1. The method I used for a considerable time with respect to some ministers, in openly exposing such as I feared or thought unconverted, in public prayer or otherwise; herein making my private judgment, in which also I much suspect I was mistaken in several instances, the ground of public actions or conduct, offending against the laws both of justice and charity.

"2. By advising and urging to such separations from those ministers whom I treated as above, as I believe may justly be called rash, unwarrantable, and of sad and awful tendency and consequence; and here I would ask the forgiveness of those ministers whom I have injured.

"3. I confess I have been much led astray by following impulses or impressions as a rule of conduct, whether they came with or without a text of Scripture. I am persuaded this was a great means of corrupting my experiences in carrying me off from the word of God.

"4. I believe further that I have done much hurt to religion, by encouraging private persons to a magisterial or authoritative kind of method of exhorting, which is particularly observable in many such being much puffed up and falling into the snare of the devil, while many others are thus directly prejudiced against the work.

"And now may the holy and wise and good God be pleased to guard and secure me against such errors for the future, and stop the progress of those, whether ministers or people, who have been corrupted by my words or example; and Oh, may he grant withal, that such as by reason of the foresaid errors and misconduct have entertained unhappy prejudices against Christianity in general, or the late glorious work of God in particular, may by this account learn to distinguish the appendages from the substance or essence, that which is vile and odious from that which is precious, glorious, and divine, and thus be entirely and happily freed from all those prejudices referred to, and this in infinite mercy through Jesus Christ; and to these requests may all God's children, whether ministers or others, say, Amen."

That so pious and devoted a minister as Mr. Davenport was believed to be by his contemporaries who knew him best, and as he doubtless was, should be left to bring so much distrust and reproach upon the most glorious revival that the country had ever enjoyed, was a mystery which will not be fully disclosed till the judgment of the great day. But it is full of instruction and warning. The great Head of the church may have seen that such a lesson of human weakness at its best estate, should be put upon record as a warning to "the generations following."

The rapid sketch which I have given of that wonderful time of refreshing, almost a century and a quarter ago, would have been one-sided and incomplete if I had omitted these statements. It is due to those into whose hands this epitome may fall, that they should be put on their guard against such outbreaks of animal excitement and enthusiasm as have marred and cut short former revivals.

After making every abatement, the years of the "Great Awakening" were precious years of the right hand of the Most High. It left the churches of New England in a far sounder and better state than it found them. It effectually shut the door against admitting unregenerate persons to the Lord's supper as a converting ordinance, which Mr. Stoddard had unhappily opened in his own church, and by his writings in others. Reasoning out of the Scriptures, Mr. Edwards, in his "Terms of Communion," showed the practice to be wholly indefensible; and I am not aware that any evangelical church has favored it since. This was a great gain. Had the practice been continued, and become universal, it would have been more than a paralysis. The churches might have retained their names, but as true churches of Christ they would not have survived.

Another important gain was, that the revival, widely extended and powerful as it was, prepared the way for freeing the churches from the "Half-way Covenant." Though in some quarters it held its ground longer, it was very much circumscribed. We shall meet with some remains of it hereafter, but dying out.

Another immense gain to the cause of Christ was, that it greatly relieved the churches from the soporific influence of an unconverted ministry. It was admitted that there were unconverted pastors over some of the churches, and regeneration had come to be thought by many no essential qualification for the sacred office. It was held, that if preachers were men of blameless lives they were not to be rejected though they did not profess to have been born again. Some of this number were the subjects of the revival, and confessed that they had preached for years without knowing what experimental piety was. In this respect the revival prepared the way for a great change for the better. It is not claimed that there can be any *certain* protection against the intrusion of unconverted men into the ministry. The strictest examination for the cure of souls cannot shut them out, for God alone knows the heart; but that none save converted men are fit to enter the ministry, is now universally held by the evangelical churches of all denominations.

Moreover, the preaching in the orthodox churches has, ever since this great revival, been more spiritual and discriminating than it was when it began. The cardinal doctrines of universal and entire depravity, regeneration by the Holy Spirit, and justification by faith alone, with other kindred evangelical topics drawn from the word of God, held from that time forth a more prominent place in the ministrations of the pulpit, than they had done for ages before.

Hence, though all that could have been desired was not accomplished, the good seed was sown broadcast over the land; and though we shall find, in the next period, that many hostile influences checked its growth for nearly half a century, it was so far from being lost where it did not spring up at once, that it was to take root and grow and ripen into other harvests, with more wheat, fewer tares, and less chaff.

CHAPTER IV.

THE REVIVAL EPOCH ABOUT 1800.

PASSING from the glorious revival period, about the middle of the last century, under the preaching of Edwards, Whitefield, the two Tennents, Dr. Bellamy, and other apostolic laborers, we find the shadows of a long night settling down again upon the churches of this land. Like Israel of old, the most of them were in the wilderness about forty years, and only kept alive by supplies of the heavenly manna, and of the water from the Rock. From 1745, to near the close of the century, the Holy Spirit withheld in a great measure those copious refreshings, which had turned so many parched fields into gardens of the Lord, and made their fruit shake like Lebanon. At no time, indeed, during that period was it all dark, all barren. All along, here and there over the wide waste, some precious revivals broke out, "like streams in the desert," to keep alive the faith, and gladden the hearts of those who mourned over the desolations of Zion. Towards the close of the period, there were more of these than I had supposed, till I met with notices of several of unmistakable genuineness between 1770 and 1790 in New England and the Middle States including the new settlements of Western Pennsylvania, and with some further south, especially as recorded in Dr. Alexander's narrative of what he himself witnessed in Southern and Western Virginia, about 1790.* These were the harbingers of that bright rising of the Sun of righteousness, which I am now approaching in these revival sketches.

It had been a long hard winter, in which the current of spiritual life was all but frozen up, and it seemed almost as if the winding-sheet which was spread over the land would never be taken off. But at the same time, precious fruits of the great harvest which had been garnered remained. None of the churches, I believe, that had renounced the Half-way Covenant in the Great Awakening, brought it back again, though it still lingered in churches which that revival, if it reached them at all, left but half reformed. I found it in Fairfield, Connecticut, where I was first settled, in 1807. Some other churches in that county had not yet given it up. It was also found in some of the Presbyterian churches, and it prevailed extensively for some time longer in the eastern and central parts of Massachusetts. If it still darkens the half-open door of any evangelical church, I do not know where it is. Other vantage ground was gained in the "Great Awakening," from which the churches did not slide back.

But although, when a brighter day dawned near the close of the century, it was not necessary to "lay again the foundation of repentance from dead works, and of faith towards God," as in the preceding reformation, the building did not go up. Dark days intervened, during which, instead of making any

* See the Life of Dr. Archibald Alexander, by Dr. James W. Alexander, chs. 2, 3, 4.

aggressive inroads upon the kingdom of darkness, the churches lost ground. The fathers and mothers who had been converted under Edwards and the other rousing preachers of his day, were passing off from the stage, and but few of the younger generation were coming on to fill their places. Many orthodox churches might be named, into which for long years no young persons, or next to none, were received.

Most of the ministers, indeed, where the great revivals in the middle of the century had been enjoyed, were sound in the faith, and preached the distinguishing doctrines of the gospel. In obedience to the word of the Lord, they kept on prophesying over the dry bones; but for the most part were constrained to ask, "Who hath believed our report? and to whom is the arm of the Lord revealed?" While they did not cease to pray, "O Lord, revive thy work in the midst of the years, in wrath remember mercy," they hardly dared to hope for so great a blessing. Such was the state of things till near the close of the century.

We are next to inquire, what were the causes of the alarming dearth and declension just mentioned, before we hail the dawn of a brighter day. In looking back upon that period, some of these causes are too obvious to be mistaken.

First came what is familiarly called, the "Old French war." While we slept, the enemy, ever awake and aggressive, had been skilfully drawing a line of circumvallation quite round the English colonies, to hem us in, by building a chain of forts from Louisburg and Quebec on the north, by the way of Detroit and St. Louis, down to the mouth of the Mississippi. And now it was, that France, aided by the warlike tribes of Indians whom she could enlist in the bloody enterprise, sought to bring all North America under the yoke of Rome. God interposed, and the attempt signally failed. But the danger, while it lasted, created universal alarm; and the necessary defence of the frontiers demanded all the force that could be raised, and absorbed the anxious minds of the whole population. In this state of things, it would have been strange indeed if the churches had been visited by revivals—if the cause of Christ had not declined, as it did.

Scarcely was that danger over, when serious difficulties broke out between the colonists and the mother country, and continued to increase till they issued in the war of the Revolution. Here, again, it would have been very remarkable if, in the midst of all these agitations of the then infant settlements, revivals had sprung up. They did not. Humanly speaking, there was no room for them. And we know that God works by means, in favorable seasons, and orders events for building up his churches, as well as for accomplishing his other great purposes.

When the war of Independence broke out, in 1775, the state of the country was, if possible, still more unfavorable to the progress of true religion. It was a struggle for colonial emancipation, with one of the most powerful nations of the world, which lasted seven years, during which the shifting and sometimes the almost despairing fortunes of the bloody contest swallowed up every other interest; so that instead of revival rejoicings, were heard the confused noise of the battle of the warriors, "the thunder of the captains, and the shouting." In such a state of things, when the American armies were wading through frost and blood to conquer national independence, and the anxious hopes and fears of the whole people were alternately swallowed up in the mighty struggle, how could religion prosper? The Spirit of God is a spirit of peace, and not of war. I know that God is able to build up his churches in the midst of wars and fightings, just as he is able to awaken and convert hardened sinners under the most unfavorable circumstances; but this is not his manner. To show that he will have mercy on whom he will have mercy, and that he can carry on his work in spite of the most hostile influences, he may work wonders. But how few revivals have ever been witnessed in the midst of a desolating war. If any, they have been extraordinary interpositions of divine sovereignty. Some may have occurred during the seven years' war; but if any, I do not know where to find the record. Certain I am, that that bloody contest was directly opposed, as all wars are, to the spiritual growth of the churches. It left them much weaker than it found them.

When it closed, and the armies were disbanded, many of the officers and soldiers brought home with them the dissipated and demoralizing habits of the camp, such as profaneness, intemperance, and Sabbath-breaking—influences as hostile to revivals as the war itself. And scarcely less so was the unsettled state of affairs throughout the country, till the new government was organized and established by the adoption of the Federal Constitution. The minds of the people were too much agitated and engrossed by conflicting political interests, to have much room for more than the ordinary routine of religious observances. Revivals were hardly expected anywhere during those years of civil agitation, and they were not enjoyed. Zion languished. While the form of godliness remained in the churches, there was but little of the power.

In the mean time, as might have been expected, *French Infidelity*, which our allies brought over with them, was sowed broadcast among our own officers and soldiers. Aided by Paine's "Age of Reason," Voltaire's assaults upon Christianity, Volney's Ruins, and other blasphemous publications, it spread rapidly, especially among the upper classes. The Illuminati, so called, of France and Germany, who were secretly associated for the overthrow of all existing religious institutions, had their affiliated societies in this country, enrolling not a few men of high social and political standing and influence. It became fashionable, in high places and low places, flippantly to prate against the Bible, and sneer at things sacred and divine. Instead of the Scriptures, French philosophy claimed to be the rule of faith and life, and ignoring all the "rights of God," was to usher in the glorious millennium of the "rights of man."

Towards the close of that period, in 1789, broke out the French Revolution, the bloodiest of all revolutions, which was not only to sweep away the throne, and level all the civil distinctions of society, but to destroy the priesthood, root and branch, abolish the Sabbath, and establish the reign of *liberty and equality* on the ruins. Though the unheard of atrocities of that *reign of terror* sent a thrill of horror through the whole civilized world, so dear was our new-born liberty to us, that the very name had a charm in it, which at first excited our fraternal sympathies, notwithstanding our abhorrence of the fiendish atrocities by which it had been sought to be acquired.

How hostile all this was to the interests of pure and undefiled religion it is needless to say; and when from this point we look back to the reaction which followed the Great Awakening, and then come down through the revolutionary war to the return of peace, which brought with it the moral camp-distemper that wars always generate, and glance at the agitations of the public mind which preceded the adoption of the Federal constitution, who can wonder that there were so few revivals, or rather, not wonder that there were any during all that upheaving tempestuous period. It seemed as if the floods of ungodliness must swallow up the church. The few survivors who remembered the days of old, when multitudes were gathered in the times of refreshing from the presence of the Lord, were ready to ask, Are the mercies of God clean gone for ever? Will he be favorable no more?

But just then when it seemed to grow darker and darker, the night was far spent, and the day was at hand. A few years before the close of the century the light of a new revival epoch began to dawn. Here and there a church rose and shook herself from the dust. Sinners were awakened, and began to inquire what they must do to be saved. So that when the old century was departing, and the new century came in, many a field that had long been languishing began to rejoice under the reviving influence. Christ by his Spirit came down, here and there, like rain upon the mown grass, and like showers that water the earth.

It is of the commencement, and progress, and fruits of that remarkable revival epoch, that I am now to speak, reserving for subsequent pages a notice of the remarkable work which God was effecting *simultaneously* in the mother country.

And here ample materials are at hand for a volume, in the narratives drawn up at the time by pastors of the churches, and published in the Connecticut Evangelical Magazine and other religious annals. Of these I shall avail myself as far as my design and limits will admit.

And here let me say, it is with no ordinary solicitude that I approach this remarkable revival epoch. The theme is high; I cannot attain unto it. O Lord, help my infirmities. It is a gloriously illuminated chapter in the History of Redemption. It were easy to collect materials more than enough. But to condense and arrange them in the best manner; to show in what respects this revival epoch differed from those in the preceding centuries, at which I have already glanced; to gather up its precious fruits, and to show its bearing upon the further advancement of the Redeemer's kingdom, is a task which, so far as I know, has not yet been accomplished by any one, and to which I feel myself very unequal. Nevertheless, the plan which I have marked out for chronicling the triumphs of the cross in these sketches, does not allow me to shrink from the attempt.

When this fresh outpouring of the Spirit began, I was just coming upon the stage, and God had cast my lot in that part of the vineyard where the gospel had been faithfully preached by ministers who were anxiously waiting for the Saviour's return. I knew them, and often heard them preach, before and during the revivals. Now, after more than fifty years, I have a distinct recollection of their countenances, their tones of voice, their earnest and solemn appeals, their going out and coming in among the people. They had diversities of natural gifts and acquired qualifications, but the same Spirit. There was no such massive pillar among them as Jonathan Edwards, to lean upon. It was not needed. There was no Whitefield to pass from town to town, from state to state, gathering his thousands in the open air, and swaying them by his soul and tongue of fire, as the trees of a forest are bowed and shaken by mighty winds. There was no voice like his to fill the open firmament of heaven with the thunderings of Sinai, and the melting tones of Calvary. But there were Bellamys to stand upon the heights and make the curses of the law reverberate from Ebal to Gerizim, and from Gerizim to Ebal. As in the primitive age, there were sons of thunder, and sons of consolation among them. There was the younger Edwards, a great master of logic, and mighty in the Scriptures. There was Griffin having just buckled on the harness, a young Melancthon, in the ardor of his first love for Christ, majestic in stature, with a voice of extraordinary flexibility and power, combining some of the finest tones of the organ with the softest and tenderest notes of the flute. I thought then, and think now, that I never heard such a voice in the pulpit. He was a great preacher in the best sense of the term, and his labors, as we shall see, were abundantly blessed in winning souls to Christ. And then there was Hallock, quite his counterpart in some respects, bred a farmer in one of the small hill towns of Massachusetts; untrained in the higher schools; meek as the meekest disciple, always readier to say, Brother, go up higher, than to go himself; but a man of good natural talents, shrewd common-sense, deep humble piety, and an irrepressible longing after souls in the bowels of Jesus Christ. He came late into the ministry, and without the slightest pretension to popular address or rhetoric, became one of the most honored, beloved, and useful ministers of his day. No one was more acceptable in that revival than he.

Nor were these more worthy or devoted than many others. There were Robbins and Backus and Mills and Gillett and Perkins and Strong and Porter and Hooker and Miller and Williams and Cooley and Hawley and Cowles, of like precious faith, whose lips the Lord touched as with live coals from off the altar, whose parishes were contiguous, and whose labors were abundantly blessed. Most of them belonged to the same district association. They held their monthly meetings for mutual improvement and prayer, in which they wrestled together and prevailed. I have named them, not as more worthy to be had in everlasting remembrance than Dwight, Hyde, Catlin, Stillman, Baldwin, Manning, Mason, Livingston, Furman, Marshall, and many others of their brethren in other parts of the vineyard that were copiously watered by the same showers, but because I knew and heard them, and witnessed the effects of their labors.

Their preaching was not in man's wisdom, but in demonstration of the Spirit, and with power. It was eminently *scriptural.* The ministers of that day read and studied the Bible more than all other books. They had received it from their Master as their only commission, and in virtue of it, as ambassadors for Christ, they besought sinners in his stead to be reconciled to God. It was surprising to notice with what facility they would quote chapter and verse from all parts of both Testaments, without turning over a single leaf. Indeed, it sometimes seemed to me as if they knew all the Bible by heart; and it is no disparagement to say, that they did know much more of it than most preachers do now. They had a great deal more of it in their sermons. Almost all their illustrations, as well as their proofs, were drawn from its rich and inexhaustible treasures. "Thus saith the Lord," was enough for them, let who would criticize, cavil, or blaspheme. They did not shun, either from fear or favor, to declare all the counsel of God, as they understood it, whether men would hear, or whether they would forbear. They did not wreathe the sword around with flowers, but left the two edges bare and sharp, to cut where they would—the deeper the better; and they applied no emollients to heal the hurt slightly.

The fathers of that day, of whom I am speaking, whatever else any of them may have lacked, were Gamaliels in the law and the prophets. They made no appeals to the passions, and there were no outcries and convulsions under their preaching, as there had been in the "Great Awakening."

The word of God, as our minister used it, was quick and powerful, sharper than any two-edged sword, and piercing even to the dividing asunder of the joints and the marrow, and discerning the thoughts and intents of the heart. Oh how we smarted under it. I remember it well in my own case, and how my heart rebelled against some of the doctrines which my Bible and my conscience told me were true, till, as I hope, I was brought to bow and submit at the foot of the cross. And as it was with me, so it was with multitudes of others. We complained of some of Paul's hard sayings, and wondered why our ministers dwelt so much upon them. We wanted to get to heaven in some easier way. But instead of abating one jot or tittle to relieve us, they pressed harder and harder, driving us from one refuge to another, till there was no hiding-place left. The law, which we had broken times without number, we were made to feel was just; its fiery penalty hung over our heads, and we must submit or die. Under such preaching it was hard to get hopes; but when embraced, they were more to be relied upon, than if they had been gained in some easier way.

Our spiritual guides and teachers never said to us, when under awakening, "Don't be discouraged; wait God's time, and he will deliver you." No, no;

but, "How long will you hold out in your rebellion against God?" They never asked us while in this state, "Don't you feel better?" but, "Why don't you submit to God, and cast yourselves upon his mercy, embracing the Lord Jesus Christ by faith, who came down from heaven on purpose to save the lost. Turn ye, turn ye; why will ye die?"

I do not say that this law work, as it has been appropriately called, was alike marked and pungent in all cases. It was not. He who worketh all things according to the counsel of his own will, opened some hearts, as he seems to have opened that of Lydia, at once to receive the truth in the love of it. But I am quite sure, that in most cases the conversions in that revival were preceded by sharp conviction of sin and of deserved punishment. It was eminently a *law* revival, issuing in the more abundant and abiding consolations of the gospel. Those loved most, who felt that they had been forgiven most.

As our pastors were careful not to encourage us that we had passed from death unto life without good scripture evidence of the change, they were very strict in their examinations for church-membership. If they thought any of the candidates did not give satisfactory evidence of having been converted, they did not hesitate to tell them so. In this way, not a few were kept back, and solemnly exhorted to begin anew, and never rest satisfied till they could obtain better evidence.

That some real converts may, under this scrutiny, have been thrown into needless alarm and distress, and kept out of the church too long, is not improbable; but others afterwards thanked their pastors, with tears in their eyes, for having dealt with them so faithfully, saying, We now see that we were building on a false foundation; and if you had encouraged us, we should in all likelihood have settled down upon it and lost our souls. On which side it is safest to err, in dealing with new-born hopes, who can doubt? If a person has been truly converted, no degree of strictness in his examination, though it should shake his hope for the time, and give him needless distress, can endanger his salvation. Born of God, his seed will remain in him, and a prayerful revision of the ground of his hope may help in the end to strengthen and establish it. Whereas, on the contrary, too much encouragement may induce one who is unconverted to settle down upon a false hope and perish, who, to human view, might have been saved by the faithful dealing of his spiritual teacher. It is not supposable that the former, when he gets to heaven, will be sorry that his pastor was so strict in examining the foundation of his hope, though it may have given him pain; but it is more than probable, that the latter may reproach his minister at the bar of God for healing the hurt slightly.

In the revival of which I am now speaking, the pastors called in no evangelists without charge to aid them. They did all the preaching themselves, helping one another as occasion required. This they did by occasional exchanges, and oftener at weekly lectures. They also sometimes went round from parish to parish, two and two by appointment. These visits by brethren who came with hearts warmed in revivals at home, were very much blessed. I remember them during the revival in B——, where I was brought up. One of the ministers preached at one service, and the other followed with an address. In the next, the order was reversed; and this was the usual way at those meetings. Besides the two regular services on the Sabbath, there were prayer-meetings in the evening, (conferences they were then called,) which the pastors generally attended, aided by some of the lay brethren. One week-day lecture was preached, sometimes two, and evening meetings were held at the school-houses, more or less, in the out districts of the congregation. Taken altogether, I think there were not so many extra meetings as are common now in powerful revivals. Perhaps there were not enough. Though I am not sure. Christians may be so much abroad as to leave but little time for home duties in the family and the closet. Is not this sometimes the case? I think it is. It is easier to sit and listen and enjoy the social meeting, than to keep the heart in a humble and devout frame for secret prayer; and I am afraid too many Christians are ready to excuse themselves for want of punctuality in the latter, by thinking that they make it up and more by going to all the meetings. And this leads me to ask, Is there not more time spent in secret wrestling with the Angel of the covenant in the earlier stages of revivals, than in the later? and if so, may not this neglect be one principal reason why many of these precious seasons are of such short continuance?

The ministers of that day held no *four-days'*, or other protracted meetings. They depended much on the preaching of the word upon the Sabbath, for the awakening of sinners; and I believe this divinely appointed means was more owned and blessed than perhaps all the auxiliary services put together, important and helpful as they undoubtedly were.

Those pastors had no seats set apart for the awakened, nor did they call upon any who wished for special prayer to signify it by rising in the meetings. Much as they rejoiced when many were turned to the Lord, they never, I believe, urged young converts to come forward and take part, till they had had some time to examine the foundation of their hopes; thinking it safer than the haste and urgency which are sometimes employed. There is doubtless such a thing as keeping back converts so long, that through diffidence they may be unwilling to pray and exhort when their assistance in the prayer-meetings would be very acceptable and edifying. This, as well as the opposite extreme, should be guarded against. Pastors want all the good lay help they can get, and every genuine revival brings some men into the church who may be trained up for these auxiliary services.

Before presenting from laborers in these revivals more minute and detailed testimonies to their character and results, I am sure I shall gratify many by drawing from the eloquent public discourses of Dr. Edward D. Griffin, an expression of his views of this great work of God, the influence of which so distinctly characterized the whole of his brilliant career, and in which he was himself one of the earliest converts.

Graduating at Yale college in 1790, at the age of twenty, the next year he was taken sick, brought to reflection, and led to consecrate himself to Christ and the ministry. He studied theology with the younger President Edwards, was licensed, and in 1792 found himself at his father's house in East Haddam, Connecticut, "the only professor of religion in a family of ten." He labored for their salvation; attended a prayer-meeting in the neighborhood; and in November, while one of his sisters "was weeping in anguish of spirit," he was making his appeals to those around him. "That," said he, "was the beginning of American revivals so far as they fell under my personal observation, and from that moment I know they have never ceased." In January he commenced preaching in New Salem, a neighboring village, where his labors were blessed in "a revival of great power, and a church was gathered where there had not been one for more than forty years," and there and in the vicinity "about one hundred were hopefully added to the Lord." Speaking of this period, he says, "I had an opportunity to see the whole field of death *before a bone began to move.* And no one who comes upon the stage forty years afterwards, can have any idea of the state of things at that time."*

* Dr. Griffin, in a note at a later period, states that long before the death of Whitefield in 1770, extensive revivals in America had ceased; and that revivals had been reported to him in Stockbridge and other parts of Berkshire county in 1772, in a part of Lyme about 1780, and in several towns in Litchfield county about 1783. Notices have also appeared of revivals in Princeton college, under Dr. Witherspoon, in 1771, 1772; in connection with the labors of Dr. McWhorter in New-

In closing his sermon preached before the American Board for Foreign Missions, at Middletown, Connecticut, in 1826, he thus celebrates the grace of God in this revival epoch:

"For many years the Christian world had been sunk in a profound slumber in regard to the duty of giving the gospel to the heathen; but for the last four and thirty years they have been waking up. He who has engraven Zion on the palms of his hands—who never wants means to fulfil his promises—has sent his heavenly influence to rouse the Christian world. He beheld the desolations of Zion, and has come to rebuild her ruined walls. He heard the groans of his people as, with harps on the willows, they were weeping 'by the rivers of Babylon,' and has come to bring them again 'to Zion with songs and everlasting joy upon their heads.' Eternal thanks to God for what our eyes have seen and our ears have heard for the last four and thirty years. Eternal

ark, 1772; of Dr. McMillan in Western Pennsylvania, 1781–1794; of Rev. Mr. Caldwell in Elizabethtown in 1772, and another in the same town in 1784; Dr. Burton in Thetford, Vermont, and Rev. Dr. Shepard, Brentwood, New Hampshire, in 1781; Dr. Wood in Boscawen, New Hampshire, 1782; Rev. Mr. Hallock in West Simsbury, 1783; Dr. Smalley, Berlin, Conn., Dr. Emmons in Franklin, and Rev. Mr. Sanford, Medway, Mass., in 1784; Rev. Mr. Waddel and Rev. Mr. Marshall in various parts of Georgia, 1784–1788; Dr. Buell in East Hampton, Long Island, 1785; Rev. Dr. Baldwin, Boston, and Rev. Moses Hallock, Plainfield, Massachusetts, 1790; and there were doubtless others, notwithstanding the pervading spiritual dearth. The great and general work of which Dr. Griffin speaks was begun in Virginia earlier than 1792, as already intimated and as appears in subsequent pages.

thanks to God for the increasing wonders which are rapidly opening on the world. And Oh—can we restrain the bursting emotion?—for ever blessed be his great and glorious name for what we have begun to see in our own land. It is more than thirty years since the Christians in Great Britain awoke, and they have been holding on their way with increasing majesty and glory, until that little island bestows annually more than a million of dollars upon strangers. It is fourteen years since New England broke her slumbers, and now the mass of her population seems drenched in the missionary spirit. I saw the day cover the plains of Europe. I saw the westward-travelling light spread itself over these eastern states. Nine years ago I saw the rays of the morning tip our Presbyterian horizon. I saw the dawn blush deeper and deeper. I knew it would not all return again to midnight. I knew the sun would rise. At length I saw his golden limb above the eastern woods, and from the course of day I knew that soon the heavenly flood would cover all the plains to Arkansas and the Pacific. Already the influence of heaven has dropt upon the wilderness, and the yell of the warwhoop is changed to notes of praise. We must not stop till every Indian tongue has joined the general song. We must not stop till our influence has cheered the whole extent of South America. And then we must go forth to the islands, and hold on our way till we meet our brethren in other fields, and unite with them in completing the harvest of the world.

"We owe the sincerest gratitude to God for giving us our existence in such a day as this. Many prophets and kings desired to see this day, and saw it not. One spirit has seized the Christian world to send the gospel, with a great company of its publishers, to all the nations of the earth. Missionary and Bible societies, those stupendous monuments of Christian charity, have risen so rapidly and in so great numbers throughout Europe and America, that in contemplating them we are 'like them that dream.' These societies have already accomplished wonders, and are constantly stretching forward to future achievements beyond the reach of imagination. On the burning sands of Africa, where Christian feet never before trod, there is the holy band of missionaries, struggling amid dangers and deaths, to lead the sable tribes of Ethiopia to stretch forth their hands to God. On the plains of Hindostan, a 'consecrated host' are translating the Scriptures into more than thirty different languages, spoken by a population greater than that of all Europe. On the borders of China they have produced a version which will give the oracles of God to one quarter of the population of the globe. In the northern islands a nation is born in a day. From the hill of Zion, from the top of Calvary, they are freighting every caravan of pilgrims with Bibles for all the countries of the east. Certainly the angel has begun his flight through the midst of heaven, 'having the everlasting gospel to preach to every nation, and kindred, and tongue, and people.'"

In his sermon, September, 1828, at the dedication of the new chapel at Williams college, of which he was then president, Dr. Griffin gives a fuller expression to his views of the influence of these revivals:

"In turning to the religious history of the college and its prospective connection with the Redeemer's kingdom, a subject opens upon us of unbounded interest.

"The year 1792, it has often been said, ushered a new era into the world. In that year the first blood was drawn in that mighty struggle which for more than twenty years convulsed Europe, and began the predicted destruction of the apocalyptic beast. In that year the first of those institutions which modern charity has planned, and which now cover the whole face of the Protestant world, arose in England.* And in that year commenced that series of revivals in America, which has never been interrupted, night or day, and which never will be until the earth is full of the glory of the Lord as the waters cover the sea. In pondering upon the destinies of this college in illumined moments—in moments of intense interest—it has been no indifferent thought, that it arose into being at that punctum of time; that it opened upon the world when those other institutions began to open which are full of salvation—when the redemption of Africa commenced at Sierra Leone and St. Domingo—when that moral change began which has swept from so large a part of New England its looseness of doctrine and laxity of discipline, and awakened an evangelical pulse in every vein of the American church.

* The Baptist Missionary Society, formed at Kettering by Andrew Fuller and others.

"It was my happiness to be early carried by the providence of God to Litchfield county, Conn., and to be fixed in that scene where the heavenly influence was to send out its stronger radiations to different parts of the country; where thrice twenty congregations, in contiguous counties, were laid down in one field of divine wonders. There it was my privilege to be most intimately associated with such men as Mills and Gillett and Hallock—names which will be ever dear to the church on earth, and some of which are now familiar in heaven. Their voices, which I often heard in the silent groves, and in the sacred assemblies which followed, and in the many, many meetings from town to town, have identified them in my mind with all those precious revivals which opened the dawn of a new day upon our country.

"During the first seven years of the existence of this college—in which *ninety-three* graduated in six classes—there were but *five* professors of religion in the institution, exclusive of two who, seven months before the close of that period, were brought into the church by the revivals in Litchfield county. In three of those six classes there was not a single professor. From the commencement in 1798 till February, 1800, there was but *one* professor of religion in college.

"The spring of 1806 was made memorable by the admission of those two distinguished youth, GORDON HALL and SAMUEL J. MILLS. Mills was the son of my early friend the Rev. Samuel J. Mills of Torringford, was known to me from a child, and received his permanent impressions in one of the most glorious revivals I have ever seen, in 1798, though he did not obtain relief till the month of November, 1801. He at once devoted himself to the cause of missions, and with a heart glowing with this desire entered upon his course of education. When he arrived in this town he found himself in a revival of religion. He could not fail to catch the spirit. He had joined a class in which, to say nothing of the living, there were such men as JAMES RICHARDS and ROBERT CHAUNCEY ROBBINS. The Spirit of God fell upon the class. In the Life of Mills it is asserted, on the authority of 'one of his most valued classmates,' that he was much engaged before the event and during its continuance, was more resorted to than any other by the awakened, and was reputed the principal instrument. And yet his modesty, and the peculiar structure of his mind prevented him from taking a conspicuous part in public meetings.

"In the course of the summer, eight or ten of that class became subjects of the work, and one or two others, among whom was Gordon Hall.

"'This revival,' says the author of Mills' Life, 'was among the most signal expressions of favor to the church.' He alludes to the well-known fact, that by means of this influence Mills prevailed to diffuse through a circle of choice spirits that zeal for missions which actuated his own breast. On Wednesday afternoons they used to retire for prayer to the bottom of the valley south of the west college; and on Saturday afternoons, when they had more leisure, to the more remote meadow on the bank of the Hoosack, and there, under the haystacks, those young Elijahs prayed into existence the embryo of American missions. They formed a society, unknown to any but themselves, to make inquiries and to organize plans for future missions. They carried this society with them to Andover, where it has roused into missionaries most that have gone to the heathen, and where it is still exerting a powerful influence on the interests of the world. I have been in situations to *know* that from the counsels formed in that sacred conclave, or from the mind of Mills himself, arose the American Board of Commissioners for Foreign Missions, the American Bible Society, the United Foreign Missionary Society, and the African School under the care of the Synod of New York and New Jersey; besides all the impetus given to domestic missions, to the Colonization Society, and to the general cause of benevolence in both hemispheres. If I had any instrumentality in originating any of those measures, I here publicly declare, that in every instance I received the first impulse from Samuel John Mills."

CHAPTER V.

THE REVIVAL EPOCH ABOUT 1800—CONTINUED.

Having thus glanced at the revivals of the period now under review, as I remember them, it is time to let the ministers whom God honored as the instruments speak for themselves, and tell us how far the views which I have given correspond with their better means of experience and observation. Their testimony I have taken where I could find it, especially from the Connecticut Evangelical Magazine, which sprung out of those revivals, and which contains quite the fullest record, I believe, that can be found in the Christian annals of the day.

In making selections from the materials within my reach, I have been obliged more or less to abridge those from which I have most largely drawn; but so as to retain all their essential features.

From Dr. Griffin, New Hartford, Conn. 1797–1799.

"The work of divine grace among us three years ago, by which nearly *fifty* persons were hopefully added to the Lord, had not wholly ceased, when the last scene of mercy and wonder commenced.

"Late in October, 1798, the people hearing of the displays of divine grace in West Simsbury, were increasingly impressed with the information. Several circumstances conspired to increase our anxiety. The glorious work had already begun in Torringford, and the cloud appeared to be going all around us. It seemed as though Providence, by avoiding us, designed to bring to remembrance our past abuses of his grace. Besides, having been so recently visited with distinguishing favors, we dared not allow ourselves to expect a repetition of them so soon.

"This was the state of the people when, on a Sabbath in the month of November, it was the sovereign pleasure of the most merciful God very sensibly to manifest himself in the public assembly. From that memorable day, the flame which had been kindling in secret, broke out. By desire of the people, religious conferences were set up in different parts of the town, which continued to be attended by deeply affected crowds, and in which the divine presence and power were manifested to a degree which had never before been witnessed. It is not meant, that they were marked with outcries, distortions of the body, or any intemperate zeal; but only that the power of divine truth made deep impression on the assemblies. You might often see a congregation sit with deep solemnity depicted in their countenances, without observing a tear or a sob during the service. Most of those who were exercised, were often too deeply impressed to eat. Addresses to the passions were avoided, and the aim was to come at the conscience. Little terror was preached except what is implied in the doctrines of the entire depravity of the carnal heart; its enmity against God; its deceitful doubtings and attempts to avoid the soul-humbling terms of the gospel; the radical defects of the doings of the unregenerate, and the sovereignty of God in the dispensations of his grace. The more clearly these and other kindred doctrines were displayed and understood, the more were convictions promoted.

"The order and progress of these convictions were pretty much as follows. The subjects of them were brought to feel that they were transgressors, yet not totally sinful. As their convictions increased, they were constrained to acknowledge their destitution of love to God, but yet they thought they had no enmity against him. At length they would come to see that such enmity filled their hearts. In the first stages of conviction it was not easy for the subjects to realize their desert of eternal death. But afterwards, even while they gave decisive evidence of being still as devoid of a right temper as those wretches whose mouths will be stopped by the light of the last day, their conviction of this ill desert was in many instances very clear. Nevertheless, even to the last, their hearts would recoil at the thought of being in God's hands, and would rise against him for having reserved to himself to decide whether to sanctify and pardon them or not. Before conviction had become deep and powerful, many attempted to exculpate themselves with a plea of inability; and like their ancestor, to cast the blame upon God by pleading, The nature which he gave me, beguiled me. This was the enemy's strong-hold. All who were a little more thoughtful than common, but not thoroughly convicted, would upon the first attack flee to this refuge. They would be glad to repent, they said, but could not, their nature and heart were so bad; as though their nature and heart were not they themselves. But the progress of conviction in general soon removed this refuge of lies, and filled them with a sense of utter inexcusableness. And in every case, as soon as their enmity was slain, this plea wholly vanished; their language immediately became, 'I wonder I ever should have asked the question, how can I repent? My only wonder now is, that I could hold out so long.' As soon as the heart of stone was taken away, and the heart of flesh given, the subjects of this happy change exhibited sentiments and feelings widely different from those above described. They were now wrapped up in admiration of the laws and absolute government of God, which had been the objects of so much cavil and disgust.

"It would not consist with the designed brevity of this narration, nor yet perhaps with propriety, to detail all the interesting circumstances in the experience of more than a hundred persons, who have been the subjects of this work. It may, however, be useful to go so far into particulars as to exhibit some of the distinguishing fruits of it. When asked what was the first thing which composed their anxious minds, they have sometimes answered, 'The thought that I was in the hands of God. It seems to me, that whatever becomes of me, I cannot bear to be out of his hands.' They do not found their hopes on the suggestions of Scripture passages to their minds, or dreams, or seeing sights, or hearing voices, or on blind unaccountable impulses. The Bible is to them a new book. Prayer seems their delight. Their hearts are peculiarly united to the people of God. But the most observable part of their character is a lovely appearance of humility. A sense of their ill-desert abides and increases upon them, after apparent renovation; a considerable time posterior to which some have been heard to say, 'I never had an idea what a heart I had, till this week.'

"It is hoped that about fifty heads of families have been the subjects of this work, a considerable part of whom rank among the respectable and influential characters in the town. The power of the almighty Spirit has prostrated the stoutness of a considerable number, who were the last that human expectation would have fixed on to be the subjects of such a change. One old man who had not been in our house of worship, and probably not in any other, for more than twenty years, has been arrested in his retirement by the divine Spirit, and still remains like the troubled sea when it cannot rest.

"It has been a remarkable season for the destruction of false hopes. Nearly twenty of those who have lately appeared to build on the rock, have been plucked off from a sandy foundation. One had supposed that she loved the God of providence because she had some sense of his daily kindness to her and her family, but was brought to see that she hated the real character of God with all her heart. Another, accustomed to contemplate moral truth in the light of a clear and penetrating intellect, had mistaken the assent of the understanding for the affections of the heart.

"From observing the effects which the light of God's presence had upon false hopes, a trembling reflection arose: How many such hopes will be chased away by the opening light of eternity. The Lord seemed to come to 'search Jerusalem with candles,' and to find out those that were settled on their lees. The church felt the shock. That same presence which at Sinai made all the church, and even Moses, exceedingly fear and quake, rendered this now a time of trembling with professors in general. Nevertheless, it was with most of them a season of great quickening, and a remarkable day of prayer."

From Rev. Jeremiah Hallock, of West Simsbury, Conn. 1798, 1799.

The manner in which God raised up some of the laborers in these revivals is worthy of devout acknowledgment. In Mr. Hallock's youthful days, in a new settlement of Western Massachusetts, he says, "I neither saw nor heard of awakenings," and "conviction, conversion, and revivals, were terms with which I was unacquainted." In 1779, at the age of twenty-one, while at work alone, he was "impressed with a sense of his dependence on God," and "of the sinfulness of his heart," which ere long "seemed so black and polluted that he could hardly avoid crying out." At length, as he afterwards wrote, "The law of God appeared just, I saw myself a sinner, and Christ and the way of salvation by him looked pleasant. I thought it was a happiness to be in the hands of God, and that I could trust my all to him. It still did not occur to me that I had experienced a change of heart." Soon after, as he was called to do military duty, and he and his fellow-soldiers had entered a barn, he "found himself surrounded by his young companions and others, exhorting them on the subject of religion," "one of whom was then awakened, and afterwards obtained hope." It was the beginning of a revival; meetings were appointed, and became frequent, full, and solemn, and as they had no minister, and Mr. Hallock was the first of the apparent converts, it often devolved on him to lead the meetings. "In looking over the daily account I kept at this time," he says, "I find that during March and April, 1780, I attended meetings most of the evenings, went sometimes as far as six miles, and spoke in them as much as a short sermon, generally from some passage of Scripture." In a few months he entered Dr. Dwight's school, then at Northampton, to study for the ministry; and in May, 1783, went to West Simsbury to study theology with a minister of his acquaintance. Here he says, "A revival of religion began. I believe about one hundred manifested a hope. Before it commenced, the church and Sabbath were almost lost; now the church was gathered, reformed, and increased." He was abundant in labors in this revival, attending and conducting religious meetings, and guiding inquirers. For nearly two years he labored in other places on which to some extent the blessing of the Spirit descended, and it was his confirmed wish to spend his life as an *itinerant* minister, but he at length yielded to the importunity of the congregation in West Simsbury, and was installed their pastor in 1785, continuing through life to visit other churches in revival seasons, and in 1801 and 1807 making mission tours of three months each in Vermont. The years immediately succeeding his settlement were a period of darkness in the churches generally. In

1795, Dr. Griffin was settled in the adjoining parish of New Hartford. They both had tasted the blessedness of revivals, and together they mourned and wept and wrestled for perishing souls and the languishing interests of Zion. One or more of the groves is still pointed out where they, with neighboring pastors, used to retire from the world to agonize for the descent of the Holy Spirit. The day of mercy was near. At length the revival burst upon them, of which Mr Hallock says:

"Through the course of twelve tedious years, before this memorable period, the religion of Jesus gradually declined among us, the doctrines of Christ grew more and more unpopular, family prayer and all the duties of the gospel were less regarded, ungodliness prevailed, and particularly modern infidelity had made and was making alarming progress. Indeed, it seemed to an eye of sense, that the Sabbath would be lost, and every appearance of religion vanish. But the God of Zion, who can do every thing, was pleased to appear and lift up the standard of the omnipotent Spirit against the enemy, and to him be all the glory.

"The first appearance of the work was sudden and unexpected. The second Sabbath in October, 1798, I exchanged with a brother in the ministry. On my return the next evening, I found a young person under deep religious impressions. The morning following I found two other youths with the one first awakened, whose minds were likewise impressed. On the evening of this day a sermon was preached by a neighboring minister. The meeting was uncommonly full, and the arrows of conviction reached some hearts.

"The next day it was affecting to see by the rising of the sun, awakened youths coming to my house, to know what they should do to be saved. On the ensuing Sabbath, the work was visible in the house of God, and the conference in the evening was full and very serious. The next day, when a sermon was preached by a neighboring minister, almost the whole parish came to meeting, and the work appeared to be going on.

"Being called one evening to visit a neighbor in distress of mind, I received from her the following information: 'I was sober and thoughtful when a child, used to attend secret prayer, thought I loved good people, and finally concluded I was a Christian. But hearing that the work of God had begun among us, I thought it became me to examine on what foundation I stood, when I found I was building on the sand. On Monday night, my hope perished.' I do not know that I ever saw any one in bodily distress manifest greater anguish. But before morning she found relief, by having, as she hoped, her will bowed and swallowed up in the will of God.

"The next week, on Wednesday, November 1, a sermon was preached, and there were but half as many present as on the week before, and we were greatly afraid that all was about to decline and die. This was indeed a trying hour. No fond parent ever watched the fever of his child at the hour of its crisis with more anxious and interested feelings, than numbers of God's praying friends watched the work of the

Spirit at this critical moment. The thoughts of its going off were more dreadful than the grave. It was not long, however, before it appeared that God had in very deed come to carry on his work, and the hearts of Zion's friends were elated with fresh hopes. The solemnity of this season cannot be communicated. It can be known only by experience.

"A brother in the ministry, among whose people the same work had begun, told me that he had seen twenty in a room, the most of them mortally sick, and at the point of death, but that the scene was not so impressive as to see a house filled with souls in distress, sensible of impending and eternal wrath, and their feet sinking in that horrible pit from whence there is no redemption. An awful silence reigned, unless when it was broken by the cry, 'What shall I do to be saved?' But it was not long before, as we hope, one and another were brought to repentance and faith. To behold poor sinners, who were but yesterday on the brink of destruction and wholly unreconciled to God, now brought to submit to him, and to hear them sing the new song, entirely surpassed all the victories of the most famous kings and generals of our world.

"The work was by no means noisy, but rational, deep, and still. Poor sinners began to see that every thing in the Bible was true, that they were wholly sinful and in the hand of a sovereign God. The first you would know of persons under awakening was, that they would be at all the religious meetings, and manifest a silent and eager attention. What are called the hard sayings, such as the doctrines of total depravity, election, and the like, were well received. Those who were once angry when these things were preached, would cease to object when thoroughly convicted, and rather smite on their breasts.

"The work was now evidently on the increase. Conferences were set up in every part of the parish, and every week, sometimes every day, would bring the animating news of some one hopefully converted. Indeed, it seemed as if it would be impossible for any thing to stand before the power of God, and that every one must bow. However, dreadful experience proves, that natural men are really morally dead: they are harder than rocks, deafer than adders, and more stubborn than the sturdiest oaks. That which will break down the rocks, and tear up the obstinate oaks, will have no effect on the carnal mind. As this was the work of the omnipotent Spirit, so the effects produced proclaimed its sovereign and divine Author. One was taken here, and another there, and often those whom we should least expect.

"One person gave me this account of his first awakening. 'I was returning on such an evening from a conference, where I had seen numbers under concern, and heard others speak of the love of God and of their hope in Christ. But nothing took hold of my mind until, as I was on my way home, these words sounded in my ears: 'Is it nothing to you, all ye that pass by?' These words were fixed in his mind, and he applied them thus: 'Is it nothing to me, that my neighbors and those of my age are troubled about their sins, and some hopefully converted to God? Have I not sins to be troubled about, as well as they? And do I not also need conversion?' A few days after, he hoped that he had received a new heart from the ascended Saviour.

"I have said that before the awakening, modern infidelity had made and was making alarming progress among us. Some who had been infidels for years, are among the hopeful converts, and are laboring to build up the faith they once sought to destroy. I heard one of them say with trembling limbs, 'I am the wretch who have murdered Christ. I have talked a great deal against the gospel, but there was always something in my heart which said it was true.' This poor man was almost in despair, but after a long season of distress, he found comfort.

"At a certain conference in which the conversation turned on the divine purposes, the subject was not attended to now for disputation, but with fear and solemnity. They did not appear to be dry, uninteresting, disputable points, but divine realities calculated to convict the sinner and refresh the saint.

"At the close of the meeting a question was asked of this import: 'Does a person who is truly seeking after God, feel afraid that any of his purposes will cut him off from salvation?' The question was answered in the negative; that the divine purposes were no more against prayer, than against an attention to common matters, and that the only reason why men brought them against prayer was, their having no heart to pray.

"Thus I have given some account of the work of God among us. There were but few in the parish who were not in a measure solemn. Almost the whole conversation, when people were together in intermissions on the Sabbath, and on week-days, was on religion. Even companies on training-days were solemn. The number hopefully born into the kingdom of God is between sixty and seventy.

"I might enlarge, but the time would fail. I have endeavored to state simple facts according to the best judgment of a fallible creature, with a mixture of joy and fear. When I find Peter, an apostle, deceived in Simon Magus, and hear him speaking of the faith of Sylvanus, using the cautious language, 'A faithful brother *as I suppose*;' it makes me tremble for fear how we shall hold out. I desire to be thankful to God, that he has allowed me to stand and behold his glorious work, though I never felt so useless since I entered the ministry. God hath wrought, and to his name be all the glory."

From Rev. Alvan Hyde, D. D., Lee, Mass. 1792.

It will be observed, that the revival here recorded preceded by about six years the distinguished outpouring of the Spirit on many churches, in 1798 and 1799. In a letter to Dr. Sprague of Albany, published in the Appendix to his Lectures on Revivals, Dr. Hyde says:

"The first season of 'refreshing from the presence of the Lord,' which this people enjoyed, commenced in June, 1792, a few days after the event of my ordination. There was at this time no religious excitement in this region of country, nor had I knowledge of there being a special work of God's grace in any part of the land. The church here was small and feeble, having only twenty-one male members. It was, however, a little praying band, and they were often together, like the primitive Christians, continuing with one accord in prayer. Immediately on being stationed here as a watchman, I instituted a weekly religious conference, to be holden on each Wednesday, and in succession, at the various school-houses in the town. These were well attended in every district, and furnished me with favorable opportunities to instruct the people, and to present the truths of the gospel to the old and young in the most plain and familiar manner. This weekly meeting has been sustained to the present time, without losing any of its interest; and when I have been at home, has carried me around the town as regularly as the weeks have returned.

"With a view to form a still more particular acquaintance with the people committed to my charge, I early began to make family visits in different sections of the town. These visits, of which I made a number in the course of a week, were improved wholly in conversing on the great subject of religion, and in obtaining, with as much correctness as I could, a knowledge of their spiritual state, that my instructions on the Sabbath, and at the weekly meetings, might be better adapted to their case. This people had been for nine years without a pastor, and were unhappily divided in their religious opinions. And as they had been in the habit of maintaining warm disputes with each other on the doctrines of the Bible, I calculated on having to encounter many trials. Contrary to my expectations, I found, on my first visits, many persons of different ages under serious and very deep impressions, each one supposing his own burdens and distresses of mind, on account of his sins, to be singular, not having the least knowledge that any others were awakened. It was evident that the Lord had come into the midst of us in the greatness of his power, producing here and there, and among the young and old, deep conviction of sin. And yet it was a still small voice. A marvellous work was begun, and it bore the most decisive marks of being *God's work.* So great was the excitement, though not yet known abroad, that into whatever section of the town I now went, the people in that immediate neighborhood would leave their worldly employments at any hour of the day, and soon fill a large room. Before I was aware, and without any previous appointment, I found myself, on these occasions, in the midst of a solemn and anxious assembly. Many were in tears, and bowed down under the weight of their sins, and some began to rejoice in hope. These seasons were spent in prayer and exhortation, and in conversing with the anxious, and with such as had found relief by submitting themselves to God, adapting my instruction to their respective cases. This was done in the hearing of all who were present. Being then a youth, who had seen but twenty-four years, and inexperienced, I felt weak indeed, and was often ready to sink under this vast weight of responsibility. But the Lord carried me along from one interesting scene to another. I was governed in my movements by what appeared to me to be the exigencies of the people.

"As yet there had been no public religious meeting, except on the Sabbath. A weekly lecture at the meeting-house was now appointed on Thursday; and though it was in the most busy season of the year, the house was filled. This lecture was continued for more than six months, without any abatement of attention; in sustaining which, I was aided by neighboring ministers, and by numbers from a distance, who came to witness this display of sovereign grace. The former disputes of the people respecting religious sentiments, in a great measure, subsided, their consciences seeming to testify in favor of the truth. The work spread into every part of the town, and was especially powerful among those who had taken their stand in opposition to the small church, and the distinguishing doctrines of grace. Many of this class were convinced that they had always lived in error and darkness, and in a state of total alienation from God. They were compelled, notwithstanding their former hatred of the prominent truths of the gospel, to make the interesting inquiry, *What shall we do to be saved?*

"The truths which I exhibited in my public discourses, and in the many meetings between the Sabbaths, were in substance the following: the holiness and immutability of God, the purity and perfection of his law; the entire depravity of the heart, consisting in voluntary opposition to God and holiness; the fulness and all-sufficiency of the atonement made by Christ; the freeness of the offer of pardon, made to all on condition of repentance; the necessity of a change of heart by the Holy Spirit, arising from the deep-rooted depravity of men, which no created arm could remove; the utter inexcusableness of sinners in rejecting the kind overtures of mercy, as they acted freely and voluntarily in doing it; and the duty and resonableness of immediate submission to God. These are some of the truths which God appeared to own and bless, and which, through the agency of the Spirit, were made 'quick and powerful, and sharper than any two-edged sword.'

"All our religious meetings were very much thronged, and yet were never noisy or irregular, nor continued to a late hour. They were characterized with a stillness and solemnity which, I believe, have rarely been witnessed. The converts appeared to renounce all dependence on their own doings, feeling themselves entirely destitute of righteousness, and that all their hope of salvation was in the mere mercy of God in Christ, to whom they were willing to be *eternal debtors.*

"To the praise of sovereign grace, I may add that the work continued with great regularity, and little abatement, nearly *eighteen months.* In this time, as appears from the records of the church, *one hundred and ten* persons of different ages united themselves unto the Lord and his covenant people. All these were examined in the presence of the church, and were received on the ground of their professing to have experienced a change of heart, and to have passed from death unto life. They appeared to exhibit the fruits of the Spirit, and to exemplify the religion of Jesus in their subsequent lives. The instances of apostasy have been but few. Many of them have finished their course, and entered into the joy of their Lord. They gave evidence of enduring to the end, and of departing this life in the triumphs of faith. Others remain to this day, 'burning and shining lights' in the church, some in this town, and some in the new settlements.

"This revival of religion produced a surprising change in the religious sentiments and feelings of the people, and in the general aspect of the town. It effected a happy union; a union which, to an unusual extent, has continued to the present time. After the shower of grace had passed over, divine influences were not altogether withholden, nor did the people lose their relish for religious meetings. Insulated conversions to the cross and standard of the Redeemer, strongly marked as being genuine, frequently occurred. In the six following years, forty-two were added to the church, including some who came from other churches."

From Rev. Ammi R. Robbins of Norfolk, Conn.

"It pleased the blessed God, in the year 1767, to afford some special tokens of his gracious presence to the peculiar joy of the precious few who loved Zion, and prayed for her prosperity. The influences of the Spirit seemed to be shed down in a remarkable manner. Many were struck with surprise, and numbers were impressed with a sense of their guilty and ruined state as sinners, and began to cry out, What must we do to be saved? But alas, it was of short continuance, as to its power and abiding influence. About ten or twelve joined themselves unto the Lord.

"A second revival, if it may be so called, began

in May, 1783, when some of God's people had been remarkably stirred up to pray for the outpouring of the Holy Spirit. Numbers were impressed in different parts of the town, without any knowledge of each other's circumstances. The seriousness became general, and the distress of many visible. As the fruits of this glorious work, there were added to the church in November twenty-seven, in January thirteen, and in March ten, making in all fifty: eighteen males, and thirty-two females.

"In January, 1799, there were indications of a third revival. Our assemblies were more solemn and attentive. The religious people about this time hearing of some revivals in two or three other towns in the vicinity, were induced to hope and ardently pray that we might have a gracious visit also. In February and March the attention became so general, that it was thought proper, at the desire of many, that religious conferences should be set up. They accordingly were in four, and sometimes five different parts of the town. A public lecture was also appointed to be preached every Thursday. Ministers from abroad generally preached on these occasions, and they were undoubtedly, by the blessing of God, the means of promoting the work. Very early there were several persons who were struck with the sense of their miserable state and condition as sinners. They were influential and very popular men in town, and of very considerable information. They were, before this, very far from all appearance of religion, much inclined to, and some far advanced in deistical sentiments, and those of the Universalists. These being hopefully subdued by an omnipotent arm, and becoming meek and humble in their deportment, gave a prodigious shock to others, especially their intimates. And they soon joined heart and hand to promote the work by conversing with others, attending and assisting at conferences; and conducting with modesty, humility, and prudence, they were used as happy instruments of promoting and spreading the revival.

"In June and July, the marvellous displays of divine power and grace were conspicuous beyond any thing of the kind we had ever witnessed. A universal solemnity spread over the town, and seized the minds of almost all, both old and young. Great numbers were bowed with a sense of the presence of the Lord. Some rejoicing and praising God, others crying out in anguish of soul, 'What must we do?' Yet they were by no means noisy or boisterous, but were cut to the heart in silent distress. Almost every day we heard of one or more who had found relief, and new instances of persons impressed with a sense of their guilty, wretched, and undone state. Some appeared almost on the borders of despair, while others were complaining of a hard and obstinate heart, and that there could be no sinner on this side of hell so vile as they. As the fruit of this revival, fifty-nine males, and ninety-four females have been added to the church. Others, several others, entertained hopes, and we trust will come in hereafter.

"Having given this brief sketch, I hope some remarks may be useful to comfort God's people, and to animate them in praying and laboring for the promotion of Christ's kingdom.

"1. It is of unspeakable importance that the means of grace be used with impenitent sinners. Jericho's walls must tumble down on the blowing of the ram's horns. Naaman must wash seven times in Jordan, that he may be cured of his leprosy.

"2. Those doctrines which the world call hard sayings, are the most powerful means in the hands of the blessed Spirit to pull down and destroy Satan's strong-holds in the hearts of sinners. No preaching and conversation seems so effectual to drive them from their hiding places and refuges of lies, as to tell them plainly, that they are eternally undone if the mercy of God is not displayed in their favor; that they have not the least claim on him, and if he does not have mercy, they are gone for ever; that they may as well despair of helping themselves first as last, and that the reason why they do not find relief, is merely because they will not yield, and bow to a holy sovereign God.

"3. When the subjects of this work were hopefully renewed, they were not usually sensible of it at the time; many of them not till days afterwards. They perceived indeed an alteration in their feelings and views, but did not entertain a thought that it was conversion. More generally they feared that God had left them, and that they had lost their convictions. They had agreed in this, that it would be just in God to cast them off, whatever he should do with others.

"One man, nearly fifty years of age, who has been a member of the church for many years, more than a year ago gave up his hope entirely—concluded there was no hope, no mercy for him—dared not come to the Lord's table, and was often filled with such agony that he could hardly attend to the concerns of his family. Now it is hoped that his captivity is turned.

"Oh, let all who love our Lord Jesus Christ and his cause, join as he has taught us, and with unceasing importunity, devoutly and humbly pray, 'Thy kingdom come; thy will be done on earth, as it is in heaven.'"

From Rev. Timothy M. Cooley, D. D., Granville, Mass. 1798, 1799.

"For a few months previous to the late revival, it was a time of great stupidity. Our youth had become much addicted to sinful diversions. In one of their scenes of amusement, God was pleased to frown upon them in a very awful manner. Two young men were seized violently ill, and carried out of the ball-chamber. A young woman, in consequence of a cold which she took on the same evening, was in a very short time taken with a fever and delirium, and brought to the brink of the grave. One of the young men, after a short illness, died. Being told by his weeping mother that he was dying, he replied with his expiring breath, 'Oh, I cannot die, I am unprepared.' These alarming dispensations of divine Providence rendered the minds of the young people solemn, and gave a check to their sinful pleasures.

"In the spring of the year 1798, professors were much awakened and ardently desired a revival of religion. I invited a number of the youth into my study, and urged upon them the necessity of the one thing needful. This was a very solemn meeting, and will probably be long remembered by some who were present.

"On the second Sabbath in June, a very plain sermon was preached from Ezek. 37:3, which was blessed to the awakening of a number of sinners. On Tuesday of the next week a number of young people met for a civil visit, and the violin was introduced, which instead of producing the usual hilarity, occasioned a flood of tears. The work of the Spirit, which had been for several days concealed, now burst forth. It was found that numbers had for some time felt a very serious concern for their future well-being, and thought they were alone in it, being ignorant of the feelings and resolutions of others. The glorious work spread with surprising rapidity through the parish. Christians were animated, sinners were awakened, and scoffers were struck silent at the powerful work of the Almighty. It was truly a remarkable season, and the most aged had never witnessed the like before. A surprising change from apparent thoughtlessness to universal alarm took place within two or three weeks. The rapidity of the work must be ascribed to the all-conquering influences of the Holy Spirit.

"Those who were first impressed communicated their feelings and resolutions to their relatives and friends of a similar age, and urged them to join them in living a new life. These private warnings were the means of spreading the work.

"Their views and feelings, while under conviction, were as follows: They encouraged themselves that by a few weeks of seriousness and diligence in duties, they should prepare themselves for regeneration. After persevering a while, they thought their prayers and cries had been sufficient to prevail with God to show them mercy. They secretly found fault with God for withholding his grace. The heart rose against divine sovereignty. Some thought hard of God for giving comfort to others, while he denied it to themselves. Such exercises discovered to them the total depravity of their hearts. They were before convinced that they had been guilty of many outward acts of sin, but now they saw something of the fountain of pollution within. They still persevered in duties, but seemed, as they expressed it, to grow worse and worse. They discovered that God's law justly condemned them, and that they must be rescued by sovereign mercy, or suffer its awful sanction.

"The views and exercises of those who obtained hope, were as follows: There was a great diversity as to the manner in which divine light was let into the mind, and at the same time a wonderful similarity in their feelings after the admission of true light. Some obtained relief by a view of the glory and excellency of Christ; others were led to see the excellency of the gospel plan and its fitness for sinners; others felt a happy and joyful submission to God as a sovereign, and were willing to be entirely in his hands. When God's time had come to show mercy, their opposition was subdued. They had new views of God, of the Saviour, of the Bible, and of Christian people. Old things had passed away; behold, all things had become new. They felt a sweet calmness of mind, but in most instances had not a thought, at the time of it, that what they experienced was regeneration. It was sometimes several days before they dared to hope they were new creatures. They rejoiced with trembling.

"The work of the Spirit has been remarkably free from enthusiasm and confusion. There have been no instances of outcries under conviction, nor of enthusiastic rants of joy after receiving comfort.

"This revival has been productive of the most happy effects. The Bible has been studied, and the distinguishing doctrines of the gospel more thoroughly understood. God has discovered his sovereignty as well as his mercy among us. Some of the most gay and thoughtless have been hopeful converts, while others who are more sober and moral are passed by. In some instances almost whole families fled to the ark of safety. In one I found seven or eight, and in others five or six, who thought they could rejoice in God. We had the pleasing sight of four sisters offering themselves to unite with the church.

"It is now three years since the beginning of this glorious work, and I can give a more ample testimony to its genuineness, than I could have done earlier. 'By their fruits ye shall know them.' Those who have made a profession of religion, and a number of others who have not yet, appear to be steadfast and unmovable, and their conversation is in a good measure agreeable to the gospel. Nearly one half of them are in youth. They in general appear to be ornaments to their profession, and by their presence at our sacramental table render the communion-season very delightful. 'The Lord hath done great things for us, whereof we are glad.' Let him have all the glory."

From Rev. Joseph Washburn, Farmington, Conn.

"About the time of my ordination, in May, 1795, an uncommon attention and seriousness became apparent throughout the congregation. The divine influences came down like the dew, and like the rain upon the mown grass, in still and gentle showers. The work was unattended with noise or enthusiasm; it caused a general solemnity through the society, and met with little or no opposition. Within the course of about one year, fifty-five persons were added to the church.

"In 1798, God began to appear in power and great glory, in a number of towns in this vicinity. Accounts of these things reached us, and became the subject of conversation among Christians, but appeared to have little or no effect.

"The first appearance of special divine power and grace was in February, 1799. It began in an uncommon attention and concern among the people of God, and a disposition to unite in prayer for the divine presence and a revival of religion.

"Soon after this, numbers in different parts of the congregation began to inquire respecting the meetings, and expressed a wish to attend. Persons of both sexes and of almost every age, and many from the distance of four or five miles, and some still further, were to be seen passing through storms and every other obstacle to attend the meetings. My house was also the almost daily resort of youth and others earnestly inquiring respecting the things of their peace. Those of the youth who were seriously impressed, now reflected on their former gayety, vanity, and sinful amusements with bitterness and entire disapprobation. An attempt which was made soon after the awakening commenced, to introduce a dancing-master, rather forwarded than checked the work on the minds of those who had been brought under serious impressions. The open opposition also, which was made by some, had a similar effect. It convinced them more and more that madness is in the heart of man, and that God is just in condemning sinners, and casting them off for ever. Sixty-one have been admitted to the church in a year, from August, 1799, to August, 1800.

"In the first stages of concern the subjects of this work were generally most affected with particular sins, and not so deeply sensible of the plague of their own hearts. But as their convictions increased, they obtained a clearer view of the spiritual nature and extent of the divine law, and a more realizing sense of the corruption of their hearts. Generally, when under deep conviction, they in a greater or less degree experienced sensible enmity and opposition of heart against the character of God, particularly his sovereignty in having mercy on whom he will have mercy. In several instances God permitted the enmity and obstinacy of the carnal heart to be manifested in an awful manner, and to an astonishing degree. While conscience like a gnawing worm preyed upon them within, a view of the divine character and the way of salvation proposed in the gospel, excited the enmity of their hearts, and every instance in which they saw any of their friends and acquaintance brought apparently to embrace the gospel, filled them with a kind of envy, with a pain which they could not describe.

"With respect to the manner and circumstances in which the hopeful converts obtained relief, and the degree of their joy and peace, there has been a variety. Some few were very suddenly relieved from their distress, and filled with adoring and admiring views of God and the divine Saviour. But the greater part were brought gradually to entertain a hope that they were reconciled to God. The hopeful converts in general have appeared very far from a disposition to think highly of themselves or their attainments, and they were ready to hope the best of others, to promote the good of all, to discharge relative and social duties, to attend carefully upon all the institutions of religion, and to manifest a tender regard for the salvation of souls and the advancement of the cause of God in the world."

From Rev. Samuel Shephard, D. D., Lenox, Mass. 1799.

"I cannot learn from any of the first settlers, that there has ever been any remarkable revival of religion in this town, until the month of June, 1799. At the time of my ordination, in April, 1795, almost all the members of the church were bowing under the infirmities of age. No person who was then in early life belonged to it. Not a single young person had been received into it in the course of sixteen years. Well might this church, like God's ancient covenant people when they sat in captivity by the waters of Babylon, hang its harps upon the willows, for it seemed indeed that when the few who were rapidly hastening down the vale of years should be removed, the name of Jesus in the holy ordinance of the supper would scarcely be had in remembrance.

"Such were the melancholy prospects of this church in the spring of 1799, while showers of divine grace were falling on other parts of Zion. But in the month of April, several members of the church manifested great anxiety about the state of religion among us, and expressed a desire that meetings might be appointed for religious conference, and special prayer for the outpouring of the Spirit. It was done, and the second meeting was unusually solemn. At the third, persons came together from every part of the town. The divine authority of the Scriptures was made the subject of conversation, and the appearance of the assembly was truly affecting. Sinners were brought to tremble in view of eternity, and professors of religion were animated, and rendered fervent in prayer. From that time the work became more general. There was an increasing attention among the young and the old for several months.

"On the twentieth of October, twenty-four persons were received into the church. This was with us a memorable day. But a small part of the congregation had ever before seen a young person brought in. The language of the church to the spectators of the scene then passing before them, was, 'We are journeying to the place of which the Lord said, I will give it you. Come thou with us, and we will do thee good; for the Lord hath spoken good concerning Israel.' The infidel and the abandoned man stood appalled, and to the friends of Zion the season afforded a prelibation of heavenly joys. The whole number who have been received into the church since the work began, is fifty-three. Almost two-thirds are females. I will close this general account with a few particular remarks.

"1. This revival was evidently the work of God. To prove this, the very sudden change in the appearance and pursuits of the people, is instead of a thousand arguments.

"2. The revival began in the church, as I believe is almost always the case when God pours out his Spirit.

"3. Such a revival strikingly evinces the importance of all the means of grace which God has instituted. Faith cometh by hearing, and hearing by the word of God.

"4. The work has been attended with remarkable regularity. God was emphatically in 'the still small voice.' No dreams and visions, no hearing unusual voices, and seeing uncommon sights, no extravagance even in gestures or outcries, appeared.

"5. Among those in this town who have been awakened to attend to religious truth, a remarkable uniformity has occurred relative to the doctrines which have been embraced, such as the total and awful depravity of the human heart, the necessity of regeneration or a change of heart as a preparation for the enjoyment of a holy heaven, the equity of the divine law in its penalty as well as precept, the divine sovereignty in the salvation of sinners as the only possible ground of hope, the necessity of gospel morality as an evidence of justifying faith, and all the doctrines essentially connected with these, were readily received by all with one consent.

"May a holy God, in infinite mercy, continue to make manifest the glory of his power, and the glory of his grace in building up Zion; for in no other way can we rationally hope to see happy individuals, happy families, happy neighborhoods, happy societies, happy towns, happy states, happy kingdoms, and a happy world."

From Rev. Alexander Gillett, Torrington, Conn. 1798.

"The first special appearance of the work among us, was on Wednesday evening, December 26, 1798, when two lectures were preached by neighboring ministers, one in the afternoon, and the other in the evening. The friends of Zion present appeared to receive a fresh anointing from the Lord, and to be awakened to a sense of their duty. Some sinners who had labored heretofore under fears about their spiritual state, were more deeply and thoroughly impressed, and brought to inquire in earnest, 'What must we do to be saved?' Thus the important scene opened, which has been truly wonderful, and expressive of divine power and grace.

"The work gradually increased from that time till May and June ensuing. A goodly number, we charitably hope, were made the subjects of the convicting and transforming operations of the Spirit of God. Forty-five have come forward, and been added to the church: twenty young persons from fourteen years and upward, nine males, and eleven females. The proportion of the whole number is seventeen males, and twenty-eight females. Thirty more have expressed a hope that they have been born again.

"It was wonderful to see what pains persons took to attend lectures and conferences. They would go through storms, cold, and bad roads, to attend the meetings. The impression was so great and extensive, and the work so new and unusual, that for a time the adversary was confounded. Opposers had their mouths shut, and stood gazing and wondering. There had been complaints heretofore of irregularities and enthusiasm, but this work was marked with the 'still small voice.' When comfort was obtained, it did not seem to arise from mere impressions on the imagination, but from such a view of God and divine things as they never before experienced.

"Previous to the new birth, the subjects of the work have had clear convictions of the native depravity of their hearts. Some have been sensible of such shocking feelings as these: 'Oh, how I wish there was no God, heaven, or hell. I would rather be like the beasts that perish, than be in the hands of such a God as this!' After they had experienced the great change, they appeared to themselves to be worse than before. They would exclaim, 'I thought I knew something of my heart before, but I knew nothing of it. How can I be a Christian? Can I be a new creature, and have my heart filled with so many vain thoughts and strange imaginations?'

"Another conspicuous feature of the work is, that when God had taken off a distressful burden, they at first had no suspicions of their hearts being renewed. They were rather alarmed at the apprehension that the Spirit of God had forsaken them. They were ready to cry out, 'I wish I could feel as concerned for myself as I have done, but I cannot.' While in this state, they have been asked how the character of God appeared. They readily answered, 'Great, excellent, glorious; there is none like him. I can't wish for any other Saviour besides Jesus Christ, or any other way to be saved but that of the gospel.'

"The doctrines made use of in carrying on this work, are another distinguishing feature of it. They are the soul-humbling doctrines of the cross, which exalt God, and stain all the pride of human glory. The divine sovereignty, the holiness, extent, and inflexibility of the moral law, human depravity, our entire dependence on God, the special agency of the Holy Spirit in conviction and conversion, and mere grace through Jesus Christ as the Mediator—these have been kept constantly in view, and proved like the fire and the hammer that breaketh the flinty rock in pieces. It has been common for awakened sinners to think hard of election and unconditional submission, and to struggle for a while against them; but they were finally brought to a thorough conviction that these doctrines, which were so terrible to them, were their only hope."

From Rev. Joshua Williams, Harwinton, Conn. 1799.

"In the latter part of January and the beginning of February, 1799, our meetings for public worship were very full and more solemn than I had ever seen before. On Friday, in the second week of February, a lecture was preached; the congregation was very large, and the effects of the word were very visible.

Another was preached in the evening, and it is believed that on this and the two succeeding days more than a hundred persons were awakened, and many of them feelingly convicted of their total depravity of heart, and absolute helplessness. It is not in my power to describe the anxiety which appeared in many. The more they saw of themselves, the more they were convinced of their desert of endless misery. Sleep almost fled from their eyes, and when they went about the necessary concerns of life, their spirits were loaded with sorrow and distress. Danger appeared on all sides, and, 'What must I do?' was a constant and earnest inquiry.

"Some were wrought upon very suddenly, and so as to make it evident that it was not of themselves, or of man, but of God. From the 14th to the 20th of April, there were eighteen instances of hopeful conversion. Several were brought under distressing conviction at midnight on their beds, and many in such circumstances that it could not be accounted for on any principle but the sovereign power and mercy of God. At this time the labor of preaching was easy indeed, but to detect the false hope to which many were prone, was a difficult and critical business. Never did I feel my own insufficiency so much as at this period. On the one hand not to wound the lambs of Christ's flock, and on the other not to encourage unfounded hopes, required the utmost caution and diligence. My usual practice was, if upon examination I found marks of a false hope, to tell the matter plainly. But if there were symptoms of a well-founded hope, I told them they must prove it to be genuine by their future holy conduct, always remembering that the heart is deceitful above all things. In July, fifty-six were added on one Sabbath to the church; in September, twenty-four more, and several others at different times; making the whole number one hundred."

From Rev. Moses Hallock, Plainfield, Mass., to Rev. Jeremiah Hallock, June 3, 1798.

"I am unwilling to miss the present opportunity to write to you, especially as the tidings I am about to convey are so glorious. It has been my favored lot to see several awakenings, but the present displays of divine power and grace far exceed what I ever before saw. At least fifty have been hopefully born of God here within a few months. And besides these, several persons appear to have obtained clear and comfortable evidence of their good estate, who, till these happy days, were in great doubt. The church seems to be greatly quickened. There are so many demonstrative proofs that the work is the work of God, that next to none pretend to gainsay it. I believe there is not a man in the town that openly opposes. None have joined the church yet, but twenty-four stand propounded. Several of these appeared to be Christians before the awakening, but dared not make a public profession till now. Twenty-two have told their experience in the meeting-house—seventeen last Friday, and five to-day—before a crowded and solemn assembly. They will probably be received on the first Sabbath of July, and sit down with the church at the Lord's table; and I expect that a number more will offer themselves before that time.

"There are two young men whose conviction has been unusually long and clear, who have received comfort within these few weeks. At some times they almost appeared in despair. I heard one of them say, with trembling limbs, '*Oh the eternity of misery that is before me!*' For a considerable time before they hopefully submitted to the divine and sovereign will, they saw and confessed the enmity of their hearts to God, and how just he would be in sending them to everlasting punishment. They told me that they felt most obstinately opposed to the way of life by Jesus Christ, and were it not that they believed in election they should be in despair. These two are men of bright natural parts and considerable reading, and bid fair to be pillars in the church some future day. These, with most of the others who have told their experience, spoke of terrible opposition of heart to God and clear views of his justice before regeneration, and how captivated and charmed they afterwards were both with the divine justice and mercy. Let God have all the glory."

From Rev. Asahel Hooker, Goshen, Conn. 1799.

"Sundry persons, whose knowledge of the subject is correct, have informed me that, previous to my settlement in this place, there never was any remarkable and extensive revival of religion among the people; and since I came here, almost nine years ago, things have remained in a most unpromising state till about the middle of February, 1799. That period was rendered memorable by the commencement of a work, the happy fruits of which are still apparent, and which I trust will be lasting as eternity. From small beginnings it made such progress in a few weeks as to have arrested general attention, while great numbers were under the most serious and impressive sense of their forlorn state as sinners. Public worship on the Sabbath and all other meetings were unusually attended, both as to numbers and seriousness. It was not long before several persons manifested a hope of having passed from death unto life. In the month of September, twenty-five persons were admitted to the church; in November, forty-eight; in January, four; making, in the whole, seventy-seven. A considerable number remain who exhibit the usual evidence of a new heart, who have not made a public profession of their faith. The change which has been wrought in many, is great and wonderful. It is the Lord's doing, and marvellous in our eyes.

"The following brief statement will enable the candid and impartial to judge for themselves whether indeed it is the Lord's work.

"1. Numbers were deeply impressed before they knew that others were in like circumstances. Often without the intervention of any means which could be distinctly recollected, the truth and reality of eternal things were brought home and fastened upon their minds with a sort of irresistible and impressive weight, pointing them to the vast importance of fleeing from the wrath to come.

"2. The first impressions on the minds of those who were subjects of the work, did not in common consist chiefly of fears of future punishment. Their deepest and most painful impressions arose from convictions of sin, by which they were at variance with themselves, and by which it was awfully realized to them, that 'there is no peace to the wicked.' Those who became eventually reconciled to the truth, and found a comfortable hope of their good estate, were led to such an acquaintance with the plague of their own hearts as convinced them, that if saved it must be not by righteousness which they had done or could do, but 'by the washing of regeneration and renewing of the Holy Ghost.'

"3. It is worthy of particular notice as a distinguishing feature of the work, that the hopeful subjects of its saving effects, notwithstanding their foregoing prejudices and opposition, have come uniformly and with one consent into the great distinguishing doctrines of grace. These are the doctrines which seem to have been specially owned and blessed by the Holy Spirit, and thence made the wisdom of God to the salvation of sinners.

"4. A considerable number had been more or less immoral and irreligious in their visible conduct. Several who were scoffers at the serious and universal strictness of pure religion, were among the hopeful subjects of genuine conviction and of saving mercy. A few who had endeavored to fortify themselves against fears of the wrath to come in the belief of universal salvation, were convinced that they had made lies their refuge.

"5. It is not common for those who entertain a hope for themselves, to be very confident of their title to salvation. There are few, if any, but seem at times to doubt whether their names are written in heaven.

Whether all those who appear to have set out and to run well for the present, will hold on their way and obtain the prize of their high calling, must be finally known by the event."

From Rev. Ira Hart, Waterbnry, in Middlebury, Conn. 1799, 1800.

"This society is but lately formed, and I am the first settled minister. While, when I came, every thing else appeared favorable, the spirit and power of vital piety seemed almost gone. Several cases of discipline existed in the church, which lay upon the brethren as a heavy burden. All saw and acknowledged the evil, and longed to have it removed; but in the general inactivity and discouragement, nothing effectual had been done. The church appeared timid, and some of the enemies of the cross exulted and cast reproach. But our sinful fears were not realized. Christ the great Head of the church caused the sweet influences of his grace to break forth when we expected trouble and disunion.

"Returning home from some places where there were revivals, I was impressed with the idea that nothing so effectually kept off the divine blessing as our neglect of those cases of discipline. The church were urged to proceed immediately, and were convinced that reformation must begin at the house of God."

[He goes on to show how this movement was blessed in bringing the church up from its depression, and awakening sinners to their danger.]

"This interposition of God," he says, "was too striking to pass unnoticed. It showed to the church and to all, that the way of duty is the way of safety, and the way in which divine blessings are usually obtained. The friends of Zion awoke, and their hearts and mouths began to be open on the subject of religion. Cases of conviction soon occurred in different parts of the society. Our lectures were seriously and solemnly attended. The Sabbath was a solemn day. Professors confessed with tears their shortcomings in duty. They looked back with grief and wonder upon themselves, and were melted down with contrition before God. The aged and the young were agreed in saying, 'It was never so seen in Israel.'

"As several of the first cases of conviction were among the youth, some of them were opposed to it, as calculated to destroy their amusements. One young man began profanely to ridicule those who were under distress of mind; but as he entered the gallery on the Sabbath, God met and pierced him with a sharp arrow of conviction. He stumbled to a seat, and amid the horrors of a guilty awakened conscience, sat trembling in view of truth and the awful iniquity of his heart, and soon after testified to the excellency of that Saviour and that religion which he before despised. This struck the young people as an admonition from heaven. They gave up their vain amusements, crowded to conferences and lectures, and a goodly number of them have, as we hope, been turned from darkness to light. It was indeed a glorious season, which will long be remembered by many as the time of their espousals to Christ.

"Considering the importance of a right judgment of ourselves, and the extreme danger of those who settle down on a false profession, I judged it not proper to encourage those who had obtained hopes, to a sudden union with the church. The duty of self-examination and a comparison of their views and exercises with God's word were strongly urged, that they might not come to the gospel feast without a wedding garment. None were admitted till the summer of 1800, when at different times thirty-five were received, and six have since been admitted. The awakening has embraced persons of almost all ages, from fifteen to sixty-five. Excepting seventeen young persons, the rest were mostly young heads of families. This gives a hopeful prospect that the rising generation will more extensively enjoy the great blessings of family prayer and religious instruction.

"The sovereignty of God has been eminently displayed in this revival. Not those whom we expected, but those whom God pleased, were called to repentance. One is taken and another left.

"From what God has done for us, it is thought all churches may learn the importance and safety of faithfully maintaining the discipline which Christ has established. If it is conducted with the prudence, vigilance, and brotherly love which the cases require, the blessing of God may be confidently expected.

"One remark more. It was common for those under serious impressions to have much opposition to the doctrines of grace, particularly the justice of God in the eternal punishment of the finally impenitent, divine sovereignty, and the electing love of God, but they found no peace till those doctrines were made the foundation of their hope. When reconciled to him through the merits of his Son, they expressed great surprise that they had never understood these plain gospel truths before, or seen their excellency and beauty."

From Rev. Ebenezer Porter, D. D., Washington, Conn., afterwards Professor in the Theol. Sem., Andover. 1803.

"Though this church had enjoyed a preached gospel with very little interruption since its formation, a period of sixty-four years, nothing that could properly be termed a revival of religion had ever taken place till the present. Many families had no altar for God. Many parents seemed to behold their dear offspring going in the ways that lead to destruction, without uttering one warning, or offering one prayer for their eternal salvation. Out of the church was to be seen a general carelessness; in it a spirit of deep slumber, a want of discipline, a want of brotherly love—a want of every thing almost, but cold, cold profession.

"There was a glimmering hope of better things for a short time, in the winter of 1801. A weekly church conference was attended regularly about two months, when it declined till it entirely ceased. It seemed as though an offended God was about to seal us up under a holy rebuke: 'Sleep on now, and take your rest.' That the only hope is the sovereign mercy of God, I had long believed, but had never so deeply felt before. Means, however, were not to be neglected.

"Early in the summer of 1802, special meetings were appointed for the youth. These meetings were attended every other week, in the form of a theological school. At each meeting, a question in the order of a system was given, accompanied with an extempore lecture, or with notice that a sermon would be adapted to the subject on the following Sabbath. At the meeting succeeding that on which the question was given, the papers that had been written by the youth were received and read publicly. These papers were so received as to have the author of each one unknown to every other. With the same precaution they were returned. These meetings succeeded, to my joy and astonishment. They substituted solid improvement for the ordinary levities of young people. They excited a relish for profitable conversation, reading, and reflection; they furnished the mind with useful ideas, rendered the more permanent by the labor of acquiring them; and what is more and most important of all, they opened an avenue for the solemn influence of truth, by a divine blessing, to reach the conscience and the heart. A respectable number usually attended on these occasions, and twelve or fifteen wrote on the same question. It was surprising to witness the progress made by them, not only in correct writing, but in doctrinal knowledge.

"Near the close of the summer of 1803, several persons became seriously impressed. Weekly conferences were revived. During the winter, the operations of the divine Spirit were discernible in every part of the society. The church, which had appeared to languish as with a wasting hectic, put on the aspect of returning health. Through the next spring and summer, though thirteen had been added to the church, we were still between hope and fear. God's people longed for, rather than expected a revival. They scarcely dared to believe that the day had indeed dawned which was to succeed a night of more than sixty years. But in the autumn, the Sun of righteousness arose upon us with healing in his wings. As in the valley of Ezekiel's vision, there was a great shaking. Dry bones, animated by the breath of the Almighty, stood up new-born believers. The children of Zion beheld with overflowing hearts, and with thankful tongues acknowledged, 'This is the finger of God.' The work was stamped conspicuously with the impress of its divine author, and its joyful effects evinced no other than the agency of Omnipotence. So manifestly was it the work of God, that opposition, however it might have rankled in the bosoms of individuals, was awed into silence. Many old professors, amidst the majesty and glory of the scene, seemed unable to contain, and equally unable to express the wonder and joy of their hearts. During a winter unusually severe, nothing could surpass the resolution with which numbers attended, to be instructed in the way of salvation. From the extremity of the season, apprehensions were entertained for persons of delicate constitutions; but the people were seldom or never more healthy.

"As the first-fruit of this precious and memorable season, fifty-four persons have been added to the church, none of whom, blessed be God, have been left to discredit their holy profession.

"It would be more important to delineate particularly the nature and fruits of this work, did it not bear so strong an affinity in these respects to the revivals already described. Without an exception, its special subjects were calm in their exercises, and embraced that system of religious sentiments commonly acknowledged and received in our churches.

"From the commencement of this work to its visible decline was more than eighteen months, and meetings, though frequent, seemed not at all to interfere with necessary temporal avocations. An increased industry could easily redeem the time devoted to this purpose from unprofitable or foolish pursuits.

"Before this revival more than ordinary attention had been paid to the rising generation, and of the number added to the church about three-fourths had sprung from professing parents. Besides the meetings of the young people, the church as a church has appointed a catechizing committee to teach the children. These catechizings have since been regularly attended during the summer season between the services on every other Sabbath.

"While infidelity is searching out every avenue for infusing its deadly poison into the minds of the young, is it not a matter of surprise that their religious instruction should not have had more share in the thoughts, the conversation, and the prayers of God's people? Do not the signs of the times summon ministers and Christians generally to exertions more united, and more correspondent with an object of such acknowledged and immense importance?"

From Judge Reeve of Litchfield, Conn., to Judge Boudinot of Newark, New Jersey.

"In the astonishing scene that has been passing at Litchfield, there has been a great diversity in such as were awakened to a serious concern as to their immortal interests, and at length have obtained a hope that they have passed from death to life. All had a sensible conviction of the depravity of their hearts, and saw that this depravity was odious and criminal, for which they deserved to experience the penalties of a righteous law, which they had broken in innumerable instances, and all agreed in choosing to be in the hands of God; but there was a wide difference in the degree of distress which took place previous to experiencing that submission of will to God which all felt. While some felt a violent opposition of heart to the law and government of a holy God, it was scarcely perceivable in others. Some were in distress but a few days before they received relief, while others remained in sorrow for many months. Instances of sudden transition from deep distress to great joy, were comparatively few. In most cases the subjects of this work who eventually obtained hope of their good estate, after having felt great anxiety of mind, and a deep sense of the odiousness of their character in the sight of God, and a thorough conviction that it would be just in him to cast them off for ever, seemed to lose their anxiety about themselves, and it was a common thing for them to complain that they were becoming stupid and had lost their convictions. Yet during this state of their supposed stupidity, it was remarkable that their sense of the corruption of their hearts greatly increased, they no longer felt any opposition to the character of God, but on the contrary, it appeared to them glorious because he was a sin-hating God, while at this time they had no apprehension that their hearts were changed; and while their Christian friends entertained the strongest hopes that they were new creatures, they left them to their own reflections without informing them of their opinion concerning them. When they began to hope, it was with much trembling, and they gradually advanced to a steady comfortable hope with great caution and much self-examination. This has been the most usual method, though there have been some remarkable instances of persons passing from the most pungent distress to the most elevated joys, and I have never heard of a case where confidence has arisen through the medium of dreams, visions, or texts of Scripture coming suddenly into their minds."

Reply of Judge Boudinot to Judge Reeve.

"If I was to copy your letter, and return it as from myself, it would be almost in every particular what has passed here. About six years ago, when our worthy pastor Mr. Griffin first came to this place, we had a revival of religion among us, and about a hundred and thirty were added to the church. After that had declined we were rather in a dull state, which in August last was very low. The administration of the Lord's supper was to take place on the first Sabbath of September. On the Sabbath preceding, it was recommended to the church to keep the Friday on which the preparatory lecture was to be preached as a day of humiliation, fasting, and prayer that God would pour out his Spirit and revive his work. If ever the verity of the words of sacred writ, 'Before they call I will answer, and while they are yet speaking I will hear,' was proved, it was in this instance. The meeting was unusually full, the Sabbath was peculiarly solemn. On Monday, our worthy pastor went out in the morning to visit in the neighborhood, without the least suspicion that any thing more than common had taken place, when, to his astonishment, in every house into which he entered, the family appeared like Cornelius of old, ready to receive the words of truth, and soon melted into tears. The flame at once caught the hearts of the truly pious among us. The next Sabbath morning a number agreed to form a society to meet at nine o'clock, and spend an hour previous to going to church in prayer to God, for his blessing on the word. They styled themselves the Aaron and Hur Society, as supporting the hands of their minister. It was not long before the blessed work pervaded every part of the congregation. No age was exempted. We have had instances of persons between sixty and eighty, some of whom had led what they called moral lives, and trusted they were going to heaven, who were brought to see that instead of being 'rich and increased in goods, and having need of nothing,' they were 'wretched and miserable and poor and blind and naked.' Others who had never troubled themselves about any of these things, were made to cry out in the bitterness of their spirit, 'What shall we do to be saved?'

"The operations of the divine Spirit have been as variable as with you. Take your own description, and you have ours correctly."

Rev. Dr. Baldwin, Boston, and Rev. Messrs. Ledoyt and Seamans, New Hampshire. 1790–1803.

About the time that Dr. Baldwin commenced his labors in the Second Baptist church, Boston, in 1790, "a revival began in which not far from seventy were added to his church, and about the same number to the First church. Another revival began in 1803, and continued more than two years, in which about two hundred were brought into his church, and about two hundred also into the First church.

The Rev. Mr. Ledoyt of Newport, N. H., wrote, in 1793, "It has been a long, dark, and cloudy night with me and the people here; but, glory to our God, the cloud is dispersing fast. His work is begun among us. Newport and Croydon are greatly blessed. I have baptized twenty-nine in four weeks. The work appears to be going on."

In 1792, a work began in New London, N. H., of which Rev. Mr. Seamans wrote, "This town consists of about fifty families, and I hope that between forty and fifty souls have been translated out of darkness into God's marvellous light, besides a number in Sutton and Fishersfield who congregate with us. Fifteen have joined the church, and I expect that a number more will come forward in a short time. We have lectures or conferences almost every day or evening in the week. Our very children meet together to converse and pray with each other. Some things in this work have exceeded every thing I ever saw before. Convictions have usually been very clear and powerful, so that industrious men and women have had neither inclination nor strength to follow their business as usual. And they freely acknowledge the justice and sovereignty of God. They also have desires beyond what I have ever before known for the universal outpouring of the Holy Spirit."

"This work continued, and the next year the church, which, at its commencement, consisted of only eighteen members, had increased to a hundred and fifteen. Some of all ages, from seventy down to eight years old, had been brought in; and what was remarkable, there were at that time in this church, thirty-seven men and their wives."

From Rev. Dr. Wood, Boscawen, N. H., to Rev. Dr. Justin Edwards.

"When I entered on my ministry in this town, in 1781, the church consisted of but twenty members in all, and the state of religion around wore a very gloomy aspect. A revival of religion had hardly been known. In consequence of our first revival, in 1782, which added to the church between thirty and forty heads of families, I was abundantly called upon to labor in the neighboring towns; and as the doctrines of grace had been but little inculcated, the churches were in a very low and formal state. In a number of instances I witnessed a change in sentiment, and a revival of the spirit of religion, which the work that the Lord had wrought among my people served greatly to strengthen and increase, till nearly the whole vicinity became revolutionized.

"When I entered on the ministry, I reflected with myself that if I should labor all my days, and be instrumental of the salvation of *one soul*, that would be more than an ample reward. But now I may say, that goodness and mercy have attended me. Since I came here we have been favored with seven or eight seasons of the special outpouring of the Spirit; the two first and the two last were very powerful. Since my settlement about four hundred and thirty have been added to the church, and I should suppose that three hundred of those have been or now are heads of families."

Dr. Wood, in a small inland congregation, fitted for college nearly one hundred students, thirty-seven of whom, in 1823, had entered the ministry, and others were studying in preparation. About thirty obtained a hope in Christ while residing in his family, and a number who there received religious impressions, afterwards joined themselves to the people of God.

From Rev. Jesse Edson, Halifax, Vermont, August, 1802.

"The first appearances of the revival began in the church; professors seemed to awake from their stupidity and coldness. The spirit of prayer was poured out upon them, and from this time there began to be a visible shaking among the dry bones, and a few individuals were raised to spiritual life. The Holy Spirit seemed to come down like a rushing, mighty wind, to melt the souls of God's children, to cause sinners to tremble, stubborn wills to bow, and hard hearts to relent. Numbers flocked to Christ as a cloud, and as doves to their windows. Fifteen were received the next communion, twenty-one the communion following; about sixty, in the whole. They were of different ages from above fifty down to fifteen years.

"The work was remarkably free from enthusiasm and disorder, and accompanied with a great sense of the evil of sin. The subjects of the work were led to see themselves destitute of any righteousness of their own to recommend them to God; that they were totally depraved, deserving nothing from God but everlasting misery, and entirely dependent on sovereign grace to pluck them as brands from the burning. The doctrines to which some of them had been particularly opposed, became sweet and ravishing doctrines.

"One instance somewhat singular, may be worthy of note. There was a respectable man who remained an attentive observer till near the close of the awakening, without any particular operation on his own mind. Going one day out of town, on a law-suit, it turned in his mind that the Bible was the best law book, the eternal rule of right between man and man. The same thought occurred to his mind frequently when going home, and when he retired for the night; but it gave him no particular alarm. When he awaked before day, the same impression was running in his mind, 'The Bible is the best law book.' He rose, made a fire, and while he sat meditating upon this impression, all at once his soul was filled with rapture, and ere he was aware, he was 'like the chariots of Amminadib.' He beheld such glory and beauty in the divine character as he could not describe, and his mouth was immediately filled with praise. He set up family duties, and continued in this sweet and comfortable frame of mind for a considerable time, without thinking of its being a change of heart; but finding his soul filled with love to God, drawn forth with peculiar affection towards the brethren, and the most earnest desire for the salvation of souls and a delight in the duties of religion, he was led to hope he had become a new man, and was admitted to the church, where he has adorned his profession.

"Another was the case of a woman who was a violent opposer in a former awakening; tried to hinder her husband, who was then a sharer, from coming forward; opposed him in family duties, and made his life exceedingly uncomfortable. She showed the utmost spite against all who appeared engaged in the work, and would rage as if she wanted means to vent her malice. She would not attend meeting, nor read the Bible, nor any good book. But God in his infinite mercy arrested her. For several months she was under the most pungent convictions. All her wickedness, bitterness, enmity, and rage, appeared to her to be pointed directly against God. The pains of hell gat hold upon her, and she was ready to give up in despair. In this extremity God met her, and brought her into the glorious liberty of the gospel, giving her to taste the sweets of redeeming love. She found peace and comfort; happiness was restored to the family, and joy and gladness revived in the hearts of God's children."

From a letter dated Rutland, Vermont, Feb., 1803.

"The Lord is making surprising manifestations of his love and power among us, in subduing the hearts of sinners to the sceptre of Jesus. It is such a time as I never saw before. We have conferences almost every evening in one part of the parish or another.

There are no outcries, but it seems like 'the still small voice.' Sometimes the work seems as if it would carry all before it. Opposition has been made in various ways, but has been totally in vain.

"In Pittsford, the town north of this, a similar work began about six months ago, since which time about one hundred have made public profession of religion.

"Thus, after eighteen years of deadness and darkness, we have really a time of refreshing; for when the Lord builds up Zion, he appears in his glory."

From Rev. John B. Preston, Rupert, Vt., July, 1804.

"I have been settled in the ministry here between six and seven years, and till within a few months past, have habitually felt that my labors were in vain, and that my strength was spent for naught. From year to year religion was declining, the church was decreasing in numbers and graces, and iniquity abounded. A little more than a year ago, the darkness reached its height, and appeared scarcely to admit the smallest beam of hope.

"In this hour of extremity, a small number of the few remaining professors agreed to meet once a week for social prayer. At first the number was very small, sometimes not more than two or three; but they appeared strong in the faith, and fervent in prayer, the Spirit helping their infirmities with groanings which could not be uttered. The meetings became increasingly solemn, so that in September, the number of religious conferences, or rather prayer-meetings, in different parts of the society were multiplied to four in a week. A day of fasting and prayer was observed about this time, and attended with a special degree of solemnity.

"But nothing very special occurred till some time in November, when on a sudden the Spirit of the Lord appeared to come down upon us like 'a rushing mighty wind.' Almost the whole society seemed to be shaken at once. Scarce a family could be found in which there were not some inquiring what they should do to be saved. Our prayer-meetings were crowded, and solemn to an amazing degree. No emotions more violent than shedding of tears, and no appearance of wildness and disorder occurred. Nothing appeared but a silent, fixed attention, and profound solemnity, the most resembling my idea of the day of judgment of any scene I ever witnessed. Infidelity retired, or was overcome by the bright manifestations of divine power and grace. Several who had been hardened in loose principles, were made to believe and tremble. One who for a number of years had been trusting to the delusive scheme of Universalism, was constrained to say, 'I know that there is one sinner who deserves eternal punishment. No man can ever have that sight of his sins and sense of his guilt which God has given me, and remain a Universalist.'

"It is impossible fully to describe the amazing change that took place among us within a few weeks, and even a few days. It was glorious to 'stand still and see the salvation of God.' The solemnity continued and increased till about the middle of February. The youth have hopefully shared very largely in the blessings that have fallen upon us. Thirty-five young men and women, the most of whom but one year ago were wholly devoted to sinful amusements, now sit with us around the table of the Lord. The whole number of additions to the church since the work began, is eighty-four. Since it commenced, we have observed not less than six days of public fasting and prayer, which the Lord has manifestly crowned with great success in carrying on his work among us.

"The truths which have been most evidently blessed in this revival, have been the divine holiness and sovereignty, the grace of the gospel, and the sinner's total depravity and dependence. And those who have obtained a hope that they were the subjects of divine grace, have almost without exception appeared fully, understandingly, and cordially to assent to all those humbling doctrines of the Bible.

"Within little more than a year, the Spirit has also been wonderfully poured out upon a number of towns, and about a thousand have been added to the churches of Christ in Bennington and Rutland counties. Bennington, Sandgate, Rupert, Dorset, Tinmouth, Rutland, Brandon, Pittsford, Benson, and Orwell, have shared the most largely in this shower of divine grace. Not less than fifty have been added to the church in each of these towns, and in several, more than a hundred. Most of the other towns have shared in some degree.

"In the county of Addison, several towns have likewise been favored with some droppings from the same cloud. In Bridport, Addison, and Weybridge, there have been considerable additions. In Hebron, there has been a great awakening the winter past, and the work now appears spreading around them. No minister was ever settled there, nor church formed, and the gospel but seldom preached. But the Lord has been pleased to pass over to their help, and to work among them for his great name's sake.

"Should not the friends of Zion be strong, and rejoice in the Lord? From the east and from the west, from the north and from the south, are heard songs, even glory to the righteous. The voice of the Bridegroom is heard in our land. The foolish and the righteous are awakening from their long slumbers. When the enemy came in like a flood, then the Lord lifted up a standard against him. Let saints rejoice in their King: let Zion arise and shine, for her light has come. The Lord is gathering in his elect from the four corners of the earth. Woe to the inhabitants thereof, who shall survive this day of the powerful manifestations of divine grace, and be found among the incorrigible number whom the Lord will destroy with the brightness of his coming."

From Rev. Dr. Proudfit, of the Associate Reformed church, Salem, N. Y., to Rev. Dr. Sprague. 1796–1802.

"We have uniformly been in the habit of dispensing the ordinance of the Supper four times in the year, and so far as I recollect, have never had a sacramental occasion without some accession to our numbers. But during this long period we have enjoyed, at different intervals, what would now be pronounced 'a revival of religion.' The refreshing influences of divine grace descended silently and softly upon the heritage of the Lord, like the showers of spring after the dreariness and barrenness of winter. A genial warmth appeared to pervade the whole church, to the joy of the generation of the righteous, and at the same time, multitudes were added to the Lord by an external profession of his name.

"One of these occasions occurred in the year 1796, when a very unusual influence apparently accompanied the outward dispensation of the word, sealing it upon the souls both of sinners and saints. A similar season occurred about six years afterwards; and another and still more memorable visitation of the Spirit was enjoyed in the year 1815.

"During all these seasons of enlargement to myself, and of spiritual joy to the children of adoption under my immediate care, and of the 'espousals of others to Jesus as their husband,' no extra efforts were used, no brethren from other towns were called in to our aid, but the work advanced silently and regularly, promoted exclusively under the divine blessing by the ordinary administration of ordinances, private and public. Yet, during the whole course of my ministry, I have never been favored with seasons more delightful in their recollection—none the results of which I anticipate with more joy on that day when the final account of my stewardship will be required."

From Rev. Dr. Thomas De Witt, New York.

"The portion of the church of Christ with which I am connected, (tho Reformed Dutch church in America,) has at different times, in several parts, been favored with gracious seasons of revival. At the time of Whitefield's first labors in America, there was already existing a powerful, extended, and well-marked work of grace, under the ministry of the Rev. Theodore J. Frelinghuysen, in the neighborhood of Somerville and New Brunswick, N. J. The blessed fruits of this work were widely spread in those parts, endured through the following generations, and may yet be clearly traced at the present time. Subsequently the ministries of Dr. Laidlie at New York, and Dr. Westerlo at Albany, tended greatly to elevate the tone of evangelical sentiment and piety in our churches, and were greatly blessed in the conversion of sinners. The ministry of the late Dr. John H. Livingston (from 1770 to 1810) is well remembered as most richly evangelical, and clothed with a holy unction, while the dew of heaven was upon it in success. At one time for several years subsequent to the revolutionary war, while alone in the field of his labor, the continued dropping from on high was on his ministrations, and numerous accessions were made from time to time of such as afterwards exhibited the character of enlightened, experimental, fruitful piety. Without referring to their ministries, it may be remarked that these were the very men most distinguished among us for their clear, discriminating exhibition of divine truth, their strict adherence to the order of the gospel, their influence upon the general welfare of the church, and their wisdom, zeal, and fidelity in the work of the ministry."

From Rev. Dr. John M. Mason, New York, to Rev. William Stoddart, of Amsterdam.

Dr. Mason was installed in 1793, and after eight or ten years of ministerial labor, wrote to his friend and class-mate, "My gracious Lord has not disowned my feeble labors. This man and that have been born in our Zion. The congregation was comparatively small when it came into my hands, containing not quite two hundred persons who had been admitted to sacramental privileges. During my ministry about six hundred have been added; and the increase, I trust, owes nothing to soothing doctrines, or to remissness of discipline. Had we chosen to open the door to the merely civil and moral, our number would have been much greater. But I wish to see *Christians* in the churches. The world and the church can never unite. If we make the foolish attempt, there will be a conflict, and either the one or the other will be prostrated."

Of Dr. Mason's labors the late Isabella Graham wrote, in 1793, "Our young Timothy is a champion for the gospel of Jesus. The Lord has well girded him and largely endowed him. He walks closely with God, and speaks and preaches like a Christian of long experience. He was ordained and installed about two months ago in his father's church. O for a thankful heart! The Lord has done wonders for me and mine; and blessed be his name, that in a remarkable manner he hedged me in to become a member of this congregation, where I am led and fed with the same truths which nourished my soul in Zion's gates at Edinburgh; and I am helped to sing the Lord's song in a strange land."

From Rev. Dr. Milledoler, President of Rutgers College, New Brunswick, N. J. 1800–1812.

"Those who are born again are said, in the sacred Scriptures, to be 'born of the Spirit,' and 'times of refreshing' are everywhere attributed to Him as their author. It is strange that the reality of revivals should be called in question by those who read the Bible, are acquainted with church history, or have any knowledge whatever of the ordinary or extraordinary operations of the Spirit of God upon the soul.

"I have witnessed two revivals during my own ministry. The first occurred between the years 1800 and 1805, while I was officiating as pastor of the Pine-street church, Philadelphia. The second between the years 1807 and 1812, while officiating as pastor of the Rutgers-street church, New York. The former continued more than eighteen months; the latter three years. Both occurred under the regular administration of the word and sacraments. Large additions were made during their continuance to the communion of those churches. The church in Rutgers-street grew in a few years from somewhere about eighty to upwards of seven hundred communicating members. This work was connected with no extra means, except an additional weekly lecture or prayer-meeting. It was attended with no extravagant demonstrations of any description whatever, but with much apparent humility, with Christian affection, and there is reason to believe, also, with much searching of heart, and of the holy Scriptures. Of those admitted to full communion at that time, few, if any, are known to have apostatized. I do not myself recollect a single instance of apostasy."

From Rev. Dr. Griffin, in Newark, New-Jersey, to Rev. Dr. Ashbel Green, Philadelphia.

"About the first of December, 1806, we were encouraged with some symptoms of revival of religion in this village, but they quickly disappeared; and in March, 1807, they were renewed, but again passed off. The death of Dr. McWhorter in July made a great impression on the congregation, which was deepened in the month of August through the instrumentality of the Rev. Gideon Blackburn, who preached several times here with great zeal and energy. The leaven was secretly and increasingly working nine months before it became evident. At a time when every thing appeared to be still around us, secret anxieties were preying upon a number of persons, which so far from being the effect of sympathy, were known only to God and themselves. In this posture things remained for about a fortnight. To a few, it was an hour of awful suspense. But in some of the last days of August, it became apparent that the desire for a revival was rapidly spreading in the church.

"As our sacramental Sabbath was approaching, this church, in connection with two neighboring churches, agreed to set apart the Friday preceding the communion, for fasting and prayer, chiefly to make supplication for the effusions of the Holy Spirit. The day, which was spent in prayer, singing, and short addresses to the people, was marked with unusual stillness, accompanied with pleasing appearances of humility, earnestness, and a sense of entire dependence. On the following Sabbath, a number of persons assembled at nine o'clock in the morning, to spend an hour in prayer for their minister, and for the blessing of God on the exercises of the day. This has become the stated practice of almost all the praying people of the congregation. Those who attended this first meeting unexpectedly found themselves animated with desires unfelt before, that God would that very day bring out his perfections to the view of the communicants, and this he did to a degree that had seldom or never been seen before. On the evening of the following Monday, at a lecture preached in a private house, evidence of the extraordinary presence of God, and the actual commencement of a revival of religion, was felt perhaps by every person present. During that, and the following week, increasing symptoms of a most powerful influence were discovered. The appearance was as if a collection of waters long suspended over the town had fallen at once, and deluged the whole place. For several weeks the people would stay, at the close of every evening service, to hear some new exhortation. At those seasons, you might see a multitude weeping and trembling around their minister, and many others standing as astonished spectators of the scene, and beginning to tremble themselves. One Sabbath after the second service, when I had catechized and dismissed the little children, they gathered around me weeping and inquiring what they should do. I know not but a hundred were in tears at once. The scene was as affecting as it was unexpected.

"Early in September many private associations for prayer were formed, and I never witnessed the communication of so earnest a spirit of prayer, and so general, nor observed such evident and remarkable answers to prayer. The agonies of parents have been such as to drive sleep from their eyes, and for weeks together have been seemingly as great as their nature could well sustain. And these parents, in every case that has come within my knowledge, have each several children who are already numbered among the hopeful converts. Many professors have been severely tried, and not a few have for a time given themselves over for lost."

"This work, in point of power and stillness, exceeds all that I have ever seen. While it bears down every thing with irresistible force, and seems almost to dispense with human instrumentality, it moves with so much silence, that unless we attentively observe its effects, we are tempted at times to doubt whether any thing uncommon is taking place. The converts are strongly marked with humility and self-distrust. Instead of being elated with confident hopes, they are inclined to tremble, and almost all are born into the distinguishing doctrines of grace.

"I suppose there are from two hundred and thirty to two hundred and fifty who hope they have been born again, and many still remain under solemn impressions. The subjects of this work are of all ages, from nine years old to more than threescore and ten, and of all characters, including drunkards, apostates, infidels, and those who were lately malignant opposers, and of all conditions, including poor negroes, and many of them hoary with age. While we gaze with wonder and delight at these glorious triumphs of the Prince of peace, and weep for joy to hear babes and sucklings sing hosannas to the Son of David, we cannot but join in the general response, and cry, 'Blessed is he that cometh in the name of the Lord. Hosanna in the highest.'"

In a letter of 1832, appended to Dr. Sprague's Lectures on Revivals, Dr. Griffin, giving a summary view of the revivals in which he had labored, says, "The first of June, 1809, I was removed by the providence of God, and by the advice of my brethren, to the Theological Seminary at Andover, and to a connection with the infant church in Park-street, Boston, as a stated preacher. The house in Park-street not being finished, and the Rev. Mr. French of Andover dying that summer, I took the pulpit, and supplied it till winter, for the benefit of the family. It pleased God to pour out his Spirit. A revival of very considerable extent ensued, calculated to fit that atmosphere to be breathed by the sons of the prophets."

Revival in Hampden Sydney College, Virginia. 1787, 1788.

The Rev. Dr. William Hill of Winchester, Virginia, on a public occasion gave the following history: "I lost my sainted mother when I was a youth, but not before the instructions which I received from her beloved lips had made a deep impression on my mind, an impression which I carried with me into a college, Hampden Sydney, Prince Edward county, where there was then *not one pious student*. There I often reflected, when surrounded with young men who scoffed at religion, upon the instructions of my mother; and my conscience was frequently sore distressed. I had no Bible, and dreaded getting one, lest it should be found in my possession. At last I could stand it no longer, and therefore requested a particular friend, a youth whose parents lived near, and who often went home, to ask his pious and excellent mother to send me some religious book. She sent me Alleine's Alarm, an old black book, which looked as if it might have been handled by successive generations for one hundred years.

"When I got it I locked my room, and lay on my bed reading it, when a student knocked at the door. And although I gave him no answer, dreading to be found reading such a book, he continued to knock and beat the door until I had to open it. He came in, and seeing the book lying on the bed, he seized it, and examining its title, said, 'Why, Hill, do you read such books?' I hesitated, but God enabled me to be decided, and to answer him boldly, but with much emotion, 'Yes, I do.' The young man said, with deep agitation, 'Oh, Hill, I envy you. You may obtain religion, but *I* never can. I came here a professor of religion, but through fear I dissembled, and have been carried along with the wicked until I fear there is no hope for me.'

"He told me there were two others who, he believed, were somewhat serious. We agreed to take up the subject of religion in earnest, and seek it together. We invited the other two, and held a prayer-meeting in my room on the next Saturday afternoon. And Oh, what a prayer-meeting! We tried to pray, but such prayer I never heard the like of. We knew not how to pray, but tried to do it. It was the first prayer-meeting I had ever heard of. We tried to sing, but it was in a most suppressed manner, for we feared the other students. But they found it out, and gathered round the door, and made such a noise that some of the officers had to come and disperse them. And so serious was the disturbance that the president, the late excellent Rev. Dr. John Blair Smith, had to investigate the matter at prayers, that evening, in the prayer hall. When he demanded the reason of the riot, a ringleader in wickedness got up and stated, that it was occasioned by three or four of the boys holding a prayer-meeting, and they were determined to have no such doings there.

"The good president heard the statement with deep emotion, and looking at the youths charged with the sin of praying, with tears in his eyes he said, 'Oh, is there such a state of things in this college? Then God has come near to us. My dear young friends, you shall be protected. You shall hold your next meeting in my parlor, and I will be one of your number.' Sure enough we had our next meeting in his parlor, and half the college were there. And there began a glorious revival of religion, which pervaded the college, and spread into the country around.

"Many of those students became ministers of the gospel. The youth who brought me Alleine's Alarm from his mother, was my friend the Rev. William Calhoun, still preaching in this state; and he who interrupted me in reading the work, is my venerable and worthy friend the Rev. Dr. Blythe, now president of a college in Indiana. Another was Rev. Clement Reed of this state; and a fifth, the late Rev. Carey H. Allen of Kentucky."

This revival included among its subjects half of the students in the college. It extended into neighboring churches, and then into those more remote, and was more extensive and powerful than had been experienced in Virginia since the days of President Davies, who died in 1761. Dr. Smith, the president of Hampden Sydney, was greatly quickened. "Two hundred and twenty persons, chiefly young people, were added to the churches to which he ministered within eighteen months; and the revival extended over Prince Edward, Cumberland, Charlotte, and Bedford counties, and to the Peaks of Otter," in the Blue Ridge.

Dr. Archibald Alexander in Central Virginia. 1789, 1790.

The history of Dr. Alexander's early life in the valley of Virginia, shows how great was the moral dearth there prevailing in the latter part of the last century, and illustrates the grace of God in raising up laborers to fulfil his own purposes of mercy. Though descended from a worthy Scotch Presbyterian ancestry, he says of himself at the age of seventeen, in 1789, "My only notion of religion was, that it consisted in becoming better. I had never heard of any conversions among Presbyterians. . . . The state of morals and religion after the revolutionary war was very bad." He engaged that year as a tutor in the family of General Posey, of which a venerated and pious Baptist lady was an inmate, who proved to him an invaluable friend. She loved the writings of Flavel, and as her eyes were weak, she often sent for him to read to her. Her conversation and this reading with other influences called his attention to religion, and Soame Jenyns on the Internal Evidences banished the prevalent French Infidelity which was assailing him. He proceeds to say:

"My services as a reader were frequently in requisition, not only to save the eyes of old Mrs. Tyler, but on Sundays for the benefit of the whole family. On one of these Sabbath evenings, I was requested to read out of Flavel. The part on which I had been regularly engaged was the 'Method of Grace,' but now, by some means, I was led to select one of the sermons on Rev. 3 : 20, 'Behold, I stand at the door and knock,' etc. The discourse was upon the patience, forbearance, and kindness of the Lord Jesus Christ to impenitent and obstinate sinners. As I proceeded to read aloud, the truth took effect on my feelings, and every word I read seemed applicable to my own case. Before I finished the discourse, these emotions became too strong for restraint, and my voice began to falter. I laid down the book, rose hastily, and went out with a full heart, and hastened to my place of retirement. No sooner had I reached the spot than I dropped upon my knees, and attempted to pour out my feelings in prayer, but I had not continued many minutes in this exercise before I was overwhelmed with a flood of joy. I was filled with a sense of the goodness and mercy of God." He passed through many fears, doubts, and conflicts before he was satisfied of his good estate, but in his later years he regarded this as the period of his conversion to Christ.

Hearing of the great revival above noticed in the neighborhood of Prince Edward, east of the Blue Ridge, he accompanied some of his fellow-students and their revered instructor Rev. William Graham, rector of Liberty Hall at Lexington, Rockbridge county, to the scene of wonders, where he passed some days; attended a communion-season at which multitudes were present, heard Dr. John Blair Smith and others preach, saw William Hill and others of the recent converts, and on their return "a revival of great power commenced, which extended to almost every Presbyterian church in the valley of Virginia." He, with several other young men, fruits of that revival, entered on study for the ministry; he was licensed to preach, October, 1791, and devoted himself to labors in the destitute and frontier settlements of Virginia and North Carolina. A private record of texts and places shows that, in the first fifteen months of his ministry, he preached one hundred and fifty-two sermons, and he says, "I never thought of any compensation for what I did." His subsequent labors and influence, especially in founding the Theological seminary in Princeton, and for nearly forty years diffusing a missionary and revival spirit among the hundreds of its members, are well known.

From a letter of Rev. Dr. Furman of Charleston, S. C., to Rev. Dr. Rippon of London, August, 1802.

Dr. Furman gives a particular account of a large union meeting held by Baptists, Presbyterians, Methodists, and others at the Waxhaws, about one hundred and seventy miles from Charleston, at which he estimated that three or four thousand were present, and about twenty ministers.

"The services," he says, "were conducted with much solemnity. Many seemed to be seriously concerned for the salvation of their souls, and the preaching and exhortation of the ministers in general were well calculated to make right impressions. Deep conviction for sin, and apprehension of the wrath of God were manifested at first, and several afterwards appeared to have a joyful sense of pardoning mercy through a Redeemer.

"A very considerable number had gone seventy or eighty miles from the lower parts of this state to attend this meeting, and since their return an extraordinary revival has taken place in the congregations to which they belong. It has spread also across the upper parts of this state. Taking it for granted that you have seen the publication entitled, 'Surprising Accounts,' by Woodward of Philadelphia, containing the accounts of revivals in Kentucky, Tennessee, and North Carolina, I therefore say nothing of them, but only that the work in North Carolina increases greatly."

Other accounts from all the states here named show the marvellous displays of divine grace. In the Kioka church, Georgia, in 1787, under the labors of Mr. Marshall, one hundred souls were brought in, and "a remarkable ingathering" in that church is recorded about 1802, "the time of the great revival which prevailed in many parts of Georgia."

Revivals in Western Pennsylvania. 1778–1805.

The aged Rev. Joseph Stevenson, who entered on his pastoral labors about fifty years since in Western Pennsylvania, writes:

"It may almost be said that the Presbyterian church in Western Pennsylvania was born in a revival. In 1778, Vance's fort, into which the families living adjacent had been driven by the Indians, was the scene of a remarkable work. There was but one pious man in the fort, Joseph Patterson, a layman, an earnest and devoted Christian, whose zeal had not waned even amid the storm and terrors of war; and during the long days and nights of their besiegement, he talked with his careless associates of an enemy more to be dreaded than the Indian, and a death more terrible than by the scalping-knife. As they were shut up within very narrow limits, his voice, though directed to one or two, could easily be heard by the whole company, and thus his personal exhortations became public addresses. Deep seriousness filled every breast, and some twenty persons were there led to Christ. These were a short time subsequently formed into the Cross Creek church, which built its house of worship near the fort, and had as its pastor for thirty-three years one of these converts, the Rev. Thomas Marques.

"From 1781 to 1787, a more extensive work of grace was experienced in the churches of Cross Creek, Upper Buffalo, Chartiers, Pigeon Creek, Bethel, Lebanon, Ten Mile, Cross Roads, and Mill Creek, during which *more than a thousand* persons were brought into the kingdom of Christ. Considering the unsettled state of the public mind at the close of the Revolutionary war, the constant anxiety and watchfulness against the incursions of hostile Indians, the toils and hardships incident to new settlements, and the scarcity of ministers, this was a signal work of the Spirit, greatly strengthening the feeble churches.

"From 1795 to 1799, another series of gracious visitations was enjoyed by the churches generally throughout Western Pennsylvania, extending to the new settlements north of Pittsburg. In this work Dr. McMillan, the first settled pastor in Western Pennsylvania, received into his church one hundred and ten, Mr. Marques one hundred and twenty-three, and large additions were made to many others.

"These works of grace prepared the way for the larger outpouring of the Spirit in 1802 to 1804. Many of the subjects of these early revivals emigrated to the surrounding counties, and became the elements of new churches, while not less than twenty of those converts prepared for the ministry, and were prominent laborers in the great revivals for which God had thus raised them up.

"In the latter part of 1801, and the beginning of 1802, the meetings for social worship, and the observance of public ordinances throughout Western Pennsylvania became remarkable in regard both to numbers and solemnity. In the spring and summer of 1802, there was a great increase of prayer and expectation of a blessing, leading many to continue all night in pleadings for the Holy Spirit's presence. In the autumn of 1802, the sacramental seasons in the various churches were attended by large numbers even from the distance of fifty miles, and deep solemnity felt by all. It is believed that more than five thousand people sometimes came together on these occasions, and remained for three, four, or five days, during which almost constant services were maintained.

"At a communion held in Cross Roads, a great multitude assembled, and nine ministers were present. The meeting-house, though large, being insufficient to contain half of the people on the Sabbath, the sacrament was administered at the tent to about eight hundred communicants, of whom forty-one were admitted for the first time. On Monday three ministers preached at different places, one in the house, and two in the encampment. This was a very solemn day. At the close of public worship it was the desire of the ministers that the people should disperse, but so intense was the feeling that few would leave. Many of the young people were deeply exercised, frequently speaking to sinners of their lost condition, of the glories of the Saviour, of the excellency and suitableness of the plan of salvation, warning, inviting, and pressing sinners to come to Christ; and all this in a manner quite astonishing for their years. Experienced Christians also were much refreshed and comforted, and affectingly recommended the Lord Jesus and his religion to those around them. Such meetings were held in various churches crowded with people from all the surrounding country, thousands were brought under deep conviction, and many hundreds professed faith in Christ.

"This work extended with more or less power over most of the churches in Western Pennsylvania and North-eastern Ohio. It continued with little abatement for two years, attesting itself to be a true work of God by its blessed fruits. From that day to this those churches have remained faithful witnesses for Christ, have established schools, founded colleges, trained hundreds of ministers, and sent forth thousands of Christians, as the nuclei of churches over the west and south."

From Rev. Thomas Marques, Cross Creek church, Western Pennsylvania. 1804.

"I took the charge of this congregation in June 1794, and preached here and in Buffalo congregation alternately until 1798. During this period there was in general a solemn attention, a considerable number were awakened, and one hundred and twenty-three were admitted to the communion, who have generally supported a profession becoming the gospel.

"In 1799, the Lord poured out the gracious influences of his Holy Spirit on the congregation, many were awakened, and twenty added to the church.

"In the spring of 1802, the Lord again revived his work, and carried it on until the first Tuesday in October, at which time the Spirit seemed like a rushing mighty wind, as on the day of pentecost. Many were alarmed with a view of their own sinful condition, and that of others around them.

"They generally had a deep sense of their undone state by nature, and their exposedness to the wrath of God. It seemed as if the sins of their childhood and youth all came up to their view, but especially the heaven-daring sin of rejecting the Lord Jesus Christ, as offered to them in the gospel. Those who have obtained relief, have scriptural views of the moral character of God, of the method of salvation through a Redeemer, of the sufficiency of his atonement, and the way in which God can be just and all his attributes remain unspotted in saving sinners according to the new covenant. They appear to acquiesce in the method of salvation through Christ, making a full, free, and hearty surrender of themselves to God and his service, embracing Christ as their prophet, priest, and king, under a deep sense of their need of him in all these offices, and of their entire unworthiness of the least favor at his hand.

"The fruits and effects of this work evidence it to be of God. Those whose tongues were dumb have learned to speak the language of Canaan. Those who were formerly Sabbath-breakers, scoffing at sacred things, and guilty of other immoralities, have not only forsaken their former evil practices, but have become regular and sober, diligently attending the ordinances of God's house, and conscientiously performing the duties of religion. Those who once depended upon their own attainments and good works for acceptance with God, have renounced all for the righteousness of Christ. Those who formerly delighted in carnal company, merry jests, profane songs, and foolish and vain conversation, now seek the company of them who fear God, and delight in holy exercises and spiritual communion. Those who formerly attended upon the preaching of the gospel either as idle spectators, or to cavil at or quarrel with it, now attend with a desire to know their duty, to enjoy communion with God, and receive grace and strength from him to enable them to live to his glory. Many have, in the most solemn, sweet, and affecting manner, spoken of the wisdom, love, and glory of God shining in the plan of salvation through Christ. They have also lamented their ignorance and want of love to him, the evil of their hearts, and the total depravity of their natures—have frequently expressed their desire after holiness and conformity to God, and their tender concern for his cause and the salvation of sinners. In short, many evidence a sweet, solemn, and humble disposition, equal to any thing we have ever witnessed in young converts. About one hundred have been admitted to the church."

Revivals in Kentucky and Tennessee about 1800.

The "Great Revival of 1800" is as well known in Kentucky and Tennessee as in the Atlantic states. Dr. Davidson, in his history of the state of the churches in Kentucky, says:

"On the eve of the nineteenth century, notwithstanding the increase of ministers and churches, the prospect was sufficiently gloomy to appall both the Christian and the patriot. The population of the state advanced with incredible rapidity, and soon outstripped the supply of the means of grace. Worldly-mindedness, infidelity, and dissipation threatened to deluge the land, and sweep away all vestiges of piety and morality. The rising generation were growing up in almost universal ignorance of religious obligation. The elder church-members were gradually dying off, and were replaced by no recruits from the ranks of the young. Except a little Goshen here and there, the shadow of night was gathering over the land. At this juncture, when hope was ready to expire, an unlooked-for and astonishing change suddenly took place. This event was the GREAT REVIVAL of 1800, so called from its wide extent and influence, and which, after all necessary allowances for the disorders which deformed it, was, beyond controversy, attended with signal benefits. A preparatory work had been going on for some time previous. The zealous labors of the Virginia missionaries, and others of the younger clergy, were not without effect, and there was yet a remnant in the land, that had neither bowed the knee to mammon nor Thomas Paine. An unusual attention to religion had been awakened in the south-western section of the state, in what was known as the Green River country, and the Cumberland settlements, a year or two previous."

A record of the Baptist churches in Kentucky states, that "in the remarkable outpourings of the Holy Spirit, from 1799 to 1803, in most parts of our land, among different denominations, about ten thousand were added to the Baptist churches within that state, who gave evidence of genuine conversion."

Of Rev. Robert Donnell, one of the fathers of the Cumberland Presbyterian church, who early entered on itinerant labors in Tennessee and North Alabama, and preached the gospel with fidelity and success for nearly fifty years, his biographer says, "He professed religion in the year 1800, in that ever memorable revival of pure experimental religion in which the Cumberland Presbyterian church had its origin."

It cannot be denied that in this revival, elsewhere so free from nervous excitement, there were, in parts of Kentucky and Tennessee, extraordinary "bodily exercises," called the jerks, falling down, etc., in the meetings, which the enlightened friends of the work lamented, and which excited its enemies to ridicule and blaspheme. But it must be remembered, that these physical agitations took place at the large camp-meetings, in which were gathered all the elements of excitement from every quarter, and which were continued day and night, till the consequent exhaustion of the multitudes in a great measure took away the power of self-control. These remarkable phenomena by no means proved that it was all fanaticism and delusion. There were beyond question many true conversions.

The Rev. Dr. Cleland wrote, in 1834, after witnessing the fruits of this work for more than thirty years, "The work at first was no doubt a glorious work of God. Many within my knowledge became hopefully pious, the most of whom continue unto this present, and many have fallen asleep in Jesus. The number of apostates was much fewer than I supposed."

The Rev. Dr. Alexander said of that work, "Many facts which occurred at the close of the revival were of such a nature that judicious men were fully persuaded that there was much that was wrong in the manner of conducting the work, and that an erratic and enthusiastic spirit prevailed to a lamentable extent. It is not doubted, however, that the Spirit of God was really poured out, and that many sincere converts were made, especially in the commencement of the revival; but too much indulgence was given to a heated imagination, and too much stress was laid on the bodily affections which accompanied the work, as though they were supernatural phenomena, intended to arouse the attention of the careless world."

REV. DR. DWIGHT, YALE COLLEGE—REFLECTIONS ON THE WORK ABOUT 1800.

I have reserved for this place the name of one whom the churches delighted to honor, Dr. TIMOTHY DWIGHT, president of Yale college, a fast friend of revivals, as well as a renowned and beloved teacher of the young men who resorted to that institution for classical education.

To go a little further back, when Dr. Dwight came into office, in 1795, many of the leading students in the several classes were deeply tinctured with French infidelity, and its bold champions were not backward to encounter the new president, at the first favorable opportunity. This was soon granted them, in a discussion before him involving the truth and inspiration of the Scriptures. They mustered all their force, and anticipated a signal victory. The day came in the class-room. It was a mortal onset for them, but a proud day for the college. In the summing up, he so scathingly exposed their ignorance, and so triumphantly overthrew them at every point, that they never wanted to measure weapons with him again. From that hour infidelity lost its prestige in Yale college, and has never dared openly to show its head since. The victory was an incalculable gain to the cause of religion in that popular seat of learning, and through the agency of its graduates who entered the ministry. It enthroned the president in the confidence of the students, and prepared them to listen with new interest to his admirable discourses from the pulpit, which, as professor of divinity, he preached in the college chapel from Sabbath to Sabbath, during the period of his presidency. It was morally impossible to sit four years under such preaching, so convincing in argument, so solemn and earnest in appeal, and so eloquent in delivery, without being instructed and profited, at least in some degree.

Nothing very remarkable, however, took place, till the spring and summer of 1802, when the revival, in its triumphant progress on the right hand and the left, reached Yale college; and there it came with such power as had never been witnessed within those walls before. It was in the Freshman year of my own class. It was like a mighty rushing wind. The whole college was shaken. It seemed for a time as if the whole mass of the students would press into the kingdom. It was the Lord's doing, and marvellous in all eyes. Oh, what a blessed change!

As the fruit of this revival, so memorable in the history of the institution, *fifty-eight* were added to the college church, and others, I know not how many, joined the churches at home. It was a glorious reformation. It put a new face upon the college. It sent a thrill of joy and thanksgiving far and wide into the hearts of its friends, who had been praying that the waters of salvation might be poured into the fountain from which so many streams were annually sent out.

The triennial catalogue shows, that for many years there had been but very few in the seminary preparing for the pulpit. In the four preceding classes, only *thirteen* names of ministers stand against *sixty-nine* in the next four years; nearly if not quite all of them brought in by the great revival.

Thus we see how dark were the prospects of the churches when it commenced. Only *thirteen* from the college in four years; less than *four* in a year, and that when there were but two or three other colleges in the country, from which any additional supplies could be expected.

It was indeed the bright dawn of a new Christian epoch, when the heavens were opened, and poured down righteousness upon Yale college, and upon scores of churches; and I may venture to say, that the influence of those revivals upon the cause of vital religion at home and abroad, has already surpassed the most sanguine hopes of those who witnessed and rejoiced in them.

At that time, when a student was converted in college, or before he entered, it was taken for granted by everybody, that he intended to devote his life to the service of Christ in the gospel. It was so at Yale, in the revival of 1802. I cannot call to mind a single convert who did not at once ask, 'Lord, what wilt thou have me to do?' and who did not set his heart upon becoming a preacher. Nearly all of them, as the catalogue shows, entered the ministry. The exceptions were very few, and mainly from causes which they could not control. How different, alas, from what we witness now! If one-half of the graduates from our colleges who profess religion enter the ministry, it is about as much as the churches and a perishing world are allowed to expect. I bless God it was not so then. Had it been, what a loss to the cause for which Christ shed his blood. And who will say that the demand for good ministers is less now, than it was then?

And why this great falling off? It is not because souls are less precious, or less in danger of perishing, in the middle of the nineteenth century, than they were at the beginning. Is it because young men obtain hopes easier under the preaching of the present day, than they did under the ministry of Hyde, Griffin, Hallock, and their contemporaries, who were so eminently doctrinal in their discourses? I cannot help thinking it is, at least in part. As he loveth much to whom much is forgiven, so he who has most deeply felt the plague of his own heart, and the justice of his condemnation under discriminating preaching—he who has most deeply felt his own perishing need of a Saviour—will feel more constrained by the love of Christ to enter the ministry, that if possible he may save some who are under the same condemnation, than if the terrors of death had not taken hold upon him when he was passing through the deep waters. Such were the preachers who came out of the revivals now under review, and who were to carry forward the work when the fathers had fallen asleep. They knew what truths had taken the deepest hold of their own minds, and made them the basis of their ministry.

Whatever view we can take of the work of God at the beginning of this century, it was a glorious period in the religious history of the country. The apostasies have been comparatively few, and besides their rich harvests in gathering souls to Christ, those revivals stand connected, in the history of Redemption, with those aggressive agencies by which He is now turning our own moral wildernesses into fruitful fields, and sending the gospel to all heathen lands.

When that era dawned, there were no Missionary societies, foreign or domestic, no Bible societies, no Tract societies, no Education societies, no onward movements in the churches of any sort, for the conversion of the world. At home it was deep spiritual apathy; abroad, over all the heathen lands, the calm of the Dead sea—death, death, nothing but death.

All the first foreign missionaries, Hall, Newell, Mills, Judson, Nott, Rice, Bingham, King, Thurston, and others who entered the field a little later, were converted and received their missionary baptism in that revival. The American Board of Foreign Missions was formed in 1810, at the urgency of the first band that went out from this country to India. But for their earnest solicitation to be sent forth with the glad tidings of the gospel upon their tongues, no such Board would have been formed; certainly not at that time; and if it had, it could not have done any thing: there would have been no missionaries to send, if God had not poured out his Spirit, and raised them up and prepared them to endure hardness as good soldiers of Jesus Christ. In these revivals the holy fire was kindled, and waked up and warmed the churches to an onward aggressive movement, such as had never been known in this country before. Other missionaries soon followed under the same Board. And about the same time, the Baptist Foreign Mission Board was organized to sustain Judson and Rice who had joined their communion, and commenced a mission in

Burmah, which has become one of the most prosperous missions of the present age. And now, behold what from these small and feeble beginnings God has wrought, in the four quarters of the world, and the isles of the Gentiles.

From the same revival source sprang home missions. It began to be felt, we have a wide and fast spreading population within our own borders that must be cared for, and then domestic missionary societies were formed to meet the want.

Nor was this enough. The churches having once waked up from their long slumbers, could not rest here. The destitute at home must have the word of God put into their hands, and it must be sent abroad with the missionaries, and translated into the tongues wherein the heathen were born, that they might read the wonderful works of God and be turned from darkness to light, from the worship of dumb idols to the worship of Him who made the world. Hence sprang the American Bible Society, and in succession its hundreds of branches and kindred institutions, that are now preparing and distributing the bread of life from one end of the earth to the other.

Nor yet again could the yearnings of Christian benevolence, once excited, rest without still further expansion. A Christian literature, in a cheap and attractive form, must be created and diffused. Small religious tracts must be written, printed, and scattered over the land; to this end Tract Societies must be organized, funds must be raised, and the press be enlisted. It was done, and through this ever active and all-pervading agency, what hath God wrought!

Having proceeded thus far with these aggressions upon the kingdom of darkness, was there any thing more to be done to pour into it the light of heaven? Yes, a great deal more, and through many other kindred agencies. So the Sabbath-school Union was formed. The Colored population, and the Sailors must be cared for, the ravages of Intemperance must be arrested on the land and on the sea.

Thus the glorious cause of religion and philanthropy has advanced, till it would require a space which cannot be afforded in these sketches, so much as to name the Christian and humane societies which have sprung up all over the land within the last forty years. Exactly how much we at home and the world abroad are indebted for these organizations, so rich in blessings, to the revivals of 1800, it is impossible to say, though much every way—more than enough to magnify the grace of God in the instruments he employed, in the immediate fruits of their labors, and the subsequent harvests springing from the good seed which was sown by the men whom God delighted thus to honor.

It cannot be denied, that modern missions sprung out of those revivals. The immediate connection between them as cause and effect, was remarkably clear in the organization of the first societies, which have since accomplished so much; and the impulse which they gave to the churches to extend the blessings which they were diffusing, by forming the later affiliated societies of like aims and character, is scarcely less obvious. Taken altogether, the revival period at the close of the last century and the beginning of the present, furnishes ample materials for a long and glorious chapter in the History of Redemption.

What if the Spirit had not been poured out when it was so greatly needed, after the long spiritual drought under which the land was suffering? Or what if a different character had been stamped upon the revival by ignorant and fanatical preachers? What if Dwight and Griffin and the other ministers of the day, whose testimony we have in these sketches, had made it an easy matter for sinners to repent and gain a hope, instead of holding up before them the character of God, the strictness, justice, and terrible penalty of his law, the entire and dreadful depravity of their hearts, the absolute sovereignty of God in having mercy on whom he will have mercy, regeneration by the Holy Spirit, and justification by faith alone—what would have been the fruits? Under smooth, superficial preaching, there might have been some real converts; but as the late Rev. Daniel A. Clark says in one of his printed sermons, "They would not have known when they were converted, WHO converted them, or what they were converted for." There is no reason to think, I am sure, that under any preaching that "heals the hurt slightly," the revivals, if they had taken place at all, would have filled and strengthened the churches by their thoroughness and the ripeness of their fruits, or their influence upon the age and the world, as those of which I have been speaking did. They went down into the depths of the soul, searched out all the deceitful hiding-places of its enmity against God, and brought the sinner helpless and self-condemned to the foot of the cross.

I have dwelt longer upon the revival epoch which opened in our own land at the commencement of this century, than upon any that preceded it, because I was then upon the stage, and passed through those remarkable years of the right hand of the Most High, so that I can speak what I do know, and testify what I have seen; because I think the work was freer from objectionable drawbacks, and a greater proportion of those who obtained hopes held out to the end, than in "the great awakening," or any preceding revival since the Reformation; because there was so little of 'Lo here, and Lo there,' to divert men's minds from the state of their own hearts, and their absolute dependence upon the Spirit of God to work in them by his renewing and sanctifying power; and because it stirred up the churches to aggressive action upon the country and the world, through the combined instrumentality of missionary and other kindred societies, as no former revival had ever done.

In looking back fifty years and more, the great revival of that period strikes me, in its thoroughness, in its depth, in its freedom from animal, unhealthy excitement, and in its far-reaching influence on subsequent revivals, as having been decidedly in advance of any that had preceded it. It was the opening of a new revival epoch which has lasted now more than half a century, with but short and partial interruptions—and blessed be God, the end is not yet. In the next chapter I shall resume the subject, and bring these sketches down to the present time.

CHAPTER VI.

THE REVIVAL EPOCH ABOUT 1800—CONTINUED.

The great Revival of 1800, as we have seen, was so quiet and orderly and free from objections, there were so many demonstrable proofs of the mighty power of God in arresting and converting men of all classes, infidels, universalists, drunkards, profane swearers, as well as multitudes of others, and there was so marked a change for the better in the state of society, that nobody could help seeing it. In some respects, as I have already shown, its distinctive characteristics were quite different from the Great Awakening sixty years before, under Edwards, Whitefield, and their fellow-laborers of like precious faith. As there were no such outbursts of high-wrought animal excitement as often disturbed public worship then, so no such fanatical divisions supervened, to rend the churches and bring reproach upon the cause. No itinerants, flaming with zeal not according to knowledge, now sprung up to distract the churches, grieve the Holy Spirit, and bring into discredit all revivals. On the contrary, the most sceptical were constrained to say, "This is the finger of God. It can't be man's work. What we have witnessed is utterly beyond all human power to accomplish." They may not have been converted, though some of them were, but their mouths were shut.

For some years after the revivals recorded in the

last chapter, though the work was not so general as at the going out of the last, and the coming in of the present century, yet there were many revivals of the same marks of genuineness, showing that God had not shut up the heavens, but was waiting to be more earnestly inquired of, again to come down and multiply the trophies of redeeming love. So that, when God again more copiously poured out his Spirit, it was not marked as a new epoch, but the same continued and extended.

It was in that interval of partial suspension, that by the grace of God, I was permitted to enter the ministry. I was ordained and settled in 1807, and by the help of God I continue unto this day to witness what I have seen, and to give a brief sketch of the revivals in this country for the last fifty years. Very brief it must be, to leave room for the Manual in the second part of this volume. This I regret the less, because if I had ever so much space, the narratives are so recent and so ample, and are to be found in so many volumes within the reach of all who take an interest in the advancement of the Redeemer's kingdom, that not much enlargement seems to be called for. Brief sketches are now more likely to be read, I think, than many repetitions of minute narratives, as repetitions to a great extent they must needs be, where the phases of revivals are substantially alike.

About 1814, as near as I can fix the date, from my own recollection and the helps before me, the clouds, laden with their rich refreshings, began again to gather over more of the churches. Those who kept near the throne in prayer, and had wisdom to discern the signs of the times, began to expect great things, and they were not disappointed. It was as if the Saviour had said, "Ye shall see greater things than these." Not greater displays of divine power than they had witnessed in the revivals a few years before at the opening of the century, but in their longer continuance, if not in their wider extent.

Many of the converts in these first revivals were now entering the ministry, and a few of them remain even unto this day. The rest have fallen asleep. I believe that not far from four-fifths of the younger pastors of evangelical churches, who were especially blessed during the succeeding twenty years, were themselves converted under the labors of Dwight, Alexander, Hyde, Griffin, Hallock, Mills, and their contemporaries, many of whose names I have given in a former chapter. They of course came out of the best schools for learning what a genuine revival is, and what preaching is most blessed in carrying on the work. When they came into the same care of souls, they would naturally refer back to their own experience and observation, when the arrows of conviction were piercing their own consciences, and the inquiry, What must we do to be saved? was sounding in their ears. They could not help it. They would adopt the same style of preaching, and substantially the same other means, as they had felt and witnessed to be mighty through God to the pulling down of strongholds; and in reviewing the history and results of their labors in winning souls, we should be disappointed not to find the same image and superscription enstamped upon the revivals under their own ministry.

How far this expectation has been realized, will appear as I proceed with these sketches.

If I do not name so many of this second generation of revival preachers in our current century, nor dwell so long and specifically upon their labors, as I have done in the earlier period, it is not because I think them inferior in talents and ministerial gifts to their fathers, nor that I think them, as a body, deserving of less honor in their Master's service, but because of their relative position and antecedents. The pioneers in any important era of human advancement are of course more prominent on the historic page, than those who are taught by them to follow in the same line and carry out their plans and principles, though the latter may be as much devoted to the cause as the former. So here, though the disciples may not have been a whit behind their masters in piety, in zeal, or in ministerial qualifications to serve Christ in the gospel, entering as they did into the labors of their predecessors and teachers, the less need be said of their labors and success in the same fields.

With few exceptions, like their fathers they did most of the work themselves. They recognized the scripture distinction between pastors and evangelists, and rejoiced that the great Head of the church was raising up and sending out evangelists to preach the gospel and plant churches in our new and destitute settlements; but they did not seek much aid from preachers without charge, since familiarly called *revivalists*.

At the same time they were glad of such assistance as God in his wisdom might please to send them. And as he in a former age raised up George Whitefield to help the pastors wherever he went, and they received him, so I must here record the grace of God in raising up, and so eminently qualifying Asahel Nettleton, to perform a similar service over a wide region where the revivals of which I am now to speak most remarkably prevailed. If there were others who were equally devoted, judicious, and helpful to pastors, I did not know them, and must leave it for those who did to name them. Mr. Nettleton's labors were so widely extended, so long continued, and so remarkably blessed, that it would be impossible for me, in my sketches of this period, not to refer to him often, as holding a high place among those whom God was pleased to honor in the conversion of souls. President Dwight, whose pupil he was, and who knew him well, is reported to have said, "Nettleton will make one of the most useful men this country has ever seen." Of course, in the inspired sense of the term, this was not prophetic; but Dr. Dwight was justly celebrated for his remarkable penetration of young men's talents and character. His judgment seemed to be almost intuitive, and it seldom failed.

If there has been, since the days of the mighty elders in the Great Awakening, a preacher more successful in winning souls to Christ within the same number of years, than Nettleton, I have yet to learn his name, and what he did. I cannot refer to all the places where Mr. Nettleton labored, nor give the exact number, but it was very large—scores, I believe, where the revivals were very powerful, and most of which sprung up in immediate connection with his untiring labors. Wherever he went, as his Memoir and Remains by Dr. Tyler show, the Lord went with him, working mightily in turning men from darkness to light, and from the power of Satan unto God. His great experience in revivals, his deep penetration of the workings of the human heart in all the stages of awakening and conviction, and with all its conflicting exercises up to a comfortable hope in Christ, gave him an advantage, of which he availed himself to the full extent of his powers, which I am persuaded has rarely if ever been surpassed, and seldom equalled in these modern times.

I verily believe that no great warrior ever studied military tactics with more enthusiasm, or better understood the art of *killing* men with the sword of war, then Nettleton did how to wield the sword of the Spirit, to deliver them from captivity to sin and Satan, and *save* their souls. I am sure no warrior ever studied his art under so great a Teacher. No matter whether Nettleton had ever met an inquirer or caviller before or not, he seemed to see just where he stood, and how to address him at a glance. If all revivalists had the talent and wisdom and piety and meekness and deep Christian experience which he had, pastors with more work than they can do when God is pouring out his Spirit might safely receive them with open arms. But the ability to do what he did as a helper, and do it so well, is granted to very few. It is one of the most difficult services in which an itinerant popular preacher ever engaged, to go in and labor with pastors of ordinary standing, in revivals. It requires wisdom, prudence, and self forgetfulness, which very few of that class possess, so as not to do quite as much harm as good, by throwing the ministers whom they came to assist into the background. Many a faithful pastor has been undermined and dismissed, unintentionally we must believe, to the great loss of the church, just in this way. Not so with Nettleton. Wherever he labored, he left the churches and their ministers stronger and more united than he found them. This was the universal testimony. I never knew or heard of an exception. Most manifest was it, that God had raised him up and kept him in this land for that very service, when he had set his heart upon a foreign mission. He labored with me three months in the most powerful revival that we ever enjoyed, and for whatever I know of the means which God has been wont especially to bless in reviving his work, I am more indebted to him than to any other man, more than to all others put together. How he was regarded by other pastors with whom he labored, we shall see in their letters and narratives as we proceed.

This renewed time of refreshing in the current century commenced, as I have said, about 1814, and as nearly as I am able to fix the dates, continued about thirty years, when the ways of Zion again went into mourning for a brief period, till the spirit of prayer was remarkably poured out upon the cities of New York, Philadelphia, and many other places, a little more than a year ago, of which more in its place.

From 1814 to 1845, the spiritual harvests were

more productive in some years than others—in some thirty-fold, in some sixty, and in some a hundred—a period which will ever be referred to as one of the most extraordinary hitherto in the religious history of our country. Not tens, nor scores, but hundreds of churches and congregations shared in those copious outpourings of the Spirit. We began to hope that these showers would henceforth continue to pour down righteousness, without any such intermissions as had so often occurred. Oh, it would be delightful to take a full survey of the great field while Christ was so gloriously triumphing everywhere, and to count the thronging trophies of his victories.

But my limits warn me to confine myself to briefer sketches. The narratives of the revivals during the period to which we have now come, if they had all been fully written out, would fill many volumes. I have enough before me for hundreds of pages; but all that I can do is to make a few selections from the mass, which is the less to be regretted as the essential leading features of these revivals, spreading over about one-third of the century, bore such striking resemblance, that to multiply testimonies would be to repeat nearly the same things. As I leave out vastly more than I shall put in, I see not how I can do better than to insert the substance of a few of these narratives, and then glean extracts from others as they come in my way.

From Rev. Gardiner Spring, D. D., New York.

Dr. Spring, in his closing sermon in the old Brick church in Beekman-street, May 25, 1856, recounting the dispensations of divine grace in connection with his ministry, which commenced August 8, 1810, proceeds to say:

"The thought has no doubt often crossed the minds of reflecting Christians, that those who have occupied a place on the earth during the last fifty years, have lived in a remarkable age of the world, not only as it respects science and the arts, and the progress of civil society, but in regard to the cause of vital piety. The period, commencing with the year 1792, and terminating with 1842, was a memorable period in the history of the American church. Scarcely any portion of it, but was graciously visited by copious effusions of the Holy Spirit. From north to south, and from east to west, our male, and more especially our female academies, our colleges, and our churches drank largely of this fountain of living waters. It was my privilege to enter upon the course of academical life not far from the meridian of this bright day. There were no subjects that interested my mind more deeply, when I began my ministry among this people, than those revivals of religion which passed over the land of my boyhood. This interest increased with time and official labors and responsibility, and exercised a most important influence upon my whole course. Sparse clouds of mercy had been hovering over the congregation during the first four years of my ministry, and not a few, especially of those in middle life, had been brought into the kingdom of God.

"The year 1814 was a year of severe labor and deep solicitude—as it drew towards its close, of great discouragement and depression. It seemed to me that I must abandon my post, and that neither my mind, my heart, nor my health were adequate to its constantly accumulating duties. My intellectual resources seemed to be exhausted, and drained dry. Many a time, after preaching, did I remain long in the pulpit, that I might not encounter the faces of the people as I left the church; and many a time when I left it did I feel that I could never preach another sermon. Yet I labored on week after week, without discovering to what extent the Spirit of God was carrying forward his own noiseless work. I perceived nothing to encourage me but an unusual enlargement and urgency in prayer, a greater facility in the selection of fitting themes for the pulpit, and more freedom and earnestness in declaring the whole counsel of God. God remarkably interposed to relieve my mind from its depression, and gave me such enlarged and delightful views of his truth, that my whole ministry received a new and cheered impulse. It was easy, also, to perceive that the spirit of grace and supplication was being poured out upon the people. The weekly prayer-meeting and the weekly lecture were full of interest. Days of fasting and prayer were occasionally observed, and a Saturday evening prayer-meeting was established by the young men of the congregation. Our Sabbaths became deeply solemn and affecting; we watched for them like those who watch for the morning, and I verily believe we anticipated them with greater pleasure and expectation than the sons and daughters of earth ever anticipated their brightest jubilee. This was the first strongly marked revival of God's work among this people; and I take this notice of it because it was so emphatic an expression of God's goodness to your young minister. Poor a thing as I have been, and still continue to be, it was this work of grace which made me what I am—which gave me entirely new views of the great objects of the ministry, and made my work my joy. I loved it before, but never so ardently as then. But for this early season of mercy, during the summer of 1814, I do not see how I could have remained among you. It was the Lord's doing, and it is marvellous in our eyes. The ingathering was not great, but it was the finest of the wheat. I may not mentiou their names.

"This was but the beginning of days of mercy. The commencement of the year 1815 was the dawning of a still brighter day. The last Sabbath of the old year and the evening services of that Sabbath will be long remembered. Eight or ten persons, during the following week, were found to be awake, and in earnest for their salvation. The whole winter was a day of the right hand of the Most High. The cloud of mercy extended itself through the following spring and summer and autumn. In the month of November the Bible-class was reorganized, the Saturday evening prayer-meeting was renewed, and God appeared to take the work into his own hands. There was complaint and hostility; there were not wanting apprehensions in the minds of some of the pastors and churches in the city, that the work savored more of fanaticism than intelligent and sober thought. But the apprehensions were groundless. The blessing was near; the sacred influence was silent as the dew of heaven. There was no outbreak and no disorder. There was prayer. There was solemn and earnest preaching. There were unexpected and unthought of instances of seriousness among the gay and frivolous, in the families of the rich as well as the poor, among the immoral as well as the moral, and many were the instances of conversion to God. The third Thursday of January was set apart by about thirty members of the church as a day of fasting, humiliation, and prayer. It was in a private house in the rear of St. Paul's, in Church-street; and such a day I never saw before, and have never seen since. It was closed under strong and confident expectation that God was near, and that his Spirit was about largely to descend upon the people. And so it was. A delightful impulse was given to the work by this day of prayer. The promise was made good, 'Before they call I will answer, and while they are yet speaking I will hear.' The weekly lecture, attended on the evening of that day, was perhaps the most solemn service of my ministry. The subject of the discourse was suggested by the words, 'Marvel not that I said unto you, Ye must be born again.' God was with the hearers and the preacher; his Spirit moved them as the trees of the forest are moved by a mighty wind. There is good reason to believe that the minds of more than *one hundred persons* were deeply impressed with a sense of their lost condition as sinners, and their need of an interest in Christ, on that evening. Enemies were silenced; members of other churches came among us to see and mark the character of the work for themselves, and all classes were constrained to confess, 'This is the finger of God.' Between one and two hundred attended the meetings for religious inquiry and conversation, and deep solemnity pervaded the whole people. There was great eagerness for religious instruction, and great satisfaction in the soul-humiliating and soul-encouraging doctrines of the cross. The work was rapid. The period of awakening and conviction in many instances was very short, so short that older Christians began to doubt the genuineness of such conversions. There was no reason for the doubt. Some of the brightest and most enduring Christians among us were those very persons whose conversion was almost as sudden as that of Saul of Tarsus. The gathering of this protracted harvest was rich, consisting sometimes of thirty and forty, and at one communion of more than seventy, filling the broad aisle of the church—a lovely spectacle to God, angels, and men.

"There have been five seasons of the especial outpouring of God's Spirit upon this people during the ministry of their present pastor. They were interspersed between the years 1812 and 1834, more or less copious, but always seasons of delightful refreshing from the presence of the Lord. If the tree is known by its fruit, they are proved to have been the fruit of God's Spirit. The subjects of this work of grace have in almost all instances run well; they have turned out intelligent and active Christians. Many of them have been called to their last earthly rest; nor shall I forget the blessedness and the blessed scenes of their last hours. Many of them are ministers of the gospel, and more the wives of ministers. Many of them are teachers and superintendents of Sabbath-schools. Many of them are ruling elders and deacons in other churches, while some remain in the honorable fulfilment of these offices among ourselves. Very many of them are scattered through this wide land, and distant churches and the distant wilderness are made glad *for them*. I never was so gratefully impressed with this fact, and with the high privilege of preaching the gospel in this sanctuary, as on an unexpected tour through Western New York and the western states on the Upper Mississippi. Everywhere I met those who remembered the young minister and the old Session-room. I heard of the death of some far away, and it was affecting to learn that in their last hours their thoughts of grateful praise were turned towards these scenes of mercy.

"It will be found, by an inspection of our records, that after the separation of the Brick and Wall-street churches, and before the installation of the present pastor, the session were faithfully employed in acts of *painful discipline*. Church discipline is not less truly an ordinance of God than church communion. No church can prosper that connives at heresy or immorality among its communicants. This unwelcome duty was faithfully pursued for several years after my settlement among this people, and has been discharged with perfect unanimity ever since. In the early part of my ministry there were some avowed infidels in the church, who were the disciples of Paine and Palmer; there were also avowed Universalists; there have been from time to time immoral men and licentious, whom no means could reclaim, and they have been cast out. It has often been at great sacrifice of feeling, and some of interest and influence, that these acts of discipline have been performed; but however reluctantly and cautiously, it is a work which has been done."

From Bishop McIlvaine, of the diocese of Ohio.

In closing a letter on revivals in 1832, Bishop McIlvaine says, "I owe too much of what I hope for as a Christian, and what I have been blessed with as a minister of the gospel, not to think most highly of the eminent importance of promoting the spirit of genuine revivals. Whatever I possess of religion began in a revival. The most precious, steadfast, and vigorous fruits of my ministry have been the fruits of revivals. I believe that the spirit of revivals in the true sense, was the simple spirit of the religion of apostolic times, and will be more and more the characteristic of these times, as the day of the Lord draws near."

The Bishop's annual address to the convention of the diocese of Ohio, in June, 1858, is chiefly devoted to the subject of the revival of religion, occasioned especially by "the blessed work of grace which God had so mercifully, and so widely and wonderfully vouchsafed to the churches of our land within the few preceding months."

"It is more than forty years," he says, "since I first witnessed a revival of religion. It was in the college of which I was a student. It was powerful and pervading, and fruitful in the conversion of young men to God; and it was quiet, unexcited, and entirely free from all devices or means beyond the few and simple which God has appointed, namely, 'prayer and the ministry of the word.' In that precious season of the power of God, my religious life began. I had *heard* before; I began then to *know*. I must doubt the deepest convictions of my soul, when I doubt whether that revival was the work of the Spirit of God. Many that have labored faithfully in the ministry, and are now at rest with the Lord; some that are still in the work; many whose mark has been strongly made upon their generation, on the side of the gospel, were the subjects of that work. Till Satan shall be bound, so that he cannot go about to deceive and devour, a work of religion more genuine, less perverted by human infirmities and devices, less dishonored by the defection of such as professed to have been born of God therein, is hardly to be expected.

"About the time of that revival, and for several years after, similar blessings were enjoyed in various communities of the land. They were, for the most part, equally simple, exhibiting numerous and decided conversions, elevating the spiritual character of Christians, and sending forth many faithful men to be ministers and missionaries of the gospel, at home and abroad."

"During this period, our Episcopal churches, under a greatly extended and more earnest and evangelical ministry, were in many places favored of God with marked manifestations of the power of his Spirit; bowing the hearts of many persons, within a short space of time, to the obedience of Christ. I have nowhere seen more fruitful 'revivals of religion,' in which the conversions were more marked, the spiritual results more beneficial and permanent. How many of our clergy can tell of such movements under their labors, and bless God for their issues of life. And how many of them can point to revivals in Episcopal churches as marking their spiritual birthdays."

Proceeding to notice a period of several years of apparent unfruitfulness, in which "it seemed as if the preaching of the word had lost its power," he says, "Then it was, just in that time of rebuke and darkness, and apparent deep discouragement, that God's hand appeared and this present work of grace began. It began in our chief commercial centres, precisely where the credit of religion had been most impaired, and the tide against it was the strongest. It began in a remarkable indication, among persons deeply immersed in business cares, of a desire to meet together for prayer. Its progress has exhibited the same simple features as its beginning. How widely it has gone over our land; how it has appeared in hundreds of our cities and villages almost simultaneously, reaching all classes of population; the same thing among all, silent, simple, subduing, harmonizing, and uniting, making people love the word of God and prayer who never cared for them before, I need not tell you. I rejoice to know that our churches, in this diocese and in others, have largely participated in the blessing, and are gathering more and more fruit therefrom. Our diocesan college is thus favored. Pray for it, my brethren, that all the youth therein may be turned to the Lord. Pray for our whole church, that no part of it may be unvisited in these 'times of refreshing from the presence of the Lord.'"

"You see a daily assemblage of intelligent people gathered from the walks of business, at an hour of the day which the world claims for its own interests, in some lecture-room or public hall, or Sunday-school-house: they pray with one another; they 'speak to one another in psalms and hymns, and spiritual songs;' they read a few verses of Scripture; they exhort one another. If a minister be present, as often is the case, he addresses them for a few minutes: they thus pass an hour; separating as punctually at its end, as they met at its beginning; and this, added to the parochial work and exercises of the churches, is all the exterior instrumentality under God, on which this remarkable movement has made its march through the land. The strong tendency is, to strengthen a sense of the value and necessity of the regular ministry, to enhance reverence for the old paths of gospel truth and ordinances, and greatly to increase the attendance upon the regular, sober services of the Sabbath, and of the judicious, faithful pastor.

"There have been, in the American churches, revivals as pure and simple, and in their sphere, as effective for good. But we read of none of such extent; reaching at the same time so many people; scattered over such a length and breadth of territory; appearing in so many denominations of Christians, of widely separated ecclesiastical institutions; leavening so many colleges, and other institutions of education; so penetrating with one and the same influence all gradations of society, from the most cultivated to the most unlettered; in cities and villages, in the counting-house of the merchant, in the workshop of the mechanic, in factories, in printing-offices, among classes of persons usually regarded as peculiarly removed from and fenced against the influence of gospel truth. How can we witness all this, and not see the hand of God, and take courage, and desire and pray for more and more of such manifestations of his grace?"

One of the revivals in which Bishop McIlvaine speaks of having labored, was in the apparently very unpromising field, the Military Academy at West Point, about 1826. Being called upon one day by a student who he thought would be as likely as any other to receive in good part a word of serious exhortation, he presented him four tracts, two of which he requested him to read for his own personal benefit, and the other two to drop where some of his *sceptical* fellow-students would be likely to find them.

The next Saturday another student called on him and said, "You do not know me, sir; my name is ——;" and then burst into tears. For some time he could not utter a word. "My friend," said Mr. McIlvaine, "if, as I trust, your grief is connected with religion—if you desire to become a servant of God, be encouraged to open your heart to me, whose heart is already open to you." "I do desire to become a servant of God," said he; and deep emotion again prevented utterance. He soon related that he had found a tract in his room, *the Death of an Infidel;* that he had not considered himself an infidel, but had been very profane, and in the habit of speaking lightly of religion. He not long after gave evidence that he had been born of God, and united himself to the communion of the church.

This young man was then intent on the salvation of his fellow-student through whom he had received the tract; and in a few days he brought him, leaning on his arm, to Mr. McIlvaine, who threw around him his arms of Christian love. "I can hold out no longer," said the student; "this is not the first time; I have been often called; I can hold out no longer. I will be a servant of God, his grace helping me, henceforth for ever." It was in reading the "Shepherd of Salisbury Plain," that he first felt his heart expanded with love to God, and bursting with the spirit of prayer. These two young men became active members of the church of Christ; they labored faithfully in tract distribution and Sabbath-schools; by one of them a school of a hundred children was raised up where the gospel had scarcely ever been preached; one of them established a weekly prayer-meeting among a people destitute of the means of grace; by the instrumentality of one of them, as many as *ten*, who had been dreadfully wicked, were hopefully converted, and so changed as to astonish their former companions. Both consecrated their lives to the ministry of the gospel, and one of them is now a bishop of the Protestant Episcopal church in the distant west.

From Rev. Dr. Archibald Maclay, New York. 1809–1820.

"From February, 1809, when eighteen members were constituted a Baptist church, and received the right-hand of fellowship from the venerable Rev.

John Williams, father of Rev. Dr. William R. Williams, till December, 1820, I think it can be truly said that we enjoyed a perpetual revival. We were few in number, but it pleased the Lord to grant a spirit of grace and supplication. We felt an ardent and longing desire for the salvation of sinners, and corresponding efforts were manifested. At that time we met in a large school-room in James-street, while erecting our first place of worship in Mulberry-street. The access to the school-room was inconvenient, but it was filled to overflowing, and became the birthplace of many precious souls. When we removed to our new place of worship, it was immediately filled, and the work of God in the conversion of sinners continued to increase. In a few years we rebuilt, on the same site, a house of double the size, and this too was filled to its utmost capacity. The Lord continued to bless the word, and conversions to God were multiplied. Almost every week, I was visited by individuals anxiously inquiring, 'What must I do to be saved? How shall I escape the wrath to come?' During this period, I am persuaded that not less than five hundred were brought out of darkness into God's marvellous light.

"A Sunday-school was established in 1810, under the instruction of Charles G. Sommers and Joseph W. Griffiths, the first that was organized in this city, or so far as I know in the United States, exclusively for religious purposes. We afterwards organized three other Sunday-schools, one of them very large, in a destitute part of the city, under the care of Mr. David T. Valentine, and all were well attended. I taught a Bible-class of young men on Monday evening, and a class of young ladies on Wednesday afternoon. I was accustomed to preach three times on the Lord's day. In the morning I usually expounded the Scriptures; expounding in this way the whole New Testament and some portions of the Old, which proved very profitable both to me and my hearers. In the afternoon I generally preached for the instruction and edification of Christians, and in the evening addressed more especially the unconverted. Our regular lecture on Tuesday evening, and our prayer-meeting on Friday evening were well attended and deeply interesting. The young people also met for prayer on Saturday evening.

"During the period that I was pastor of the church, eighteen brethren were licensed to preach, and became useful ministers of the gospel; and six or seven other brethren who were dismissed from us to other churches, also became preachers. Some of these are still living, and have labored in the cause of Christ for nearly half a century.

"In my ministry it has been my aim to keep back nothing profitable to my hearers, but to declare unto them 'all the counsel of God.' The leading theme of my preaching has been Christ, and him crucified, as the only Saviour of lost sinners. I have shown the universal and total depravity of men; that every unconverted sinner is under the dominion of a carnal mind, which is enmity against God and not subject to his law; that a change of heart, a heavenly birth, is absolutely necessary to see the kingdom of God and enter therein; that the same power that created the world, and raised our Lord from the dead, must quicken the sinner dead in sins, and make him alive to God; that if saved from sin and hell, it must be by free, sovereign, efficacious grace, through faith in the Lord Jesus Christ; and that nothing can meet the necessities of a sinner awakened to a sense of his guilt by the teaching of the Holy Spirit, but what satisfied divine justice, the full atonement of Jesus Christ.

"To guard my hearers against self-deception, I have insisted that true religion demands nothing short of entire conformity to the image of Christ, and obedience to all things that he has commanded.

"Those that were converted to God during this revival, were brought generally to see and feel deeply the evil of sin as committed against God, and their just exposure to the wrath to come, and were led to renounce all dependence on works of their own, and rely alone for life and salvation on the great Redeemer.

"Many of those who embraced the gospel at this period were young. One was only seven years old. She came to me in my study in great distress, asking if God could save her, for she had lived seven years without loving him, and all the time sinning against him. She united with the church, and has lived to train up a large family in the fear of God. Her grandmother found Christ after she was ninety years of age. The great body of those who made a profession of religion, have continued in the faith, rooted and grounded in love, and have not been moved away from the hope of the gospel."

From Rev. Dr. Hyde, Lee, Mass.

"In the summer of 1821, there was an increase of solemnity in the church and congregation, and some were known to be anxious for their souls. The church often assembled for prayer, and in the month of August we observed a day of fasting. The hearts of many seemed to burn within them, and there were increasing indications from the rising cloud, of abundance of rain. At this interesting crisis, the Rev. Asahel Nettleton spent a few days with us. He preached five sermons to overflowing assemblies, and his labors were remarkably blessed. The Spirit of God came down upon us, like a rushing mighty wind. Conversions were frequent, sometimes several in a day, and the change in the feelings and views of the subjects was wonderful.

"At the suggestion of Mr. Nettleton, I now instituted what are called *inquiry meetings*, and more than a hundred persons attended the first. These meetings, as I found them to be convenient, were continued through the revival; and I have ever since made use of them, as occasion required, sometimes weekly for many months in succession. The church have always been requested to assemble for prayer in the upper room of the large school-house, in which these meetings have been held. In these meetings the ruined and helpless state of sinners, the exceeding wickedness of their hearts, and the awful consequences of neglecting the great salvation, have been impressed on the minds of the inquirers. They have not been directed to take any steps preparatory to their accepting of Christ; but repentance towards God and faith in

Christ have been enjoined upon them as their immediate duty and only safe course. No language can describe the deep feeling which has been manifested at some of these meetings. The work continued till the close of the year, and the church received an accession of eighty-six persons as the fruits of it.

"Between this revival, and that which took place in 1827, the seasons of prayer in the church were frequent, and occasionally whole days of fasting and prayer which all the people were invited to attend, were observed. The church also by a large committee visited every family in the town, and conversed with parents and children on the concerns of their souls, closing these interviews with prayer. This has been repeatedly done, and sometimes the whole has been accomplished in one day.

"On the Sabbath preceding the first day of the year 1827, I invited the people, as it had been our practice, to assemble at the rising of the sun in the sanctuary, for the purpose of prayer and praise. Several hundreds attended, and an uncommon interest was evidently felt in the meeting. Another display of the all-conquering grace of God commenced, which was very powerful, and continued through the winter and spring. In the course of a few months it was found that thirty new domestic altars were erected. As the fruits of this revival, one hundred and twenty-five were added to the church.

"The year 1831, which was a year memorable for the effusion of the Spirit in almost every part of the land, this people were not passed by. For a number of months the excitement was very great, and our meetings were frequent, crowded, and solemn. Some instances of conversion were more striking than any I had ever witnessed. The almighty and sovereign power of God was remarkably displayed, evincing the truth of his own declaration, 'I will have mercy on whom I will have mercy.' This revival was followed by the addition of forty-four members to the church.

"Of the whole number received during my ministry, six hundred and seventy-four, none have been admitted under two or three months after they began to hope they had passed from death unto life; and many chose to wait longer. Whenever we have been favored with outpourings of the Spirit, meetings have been appointed with particular reference to the young converts, at which they have been freely conversed with respecting the ground and reason of their hope, that they might test their character by having the great truths of the gospel presented clearly to their view. A confession of faith has also been read and explained to them, and their full assent to it has been obtained, before they offered themselves to the church.

"I have never countenanced the praying of women in promiscuous assemblies, whether great or small, from a full conviction that the practice is contrary to the spirit of the word of God. Neither have I seen it to be proper, even in seasons of the greatest excitement, to call upon impenitent sinners, either in public or private meetings, or in the inquiry room, to manifest their determination to seek religion or to give any pledge that they would do it. It would be a departure from the practice of Christ and his apostles. In their preaching they inculcated repentance and submission to God as the immediate duty of sinners."

From the Rev. Dr. Porter, Farmington, Conn.

"The year 1821 was eminently, in Connecticut, a year of revivals. Between *eighty* and *a hundred* congregations were signally blessed. From the commencement of the year a new state of feeling began to appear in this town. On the first Sabbath in February I stated to the assembly the tokens of the gracious presence of God in several places in the vicinity, and urged the duties peculiarly incumbent on us at such a season. Professors of religion now began evidently to awake. In their communications with each other and with the world, they were led spontaneously to confess their unfaithfulness; and about the same time a few without the church were pungently convicted.

"In this state of things, Rev. Mr. Nettleton made us his first visit. His preaching, on the evening of the Lord's day, from Acts 2 : 37, was set home by the power of the Spirit upon the hearts of many; and his discourse on the Wednesday evening following, from Gen. 6 : 3, was blessed to the conviction of a still greater number. As many as *fifty*, it was afterwards ascertained, dated their first decided purpose of immediately seeking their salvation from that evening.

"At a meeting of the anxious, on the evening of February 26, about a hundred and seventy were present. Here were persons of almost every age and class, some who a few weeks before had put the subject of personal piety at a scornful distance, and others who had drowned every thought of religion in giddy mirth, now bending their knees together in supplication, or waiting in silent reflection for a minister of the gospel to pass along, and tell them individually what they must do.

"From this time, so rapid was the progress of the work, that at the next similar meeting, March 12, a hundred and eighty were present, of whom fifty supposed that since the commencement of the revival, they had become reconciled to God; and a week afterwards, I had the names of more than ninety who indulged the same persuasion concerning themselves.

"The state of feeling which at this time pervaded the town, was interesting beyond description. There was no commotion, but a stillness in our very streets; a serenity in the aspect of the pious, and a solemnity apparent in almost all, which forcibly impressed us with the conviction that in very deed God was in this place. Public meetings, however, were not very frequent. They were so appointed as to afford the opportunity for the same individuals to hear preaching twice a week, besides on the Sabbath. Occasionally there were also meetings of an hour, in the morning or at noon, in private dwellings, at which the serious in the neighborhood were convened on short notice, for prayer and conference. The members of the church also met weekly for prayer, and commonly on the evenings selected for the meetings of the anxious. From these meetings, the people retired directly, and with little communication with each other, to their homes. They were disposed to be much alone, and to take the word of God for their guide.

"The topics principally insisted on in this revival, were the unchangeable obligations of the divine law, the deceitful and entirely depraved character of the natural heart, the free and indiscriminate offers of the gospel, the reasonableness and necessity of immediate repentance, the refuges and excuses to which awakened sinners are accustomed to resort, and the manner, guilt, and danger of slighting, resisting, and opposing the operations of the Holy Spirit.

"Among the first subjects of the work, there was a large proportion of the more wealthy and intelligent. A considerable number of youths belonging to this class, had just finished a course of biblical instruction, for which I had met them weekly for more than a year, who, with scarcely an exception, at the very commencement of the revival embraced the gospel which they had learned, and by their experience of its power commended it to the families to which they belonged. I suppose that within three months, there were about two hundred and fifty persons who hoped they had passed from death unto life. On the first Sabbath in June, a hundred and fourteen were added to the church; and at subsequent periods a hundred and twenty more. Many have died, and many have removed from our immediate connection; but those who remain, now constitute the chief strength of the church."

From Rev. Dr. Tenney, of Wethersfield, Conn. April, 1822.

"Previous to the revival, our church consisted of about *two hundred and sixty* members. As its fruits, precisely *two hundred* more have been added, of whom *seventy-nine* are heads of families. Sixty-two are males, and thirty-two are young unmarried men. A number of others have indulged hope. Generally the subjects of the work still appear well.

"Some instances of conversion have been strongly marked. The awakening of some has been sudden and powerful, and has soon issued in triumphant peace. In others it has been as the 'still small voice.' One individual who had been a total disbeliever in revelation, began to examine the subject of religion with all the coolness of a mathematician; till, in the course of a few weeks, the great truths of Scripture bore upon his conscience with insupportable power, and had almost that 'keen vibration through his soul, which makes hell;' and his heart yielded to God. One aged man said, If I have been born of God, it was on the day when I was seventy-six years old. Another said, It was the day when I was sixty-eight. In one family, a mother of *eleven* children, who had long gone to the table of Christ mourning that of her great family there was not one to accompany her, now hopes that *eight* of her children are the children of God. In another family consisting of parents and seven children, all have indulged hope, except one son who was absent at sea. A widow, the mother of seven children, some of them pious before, now has hope of all the others. The whole family now belong to the church.

"Greatly are we indebted to a number of neighboring ministers whose labors were of great use. Peculiar are our obligations to the Rev. Asahel Nettleton, who was much with us, and whose labors were eminently blessed, reminding us of 'the chariots of

Israel, and the horsemen thereof.' Though in this work there has been the strongest coincidence between the means used and the success, and between the prayerfulness of Christians and the conviction and conversion of sinners, yet God has displayed his glorious sovereignty, as well as faithfulness. The work is emphatically his. To him all the glory is due. To him let it be given, now and evermore."

From Rev. Dr. Ashbel Green, late President of the College of New Jersey at Princeton, to Rev. Dr. Sprague.

After glancing at the earlier history of the college, Dr. Green says, "In the spring of 1782, when I became a member of the institution, the walls of the building were still perforated in a number of places, the effect of the cannon balls which had passed through them from the artillery of the American army, to drive out a British foe that had taken shelter there.

"While I was a member of college there were but two professors of religion among the students, and not more than five or six who scrupled to use profane language in common conversation. To the influence of the American war succeeded that of the French revolution, still more pernicious. The open and avowed infidelity of Paine, and other writers of the same character, produced incalculable injury to religion and morals throughout our whole country; and its effect on young men who valued themselves for genius, and were fond of novel speculations, was the greatest of all. Dr. Smith, then President of the college, told me that one man who sent his son, stated explicitly in a letter that *not a word was ever to be said to him on the subject of religion.* The youth was refused admittance. The tendency to dissipation and dissolute morals which had long prevailed, had risen to a most fearful height when I was called to the presidency in the autumn of 1812."

After two years of faithful and abundant labors to effect a reformation, he perceived that "there was a marked attention to the religious duties of the college. Every religious service was attended with a solemnity that was very impressive. In the second week of January, 1815, without any unusual occurrence in providence, without any alarming event, without any extraordinary preaching, without any special instruction, or other means that might be supposed peculiarly adapted to interest the mind, the effect became more apparent. In about four weeks there were very few individuals in the college who were not deeply impressed with a sense of the importance of spiritual and eternal things. There was scarcely a room, perhaps not one, which was not a place of earnest secret devotion. For a time it seemed as if the whole of our charge was pressing into the kingdom of God. The result was, that of one hundred and five students, there were more than forty in regard to whom favorable hopes were entertained that they were the subjects of renewing grace.

"The means which were employed and blessed of God in producing the revival, were chiefly the study of the holy Scriptures, accompanied with comments on the portion read, and practical application of the leading truths contained in it. God has remarkably honored and blessed his word. Appropriate addresses were frequently made, and the public exercises were conducted with a special view to religious edification.

"The few youths who were previously pious had for more than a year been earnestly engaged in prayer for this event. When they perceived the general and increasing seriousness, several of them agreed to speak privately and tenderly to their particular acquaintances on the subject of religion; and what they said was in almost every instance not only well received, but those with whom they conversed became earnestly engaged in those exercises which it is hoped have issued in genuine piety.

"In preaching on the Lord's day morning, subjects were selected suited to the existing state of the college; a weekly lecture, intended for the students exclusively, was given every Tuesday evening; a prayer-meeting was held every Friday evening, at which one of the theological professors commonly made an address; a prayer-meeting was every evening held by the students themselves, at which a large proportion of the whole college attended; smaller and more select associations for prayer were also formed; the individuals whose minds were anxious were, as often as they requested it, carefully conversed and prayed with in private; writings of approved character on doctrinal and practical religion were recommended, and a short system of *Questions and Counsel** was drawn up by myself for the use of those who appeared to have entered on a life of practical piety.

* These Questions and Counsel constitute No. 113 of the American Tract Society's series.

"The fruits of this revival were happy and lasting; for although a number lost their impressions, yet there are a goodly number now in public life who are bringing forth the fruits of that renovated nature which was imparted to them by the gracious Spirit of God in this revival. I once counted the number of ministers of the gospel whose conversion was believed to have taken place at that time. I forget what the number was, but I remember I thought it greater than that produced on any similar occasion in Nassau-hall.

"There were two other periods during my presidency, at which hopes were excited that we were on the eve of another general revival. But though the favorable appearances passed away without realizing this hope, it was not without leaving several monuments of divine grace, some of them very remarkable. May God soon grant a general revival to an institution consecrated by its founders to the promotion of science in union with piety, and in behalf of which many fervent prayers, both of the living and the dead, have ascended to the throne of mercy."

From Rev. Dr. John McDowell, Elizabethtown, New Jersey. 1812–1825.

In a letter to Rev. Dr. Sprague, Dr. McDowell gives a record of revivals in 1772 and 1784; and one in 1807, which apparently commenced in connection with "a powerful sermon on prayer by the Rev. Dr. Gideon Blackburn," and continued about eighteen months, as the fruits of which about one hundred and twenty were added to the church. He proceeds to say:

"Another revival visibly commenced in December, 1812. It was on a communion Sabbath. There was nothing peculiarly arousing in the preaching. I was not expecting such an event. I saw nothing unusual in the appearance of the congregation; and it was not until after the services of the day were ended, when several called in deep distress to ask me what they should do to be saved, that I knew that the Lord was specially in this place. This was a day of such power, (though I knew it not at the time,) that as many as *thirty* who afterwards joined the church, were then first awakened. And it is a remarkable circumstance, that the same powerful influence was experienced on the same day in both of the Presbyterian churches in the neighboring town of Newark. It was also communion-season in both those churches. This revival continued about a year; and the number of persons added to the communion of this church as its fruits, was about one hundred and ten.

"About the beginning of February, 1817, this church was again visited with a great revival of religion. It commenced most signally, as an immediate answer to the united prayers of God's people. The session, impressed with a sense of the comparatively low state of religion among us, agreed to spend an afternoon together in prayer. The congregation were informed of this on the Sabbath, and a request made that Christians would at the same time retire to their closets, and spend a season in prayer for the influences of the Spirit to descend upon us. The season appointed was the next afternoon; and that evening was the monthly concert of prayer, which was unusually full and solemn; and before the week was out, it was manifest that the Lord was in the midst of us, in a very special manner. Many cases of awakening came to my knowledge, and the work soon spread throughout the congregation. This revival was marked, not by the deep distress of the preceding, but by a general weeping in religious meetings. There was doubtless much of sympathy. A larger proportion than usual of the subjects were young, and many of them children. Some were long in darkness, but most of them, much sooner than in either of the former revivals of my ministry, professed to have embraced the Saviour. The number in the congregation who appeared to be seriously impressed, amounted to several hundreds. The special attention continued about a year; and the number added to the communion of the church was about one hundred and eighty.

"At the close of the year 1819, it pleased a gracious God to grant to this church another season of special refreshing, which continued about a year; and the number added to the communion of the church as its fruits, was about sixty.

"In the early part of the year 1824, there was a considerable increase of attention to the subject of religion, which continued through the year 1825. About sixty were added to the communion of the church during this time, as the fruits of this special influence. But the work did not terminate with this ingathering. These were but as drops before a mighty shower. About the beginning of December, 1825, the work was greatly increased. It commenced visibly on a day of fasting and prayer, appointed by the synod of New Jersey, on account of the absence of divine influences from their churches generally. Within a few weeks many were awakened and brought to seek the Lord. This revival, with few exceptions, was not marked by deep distress, and the subjects of it generally, soon professed to hope in Christ. It continued through the year 1826, during which time about one hundred and thirty were added to the communion of this church, as its fruits."

REVIVAL IN PITTSFIELD, MASS., AS WITNESSED BY THE AUTHOR, IN 1821.

The most extensive and powerful revival that I have ever witnessed, took place in Pittsfield, Mass., in the summer of 1821. We had enjoyed a cheering time of refreshing the year before, which brought in about fifty additions to the church; but it reached very few of the prominent and influential members of the congregation, and there were but few of that class then in the church. That first revival had apparently come to a close, and the fruits had been mostly gathered in, before the opening of the spring of 1821. The strong men had not bowed themselves at the foot of the cross, and we were afraid that before another such season should return, many of them would be in their graves.

It was about the middle of May, that the Rev. Asahel Nettleton, who had been for several years laboring in revivals with wonderful success, came unexpectedly to make me a visit, and as he said, "to rest a while;" for he was very much worn down by his almost incredible labors.

His fame as a revival preacher had come before him. Though he kept himself close, it soon became known that he was here, and many were anxious to hear him, as much from curiosity perhaps as any thing else. Though I knew his need of the rest which he came to find in the bosom of my family, I rather urged him to gratify them by preaching once, if no more. He declined, till after two Sabbaths, I think, when, as I was providentially absent, the funeral of a child on a week-day brought him out. There was a large gathering, and I presume he saw something which indicated the return of the Holy Spirit, though nobody else did. The next Sabbath he preached once, and it seemed evident to him at least, that the Spirit was moving upon some during the services of the day. These indications gradually increased, till the church began to be encouraged with the hope that we might have another revival, which all felt was greatly needed; for many more were left, than had been taken the preceding year. Mr. Nettleton saw by this time, if not before, that here was harvest work to be done, and that he must not rest too long. He remained with us about three months, including one or two short visits to neighboring fields, which were white for the reapers.

I published a narrative of the work the next year in the Christian Intelligencer, the substance of which I shall repeat, though I have it not now before me. And I shall venture to give it more at length, than I can find room for any other revival of those remarkable years of the outpouring of the Spirit—not because the number of converts was greater, or so great as in some other places, but because I was an eye-witness and a coworker in the field of divine wonders; and also, as at the critical stage of the revival the great adversary did his best to stop it, to show how signally God defeated him.

The revival did not break out suddenly, as has been often the case, but there was a growing solemnity visible in the congregation, which quite early in June encouraged us to let it be known, in a still way, that we should be happy to meet any who might be disposed to come to my house for a short meeting the next evening. It was understood to be for inquirers, if there were any. A larger number than we had dared to expect came, and it was noticeable that most of them were from the more prominent and leading families in the village. We could not help regarding this as a favorable omen, most of them having been passed by in the former revival. It was a sort of *test* meeting, and from that time the work advanced and spread rapidly; but not without exciting opposition on the part of some who were capable of wielding a wide influence.

Something they thought must be done to check the epidemic, before it should come into their families, and get beyond control. What should it be? It would not be safe to come out openly, as so many were already asking what they must do to be saved. St. John's day, as it was called, (June 25,) was near at hand; and it was resolved to hold, in Pittsfield, a grand festival of all the masonic lodges round about. We could not say that the ruling motive on the part of those who sent out the invitation, was to put a stop to the revival; but the movement was so sudden, that, taken in connection with all the circumstances, it looked very much like it.

A very popular speaker, who had once been an approved minister of the gospel, was engaged to come and deliver the oration. We were distressed. We exceedingly feared that such a gathering would divert the minds of the people from the great salvation which was then so freely offered; but we could not prevent it. The occasion called for earnest prayer for direction, and that God would graciously interpose and prevent the dreaded consequences. One thing we could do. The orator chosen had, as I have just said, once been a minister. We—Mr. Nettleton and myself—addressed him a joint letter, saying we understood he had engaged to come; that there was a very interesting revival in progress here, which we presumed he had not heard of; that we did not write to dissuade him from coming, but that we hoped he would give his discourse such a shape as to interfere as little as possible with the work of the Lord. He came. The day was very fine. The anniversary was very largely attended by the masons from all quarters. The church was crowded. We were there, and greatly relieved. The discourse was more like a sermon than a popular oration. There was nothing in it to which we could object, but a good deal which was rather calculated to promote the revival than to check it. We thanked God, and took courage.

The masons were astonished. What could it mean? They were so excited, that they could not help expressing their disappointment to the speaker, and asking him what he meant. He excused himself by saying that he had been induced to give that religious shape to his address by a letter which Mr. Nettleton and I had written him. This brought down upon us a storm of vituperation for our interference. But the Lord was on our side. He had undertaken to accomplish a great work in Pittsfield, and neither earth nor hell could prevent it. We could not see that the masonic festival hindered the revival at all.

But the disappointment and opposition were soon manifested in another form. The people of the town had been in the habit, on the fourth of July, of celebrating the declaration of American Independence, ever since it was declared; and at the close of each festival with toasts and speeches and drums and cannon, to appoint a committee to make arrangements for the next year. Such a committee had been appointed the year before. As the revival was now becoming general and powerful, we were very desirous of having a religious celebration, and inviting our friends in the county to come in and enjoy it with us. I accordingly inquired of the committee whether it was their intention to have the usual festive celebration; stating that, if it might be dispensed with under the present unusual circumstances, we should be glad to substitute a religious service, and that we found a great many were in favor of it. The committee cheerfully assented to the proposal, and we made our arrangements accordingly.

Thus, as to the regular arrangements, the matter was settled in our favor; and we supposed there would be no interruption. But we were mistaken; those who wanted the customary noisy celebration, determined not to be deprived of it. So the *young men* resolved to have an oration and a dinner at the usual hours. How far they were encouraged by some older men opposed to the revival, did not openly appear; but that they were to some extent, was not doubted at the time. The oration was delivered in the forenoon, and at two o'clock our public meeting was held. The meeting-house had never been filled with a more serious and respectable congregation. The day was fine, and a large number of our friends from abroad were there. I tried to persuade Mr. Nettleton to preach; but as he positively declined, I was obliged to make the best preparations I could. My text was, "*If the Son shall make you free, ye shall be free indeed.*" John 8:36.

Though there was some noise outside from the commencement of the services, it did not appear that there was any intention to disturb us, till the sermon was about half through. Becoming impatient when the guests had finished their dinner, and loaded the four pounder, and got primed for the toasts, they first sent their band with drums and fifes to march round the house, and warn us that it was time to close and leave the ground. One or two gentlemen went out to remonstrate, but they were disregarded. I went on with my discourse, and I believe made myself heard.

Finding that their martial music did not succeed, they determined next to try what powder would do. The first discharge was so unexpected, that it almost started the whole congregation from their seats. The high-sheriff of the county, with one or two of our most respectable citizens, went out to persuade them to desist; but they would not. Many within turned pale, but none of the audience retired. By the third round they were entirely composed, and a more solemn assembly I never looked upon. How many rounds were discharged I cannot remember, but as the cannonading went on, and I drew towards the close of my written discourse, it came so aptly in my way that I couldn't help adding something to the improvement, by contrasting *the liberty* wherewith Christ makes his children free, with *the bondage* of Satan's servants without. This I suppose added ten or fifteen minutes to the length of my discourse, after which Dr. Shepard of Lenox closed with prayer, and the evening lecture was appointed from the desk. The great audience then retired as if nothing had happened, only more deeply impressed.

As we went out, the sheriff expressed his determination to make the disturbers smart for it; but I begged him to do no such thing: "They have not injured us, but shot themselves dead, and don't meddle with their remains: 'The Lord of hosts is with us, the God of Jacob is our refuge.'" And so it proved. It needed no enemy to spike their cannon, or to scatter them. Whereas, on all former celebrations here, the noise was kept up to a late hour in the evening, the green was now entirely forsaken by sundown, and the stillness of the evening throughout the village was like the Sabbath. The lecture at half-past seven was crowded, and unusually solemn.

It was on that occasion, that Mr. Nettleton took for his text those urgent words of the angels to Lot, "Up, get ye out of this place, for the Lord will destroy this city;" and so vivid was his description of that sudden and awful destruction, that not a few of the audience involuntarily turned their faces to the windows, as if the storm of fire and brimstone had actually come down upon the place.

Taken altogether, the triumph of the day and the evening was truly sublime. It was wonderful to witness with what power the Spirit of God triumphed. A new impulse was given to the revival. From that time, there was no more open opposition to the work. Whatever any might have felt, they were afraid to show it. Some of those who had been active, if not ringleaders in the disturbance, were afterwards hopefully converted. The work went on with great power through the months of July and August, and extended far into the autumn. It was such a summer as Pittsfield never saw before, nor since.

The narrative would be quite incomplete if I were to close it here. In all revivals God works by means and instruments, and some may be glad to know what course was here adopted.

In the first place it was fully understood between Mr. Nettleton and myself, that as I was the pastor, he was to be the helper, and not the main director. He could not have been persuaded to make the appointments, and tell me when and where I should aid him. He was not the man for that anywhere, and if he had been, I certainly should not have come into any such arrangement. I always consulted him as a matter of course, for he knew incomparably better than I did, what means had been most successful in the progress of revivals. But it was my parish, and not his. In placing me here, the Head of the church had devolved upon me a responsibility, which I did not feel at liberty to throw off. And with this understanding, I do not believe that any two preachers ever labored more harmoniously together than we did.

Our general course of preaching and incidental labors was as follows: Three discourses on the Sabbath, one of which was always in the evening. Two public lectures on week-day evenings, preceded by a short prayer-meeting a little before sundown; occasional lectures and prayer-meetings in the outdistricts, one object of which was to bring as many as we could to attend the central lectures; an inquiry meeting every Monday evening, and a church prayer-meeting at the same hour. Besides these, a great many smaller neighborhood meetings were attended, connected with visiting from house to house as we could find time. I also held a meeting once a week with as many aged members of my flock, who were not professors of religion, as I could collect, and there is reason to hope that some of them were brought in at the eleventh hour.

In our discourses in season and out of season, we did not shun to declare "all the counsel of God," as we understood it. Mr. Nettleton's preaching was "not in the enticing words of man's wisdom, but in demonstration of the Spirit and with power." It was plain, earnest, direct, searching, driving the sinner from all his refuges; now making the law thunder as but few preachers can, and then from a full heart pouring out the melting invitations of the gospel. Though there were diversities of operations, for the most part the converts were led to Calvary by the way of Sinai. They experienced a law work before they closed in with the terms of the gospel. "When the commandment came, sin revived, and they died;" and when the Spirit raised them to a new life, they lived all the better for it.

The subjects of the work were chiefly heads of families; some of them below, and not many of them much above middle age. They were in the midst of life, and more than any equal number of the congregation exercised a controlling influence in the community. Among them were our principal lawyers, doctors, merchants, and men of standing and business in the town. And it was very interesting to notice how, as they were brought out one after another, they went at once and reported to their friends of the same class what a Saviour they had found, urging them to come to the meetings and see. It reminded us of the manner in which the disciples of Christ were brought to him one after another, as recorded in the first chapter of John. "John (the Baptist) stood, and two of his disciples; and looking upon Jesus as he walked, he saith, 'Behold the Lamb of God! and they followed Jesus. One of the two who heard John speak and followed him, was Andrew, Simon Peter's brother. He first findeth his own brother Simon, and saith unto him, We have found the Messias, which is, being interpreted, the

Christ. And he brought him to Jesus. The day following Jesus would go forth into Galilee, and findeth Philip, and saith unto him, Follow me. Philip findeth Nathanael, and saith unto him, We have found him of whom Moses in the law and the prophets did write, Jesus of Nazareth, the son of Joseph. And Nathanael said unto him, Can any good thing come out of Nazareth? Philip saith unto him, Come and see." So it was here, and so it ought always to be in a revival. Just as soon as Andrew finds the Saviour, he should go and bring in Peter. So Philip should find Nathanael, and bring him also to Christ, that they may all rejoice together in their discipleship.

In the progress of the revival, a great many incidents occurred which heightened the interest of the work, but I have room for only two.

One Monday morning early, a colored woman about forty years old came to my house bowed down as if by some great calamity. "Dinah," I said, "I am glad to see you; but what is the matter?" "Oh, I don't know, but I feel dreadfully." "How long have you felt so?" "Ever since yesterday, when you was preaching it seemed as if a knife was stuck right into my heart." How could I help calling to mind instantly, Peter's sermon on the day of pentecost? "When they heard this, they were *pricked* in their hearts, and cried out, Men and brethren, what shall we do?" Here was a poor woman who had been brought up a slave, and could not read a word, feeling just as they did, and using nearly the same language, without knowing or suspecting it. How could

I doubt, how can anybody doubt, that if it was the Spirit of God that pricked the hearts of Peter's hearers, it was the same Spirit that seemed like a knife piercing Dinah's heart; corresponding too as it did with that other scripture, "The word of God is quick and powerful, sharper than any two-edged sword." Though Dinah could n't tell what ailed her, I soon found that she was in deep distress for her soul. She of course needed a great deal of instruction; but in a few weeks she was brought out of darkness into marvellous light, joined the church, and adorned her profession to the day of her death.

The other was the case of an ignorant, swearing, intemperate man, one of the vilest of the vile, who rarely, if ever, attended public worship anywhere. One Sabbath afternoon, in the midst of the revival, he strayed into the church; he could not tell why; took his seat near the door so that he could easily slip out, but remained quiet till the sermon commenced. The words of my text were, *It is the last time.* As he said afterwards, it struck him to the heart, and threw him into the greatest agitation. His first thought was, that he would go at once to the tavern and drive it off with a dram. But somehow he found himself fastened to his seat till the meeting closed, and then he knew not where to go, or what to do. The arrow had struck too deep to be extracted by any but a divine hand. A scene of terrible distress followed. For a number of days he was almost in the horrors of despair. Prayer was offered continually for him, and he was assured that the mercies of God were not clean gone for ever, if he would repent and cast himself upon Christ to wash away his sins. How long he remained in this condition I do not remember, but at length light began gradually to break in upon his mind. He embraced a humble hope that God had brought him up out of the horrible pit and the miry clay, and after a probation of several months he gave such evidence of a saving change that he was received into the church, and as those who knew him best believed, he died a true penitent.

Though the revival commenced early in the summer, as I have already stated, none of the subjects of it were received into the church till at our regular communion-season, the first Sabbath in November. My judgment was and still is, that as a general rule, it is best that hopeful converts should take considerable time to test the genuineness of their hopes, before making a public profession. It appeared to me that the candidates for membership, as a body, needed a good deal of instruction to prepare them for an intelligent profession of their faith in Christ.

Accordingly, besides conversing with them individually touching the reasons of the hope that was in them, I called them together in a body, and spent several evenings in explaining to them our confession of faith and covenant, article by article, and exhorting them to be fully persuaded in their own minds, of the scriptural basis of our creed, before subscribing to it; and I have reason to think that no evenings were more profitably spent than these. They afforded full scope for asking and answering questions, and examining proof-texts; and I am not aware of a single case of departure from "the form of sound words," as we believed them to be, in our articles.

When the converts presented themselves for admission, they were examined one by one, by the pastor and a committee, in presence of as many of the church as chose to attend, to which no one of the number made any objection. When the time arrived for their admission, *that Sabbath-day was a high day.* Nothing like it had ever been witnessed in the history of the church. I think the number who came forward was *eighty-five;* and to see the long broad aisle filled, from the communion-table down to the door, with disciples hastening as it were to meet their Master for the first time at his table, was a spectacle which caused the aged fathers and mothers to weep for joy, and filled the great congregation with wonder and awe. While there were persons of all classes and different ages standing together to take upon themselves the vows of their consecration, what made the scene uncommonly impressive was, that there were so many husbands and wives of our most influential families—so many men in and out of the professions, who, from their position in society, would have it in their power to exert so wide an influence in the cause of Christ, and for the good of the town.

Though in the providence of God I was called two years after to leave my beloved charge, and labor in another field,* I was near enough to keep myself advised of the Christian walk of that large band of professors; and having long since returned to reside in Pittsfield, it affords me the highest satisfaction to

* The presidency of Amherst college.

be able to say, that now, at the end of thirty-seven years from the time of their public espousals to Christ, there has not, so far as I can learn, been a single case of apostasy from the faith once delivered to the saints, nor of yielding to the mastery of any of those habits which disgrace the Christian name, and drown men in destruction and perdition. There was indeed one of the number, who for a time was in great danger of being brought into bondage again to bad habits from which he had been reclaimed, insomuch that the church stood in doubt of him, but he did not utterly fall away; he was reclaimed, and gave evidence that God had restored him from his backslidings, and that he died in the faith.

To the foregoing account I venture to append a few brief extracts of a letter to the editor of the Charleston, S. C., Intelligencer, from a gentleman who was present at the meeting on the fourth of July.

"The opposers of the revival, finding that a religious celebration was agreed on, resolved to have a political celebration. They occupied the church in the morning. At two o'clock they who loved the Lord began to assemble in the same place. The church was crowded. While the people were assembling, and as they passed near the rioters, crackers were repeatedly exploded to annoy them. The service began and went sweetly on. Mr. H——, pastor of the church, took his text from John 8:36, "If the Son shall make you free, ye shall be free indeed.' Towards the close of the sermon the word *fire* was heard, and our ears were suddenly stunned by the report of a cannon. It was the attack of the adversary, and well kept up. But unfortunately for him, every shot preached louder than ten thousand thunders. Meanwhile the drums beat, the fifers played as they marched back and forth before the church-door, animated by the music of the cannon, and the hope of a glorious triumph over the cause of God.

"Some few Christians of delicate frame and quick sensibilities were agitated and alarmed, and others, though not intimidated, dreaded the consequences of this violent attack; but generally there were high hopes that it would be overruled for good. And so it was. So skilfully did the preacher allude to, and apply his discourse to the conduct of the opposition out of doors—such advantage did he take of every blast of the cannon, and every play of the drum, by some well-pointed remark—that it went like a two-edged sword to the hearts of listening sinners. Indeed, Mr. H—— afterwards informed me, that, had he previously showed the heads of his sermon to the riotors, and requested them when he reached such a point to *fire*, and when he reached another point to *fire*, they could not have more effectually served the purpose of the discourse. One gentleman who had previously been somewhat serious, told me that every shot of the cannon pierced his soul—filled him with indescribable horror, and by the blessing of God brought him to such a hatred and detestation of sin in himself and others, as constrained him quickly to fly to Christ.

"I confess I trembled for the ark of God. After the sermon was concluded, I went and expostulated with the ringleader, whose companion I had once been in wickedness, and over whom I thought I might have some influence. I sat near Mr. Nettleton, and so delighted was he with the discourse, and so accurately did he foresee the result, that whenever an apt allusion dropped from the lips of the speaker, he would turn round with a holy smile and whisper, *That is good, that is good.* Nothing could be more appropriate, or more naturally rise out of the text, than Mr. H——'s description of the miserable bondage in which those out of doors were serving their master.

"This was an eventful day for Pittsfield. From that time Immanuel gathered his trophies from among great and small. They who thought to crush the work of God were bitterly disappointed. The fruits of this revival were *one hundred and forty converts.* Praise the Lord."

CHAPTER VII.

THE REVIVAL EPOCH ABOUT 1800—CONTINUED.

BRIEF NOTICES OF REVIVALS—1815 TO 1825.

"IN the summer of 1815, there was a great revival in the town of Salisbury, Conn. The subjects were of different ages, but generally youth. As the fruits of this revival, more than two hundred were admitted into the churches.

"In the summer of 1816, the revival reached Torrington. At the communion in November, the first fruits were gathered into the church, and the number of hopeful converts was about seventy.

"About the same time, the Holy Spirit visited the town of Waterbury in a signal manner, with his convicting and converting influences. It embraced all the variety of operations, from the still small voice to the most powerful threatening of a broken law, and embraced all ages from youth to grey hairs. More than one hundred were the fruits of this revival.

"In the fall of 1817, there was a revival in the parish of Rocky Hill, Conn., as the fruits of which, Dr. Chapin the pastor says eighty-four persons became members of Christ's visible church.

"In the fall of 1818, a revival was enjoyed in the small society of Ashford, and eighty-two were added to the church.

"In the spring of 1819, there was a happy revival

in the town of Bolton. The convictions of the subjects of this work were deep, increased rapidly, and were of short continuance. Unconditional submission was urged as the ground of their acceptance with God. As soon as this was exercised, in most instances the sinner was filled with joy, and fifty-nine were added to the church.

"The same year, 1819, was a remarkable year of the right hand of the Most High, in the county of Saratoga, New York. The work commenced in the summer, at Saratoga springs, and about forty made a profession of religion, including some of the most prominent persons in the village.

"About the same time, there was a remarkable revival in Stillwater. In February, a hundred and three were added to the church, and about a hundred more were rejoicing in hope, expecting soon to be received.

"In Ballston too the work was very powerful, and at two communion-seasons a hundred and eighteen were added to the church, while the work was still increasing.

"In the adjoining town of Milton, the work was overwhelming. In less than two months, more than a hundred and fifty were brought to rejoice in hope. In Amsterdam, there were about fifty hopeful conversions.

In a letter dated Union college, April 28, 1820, Mr. Nettleton writes, "I have no time to relate interesting particulars. I only add, that some of the most stout-hearted and heaven-daring rebels have been in the most awful distress, and within a circle whose diameter is about twenty-four miles, not less than *eight hundred* souls have been hopefully born into the kingdom of Christ since last September. In Malta, there were such displays of the power of God's Spirit in crushing the opposition of the natural heart, as are very seldom seen. The Deist and Universalist, the drunkard, the gambler, and the swearer, were alike made the subjects of this heart-breaking work. It was a place of great spiritual dearth, and like the top of Gilboa, had never been wet by rain or dew; but the Lord now converted that wilderness into a fruitful field. A church was soon organized with eighty-five members."

In the same year, 1820, was a powerful revival in New Haven, and about three hundred were added to the churches. It extended to most of the neighboring towns. Out of thirty-one congregations in the county of New Haven, at least twenty-five were visited, during the winter and spring, with the special presence of the Lord, and it was estimated that within these limits between *fifteen hundred* and *two thousand* souls were called out of nature's darkness into marvellous light.

In North Killingworth the revival was very powerful. It commenced about the last of August in a Bible-class, and rapidly spread over the town. The hopeful converts were a hundred and sixty-two, a hundred and seven of whom united with the church at the communion-season in January, and soon after twenty-five more.

In 1822 and 1823 were many extensive revivals in the eastern part of Connecticut, of which Mr. Nettleton gives the following summary view:

"Most of these churches have in years past been favored with seasons more or less reviving, but never with such a general and powerful refreshing from the presence of God. The following towns have shared in the work. In Somers, one hundred and fifty have been made the subjects of divine grace. In Tolland, one hundred and thirty. In South Wilbraham, one hundred. In North Coventry, one hundred and twenty. In South Coventry, North and South Mansfield, about one hundred in each. In Columbia, forty. In Lebanon, ninety. In Goshen, thirty. In Bozrah, seventy. In Montville, ninety. In Chaplin, fifty.

"The work has recently commenced, and is advancing with power in Hampton, and within a few weeks fifty or more are rejoicing in hope. Also, within a few weeks past, the Spirit of God has descended with overwhelming power in Millington and Colchester. In the former place about seventy, and in the latter sixty are already rejoicing in hope. They have never witnessed the like in the power and extent of the work. In the above cluster of towns, all contiguous, more than *thirteen hundred* souls have hopefully received a saving change since the work began. Of these, more than eight hundred have already made a profession of religion. In Chatham also the work is interesting, and about seventy are rejoicing in hope. The Lord has done great things for Zion, whereof we are glad; and let all her friends humbly rejoice, and bow, and give thanks, and exalt his name together."

The above items from memoranda in the life of Dr. Nettleton, whose labors were extended to other parts of the northern states, and for three successive winters, 1827–1829, to Virginia, are scarcely a tithe of the places where revivals spread, and where the Spirit wrought mightily in the conversion of sinners. Hundreds and thousands of churches, connected with the various evangelical denominations in all parts of the country, were visited and blessed by the gracious outpourings of the Spirit, notices of which constantly appeared in the weekly and other periodicals for a score of years, but which the design and limits of this work do not require or permit me to notice more in detail.

In Central and Western New York, the revival was very extensive and powerful. In Troy, Utica, Auburn, Syracuse, Rochester, Buffalo, and many other places, the revivals between 1820 and 1825 surpassed all that had been seen before. They were noticed in the religious newspapers of the day, and through some other channels of religious intelligence, but I have not been able to find narratives of them in more permanent forms.

SOME THINGS TO BE REGRETTED.

But glorious as these revivals were, I believe that in the retrospect nearly all the ministers who were then on the stage can recollect some things to be regretted, which were at length in some places introduced, as there were in the "great awakening" of the last century, and which, considering the imperfection of the best of men, are liable more or less to mar every great revival. I cannot do less than glance at them in these brief historical sketches.

None but the decided enemies of vital religion could then say, or can now say, that those mistakes were so many and so wide spread anywhere as to destroy the good there was in them in that remarkable day; though there were some things to be guarded against and avoided, which in a greater or less degree interrupted the good work, and gave some occasion to such as sought occasion to oppose it. It could not be denied that in several places the pressure was for a time so high, under certain revival measures, as to disturb the calm and regular action of men's minds. Outbreaks of nervous excitement were so far from being checked, that they were rather encouraged in the prayer-meetings, if not in the more public assemblies.

It having been found that four-days' meetings were remarkably blessed, they were in many cases multiplied and repeated till they were fairly worn out. It came to be thought, in some churches, that when religion was at a low ebb, they had only to arrange for a protracted meeting, and were almost sure of a revival. Accordingly when four days did not do it, the meetings were continued indefinitely—six, ten, fifteen, twenty, and in some cases much longer—till all who attended them were exhausted in body and mind; and whatever forced excitement was at last produced, was unavoidably followed by a speedy reaction, which left the church and congregation in a far less impressible state than the meeting found them. I presume that few if any of those churches would now repeat the experiment of very long protracted meetings. In consequence of such failures as were witnessed, unreasonable prejudices have ever since existed in some quarters against all such meetings.

The great demand for preaching in western revivals, brought out a number of zealous young men with but little experience, who felt it their duty to enter into the work, and help the pastors wherever their services were desired. They soon took the name of Evangelists, or Revivalists as they were more commonly called. Some of them, in process of time, became zealous overmuch. They introduced measures which many pastors of riper judgment and more experience in revivals could not approve. And as their zeal increased, they wanted to go to places where they were not sent for. Nor would they be hindered for want of *regular* invitations. Influential members of the churches who sympathized with them were approached, and enlisted to overrule the judgment of their ministers, and wring from them a reluctant consent. If the ministers would not yield, they must be broken down, as the phrase was. This was often attempted, and sometimes succeeded. Nor would the Evangelist long consent to labor under the advice and direction of the pastor. He must give up the reins, and stand aside and look on, or take a subordinate part in the revival. The consequence was, that divisions were created in the churches, part holding with the pastors and part with the Evangelists; and though scores of converts might be announced, some churches were actually weakened, and to such a degree that if not quite broken up, in what has since been called the 'burnt district,' they have scarcely recovered to this day. Not only were good ministers driven from their congregations in this manner, but such prejudices against revivals were created by these extreme measures, that it has taken a whole generation to remove them.

Some of these Revivalists found their way into the border congregations of New England. And though they did not find so free an entrance as they desired, they visited and labored in towns enough to test their extreme measures by the fruits; and while in looking back we do not feel warranted to say they did no good, it is certain they caused many unhappy divisions, and that their success was nothing like what they proclaimed upon the housetops. Places might be named where they counted scores if not hundreds of converts, but few of whom could be found, ten years after, to have joined and adorned the Christian profession in any of the churches. One great object was to gather in the converts as soon as possible, and the consequence was, that not a few petitions were erelong presented for dismissions back again to the world, by persons thus hastily admitted. They said, We thought we were converted when we joined, but are now convinced it was mere animal excitement: we have no more religion than we had before, and have no right to be counted as Christians, and come to the Lord's table.

This is not the place to decide what ought to be done in such cases. But it is obvious, upon a moment's reflection, that they must be extremely embarrassing. Nor is it uncharitable to express the fear, that many who are thus hurried in, and who do not ask to be released, have the form of godliness without the power, and by remaining weaken the churches instead of strengthening them. These were serious drawbacks upon the revivals of the period now under review. In some cases they put a stop to them. Nevertheless, as I have already said, they were unquestionably glorious years of the right hand of the Most High.

REVIVALS IN COLLEGES AND SEMINARIES.

It is ground of devout thanksgiving to God, that within the last fifty years our *colleges* have been much oftener visited by the special outpourings of the Spirit, than during any former period; and that a very large proportion of the most able and successful ministers and missionaries have been converted and nurtured in these institutions. In Yale, I believe there have been ten revivals at least. In Williams and Amherst there have been nearly as many, and others have shared richly in these blessings. From what sources could faithful ministers have been obtained, if these institutions had not been thus visited?

Nor must we forget to magnify the grace of God in the effusions of his Spirit upon our academies, high-schools, and other kindred educational seminaries, both male and female. It would be safe to say, that within the last forty years, there have been hundreds of revivals in these nurseries of the churches and of the state, the like of which have never before been enjoyed in this or any other age or country.

In many of the Female seminaries especially, they have been remarkable, frequent, and powerful; upon some of the largest of them, the Spirit has been poured out almost every year. Among these the Mount Holyoke seminary in South Hadley, Massachusetts, was so highly favored under the instruction and religious training of that remarkable woman MARY LYON, its founder, and her associates, that I cannot refrain from copying the following letter of one of the teachers, Miss Whitman, written by request to President Hitchcock in 1846, which I find in the new edition of Miss Lyon's life.

"The school has been in operation nine years, and each year since its commencement there has been decided religious interest, unless we except the first and the eighth, several times amounting to a deep and extensive work of grace. Among the pupils of the first year, there were but ten or twelve who were not hopefully pious; and although there was a general consistency of character and deportment, and great zeal in building up the new institution, there was no marked religious interest.

"The second year, the number regarding themselves as unconverted was about thirty. During that year, God manifested his acceptance of the consecrated institution, not by a visible cloud, but by a baptism of the Holy Ghost. The work was very rapid, and advanced with great power. It occurred in connection with the fast for literary institutions. The whole school bowed beneath its influence. The breathings of the Spirit were felt in every heart. The lukewarm professor and the openly irreligious alike trembled for their personal safety. The light footstep, the hushed voice, and the solemn countenance indicated the thoughts of all hearts. Many a slumbering professor awoke to newness of life. During the three days succeeding the last Thursday of February, which had been sacredly observed by the teachers and scholars as a season of fasting and prayer, about one-half of the impenitent indulged the hope of having passed from death unto life.

"Saturday of the same week was a day of recreation. In the afternoon, nearly the whole school with one accord came together, filling to its utmost capacity the reading-room, where the meeting was held. After continuous prayer for an hour, the meeting was appropriately closed by one of the teachers. No one rose to leave the room. The feeling pervaded the circle that prayer must be continued until every soul was converted. Another prayer was then offered, after which the same teacher proposed that they should all retire to their rooms for half an hour, and then those who desired, should meet again in the same place. At the end of the half hour the burdened souls came together to plead once more for their companions who were still out of Christ. But one, that year, remained destitute of the Christian hope. Many were the prayers offered for that halting one, and in after-years it was found that praying breath had not been spent in vain. She has since died in a peaceful hope of divine acceptance, referring its origin to that second year of the Holyoke seminary.

"Thus did this young seminary receive its baptism of the Spirit. Thus did God condescend to manifest his acceptance of the offering. Thus did he receive as his own the seminary which had been privately and publicly consecrated to him by the donors, the trustees, and most of all by her who, standing at its head, was often heard earnestly pleading, that not one of all who should enjoy its privileges down to the dawn of the millennial day, should fail of eternal life.

"This revival gave the school that religious character which its founders desired. Its effects were felt for several successive years, but especially in the next, which was the third in the history of the seminary. That year, *all indulged the Christian hope.* The work was gradual, and there was a continued interest from the first week of the school till the close of the year. The presence of the Spirit was manifested from the first, by attention to instruction, the tearful eye, and exhibition of tenderness of feeling whenever the subject of personal religion was introduced. The number of cases of hopeful conversion this year was nearly the same as the preceding, or about thirty. The fourth year, the religious interest still continued, somewhat diminished in its power, yet manifest through the year. Christians were not so generally and deeply affected as at some former times, yet there was an interesting growth and maturing of Christian character; six or eight only remained at the close of the year without hope. The fifth year, our building was enlarged, and our numbers greatly increased. There were in many cases a decided and interesting development and settling of religious principle, and also several cases of hopeful conversion of an unusually marked character. The number expressing hope was perhaps about seventeen, being nearly half who entered without hope.

"The following year, the sixth, was one rich in blessing. A more careful division of responsibility and labor among the teachers was made, and from the commencement of the year, there was an increased personal effort in relation to every member of the family. God crowned these efforts with abundant success. From the first there was an attentive listening to instruction, and truth seemed to be taking a deep hold of the understanding and conscience. But it was not till March, that the Spirit of the Lord came upon us with great power, and at once a large number stood up on the Lord's side, having received the breath of life. The work was sudden, rapid, and powerful. We could only stand still and see the salvation of God. Some cases of conversion were of a very marked character, and of great interest. Of the sixty-six who entered the school without hope, only six remained destitute of it. The missionary interest this year received a new impulse by the departure of Miss Fisk, one of our teachers, on a foreign mission, and there was an increase in the missionary contributions. During the seventh year, there were about thirty cases of hopeful conversion. In our last term, there were about twenty, and a number have occurred the present term."

During the twelve years which have since transpired, that consecrated school of some three hundred pupils has been almost equally blessed by annual revivals. The spirit of the founder has rested on her successors whom she trained up for the service.

REVIVALS ON MISSIONARY GROUND.

While God was pouring out his Spirit so copiously upon the church in this country, as we have seen, he was strengthening the hands and encouraging the hearts of her missionaries in foreign lands, by precious refreshings from the same inexhaustible fountain.

To begin with the Sandwich islands. When the first missionaries of the American Board landed there, in 1820, they found the natives sunk in the most deplorable ignorance and barbarism. A more hopeless missionary field could scarcely be found in the whole heathen world; but God had gone before them, and moved those wretched islanders to cast away their idols, they knew not why, as the first step towards receiving the gospel. Much earlier than the strongest faith had dared to anticipate, God poured out his Spirit in a most wonderful manner. The missionaries stood still in amazement, as they witnessed the power and progress of the work. They had seen great revivals in their own country, but they "never saw it on this fashion." Almost the whole population was simultaneously moved by an invisible mighty impulse, which they could not withstand. Such a revival, it is believed, had not been witnessed for *seventeen hundred years*. "So mightily grew the word of God and prevailed." I have no room for statistics, if I had them all before me. They will be found in the reports and correspondence of the missionaries with the American Board at that period. Suffice it to say, that the converts were numbered by thousands, so that within a very few years a larger proportion of the natives, hopefully born again, were received into the churches, than could be numbered in any Christian land. The church in Hilo was for a great many years, and is now *the largest evangelical church in the world.* Several powerful revivals have been enjoyed in those islands since the first and the greatest. Christ has taken possession of them as a part of his inheritance; and how any, who claim to be Christians even in the most "liberal" sense, can with this history before them doubt that he is able to subdue all things to himself, surpasses my comprehension.

From the Sandwich islands let us pass over the great seas to Burmah, where the sainted Judson endured all the lingering sufferings of martyrdom, up to the very point of the spear, from which he was scarcely saved by the almost superhuman efforts of his heroic wife. Next to that at the islands, the mission among the Karens, under the Baptist Foreign Board, has, I believe, been the most prosperous of any in modern times. I do not pretend to give dates in these sketches, nor the number of converts from heathenism at any of the stations. It is unnecessary to my purpose, which is to show that God has been, and is carrying on his work of saving sinners chiefly by revivals where missions are planted on pagan ground, as we have seen he does in Christian lands. Suffice it to say, that there have been several marked revivals among the Karens—perhaps it would come nearer the actual state of things to say there has for several years been a connected series of them there—in which thousands have been brought out of darkness into God's marvellous light. "Two thousand and thirty-nine," say the Missionary Union, "were brought into connection with the Aracan churches by baptism, in 1844. The average annual accessions in the last five years exceed fourteen hundred. The number baptized from the beginning, is sixteen thousand. The number of hopeful converts through the preaching of the cross of Christ by missionaries and native preachers of this Board, is more than twenty thousand." This I copy from the Retrospect of 1851, and large additions have since been made to the churches. What hath God wrought in pagan Burmah!

Although no such very extraordinary success has been reported from other Protestant missions, there has been enough to show that "God is not slack concerning his promise." There have been repeated revivals in the missionary schools at Ceylon and other parts of India, of the same type as in our schools and academies at home. Also in the schools of our missionaries among the Nestorians. There are revivals still in progress, of greater or less extent and power, as there have been for some time past under the labors of the American missionaries among the Armenians of Asia Minor. So also among the Zulus in South Africa, as there had been long ago among the Hottentots. In Western Africa too, the Methodist, Baptist, Episcopal, Presbyterian, and Congregational missionaries have been cheered by special refreshings poured upon their respective fields of labor, from the river of God which is full of water. So it has been with the Choctaws, Cherokees, and other pagan tribes of our North American Indians. Wherever they have been christianized, and churches established among them, it has been by the mighty power of God's Spirit in revivals. I cannot call to mind an exception. So it was in the days of "the apostle to the Indians" John Eliot, the Mayhews, and other first missionaries to the tribes on Martha's Vineyard and the New England shore. The Holy Spirit was poured out, churches were established, and there were at one time fifteen or twenty congregations of praying Indians, as the natives were then called, who renounced heathenism and attended public worship.

In like manner, about the middle of the last century there were revivals under the labors of that devoted missionary David Brainerd, whose name will be had in everlasting remembrance for his labors among the Indians, in the depths of their forests and their barbarism at Crossweeksung and the forks of the Delaware.

I might add others to this list of examples on heathen ground, but I have named more than enough to show that the divine economy for spreading the gospel in heathen lands has been by revivals. I nothing doubt that if they could all be chronicled in their full extent since the world began, they would fill some of the longest and brightest chapters in the History of Redemption, down to the present hour.

THE REVIVAL OF 1858.

To return again to our own land. I have brought these sketches down to about 1845, when there were but few powerful revivals, and for some years these sacred visits seemed to be becoming less and less frequent. Many churches here and there were refreshed, and many souls brought in; but to an alarming extent the young were growing up without hope and without God in the world. There was increasing coldness and worldly conformity in the churches. From some of the watch-towers of Zion the alarm indeed was sounded. There was weeping in secret places over the general decline, and many prayers were offered for the return of the Spirit. But to the question, "Watchman, what of the night?" there was no cheering answer. It was very dark, and seemed to be growing darker. As in the days of the prophet Israel was mad upon her idols, so we had our idols of gold and silver. A *money* mania pervaded not only all our commercial cities, but the whole country more or less, involving all classes. The old paths to competence by the moderate gains of industry and frugality were being more and more forsaken, as no longer suited to this progressive age. Speculation in stocks, in city and village lots, in wild lands, in paper villages and flourishing marts of business, and in every thing that promised sudden and extravagant gains, had reached the crisis of fever-heat, and filled the dreams of thousands upon thousands with uncounted treasures, with fairy mansions, and all the delights of "the lust of the flesh, the lust of the eye, and the pride of life." Would that it had been but an Arabian night dream, instead of the actual every day state of the scrambling multitudes.

And then such a highly inflated and insane grasping for riches could not fail of creating temptations, to an alarming extent too strong to be resisted, in the large business transactions of the country. Hence those enormous frauds which have made the ears of the nation tingle, and by which multitudes of widows and orphans have been swindled out of the small hard-earned investments, on which they depended for their daily bread. It was painfully manifest that without some check to this all-absorbing worldliness, there was no reasonable prospect of such a return of the years of the right hand of the Most High as we had once enjoyed, under the opening heavens pouring down the Holy Spirit and reviving his work. The church was fast falling into the current which swept madly on, and threatened, if possible, to swallow up the very elect. To change the figure, we were descending an inclined plane with all the steam on, and no brakes to check the engine and save the train from being dashed to pieces.

Just then, in the summer of 1857, God interposed in a way which but few if any would have chosen or thought of. When men were saying, "Soul, thou hast much goods laid up for many years; take thine ease, eat, drink, and be merry;" when they were building their castles in the air, not easy to be numbered; when the common talk on change was of hundreds of thousands and millions; when, in short, all were saying, "To-morrow shall be as this day, and more abundant," then suddenly came the crash, as if thunders from a clear sky had simultaneously broken over the whole land. Like a yawning earthquake, it shook down the palaces of the rich, no less than the humble dwellings of the poor, and swallowed up their substance. Men went to bed dreaming all night of their vast hoarded treasures, and woke up in the morning hopeless bankrupts.

Happily these overwhelming losses brought many prosperous business men to a stand, who had given themselves no time to think about laying up treasures in heaven; and under the wise and merciful orderings of Providence, this prepared the way for a new revival epoch, differing in its commencement and some of its aspects from any that had preceded it.

It is quite too early to speak with confidence of the extent and fruits of this most remarkable revival. Its rise and progress have been so fully registered in the religious and secular journals of the day, that repetitions are not called for, if we had room for them. But as I have sketched the leading characteristics of former revivals which have come under review, it is in place to inquire in what respects, if any, this work differs from them. That there are some striking differences must be patent to all who are conversant with this branch of the history of Redemption.

1. In *its commencement.* How and where did it begin? The kingdom of God came not with observation. Such a visit at such a time was not looked for. On the contrary, many feared that the financial disasters of the country had so absorbed the minds of the whole people both in and out of the churches, as to leave no room for the concerns of the soul. But it would seem that the mighty crash was just what was wanted in the great marts of business and speculation, to startle men from their golden dreams, and

lead them to seek for durable riches and righteousness. The horseleech epidemic had spread so wide, and reached such a crisis, that no ordinary means could arrest it. There is no reason to believe, I think, that this revival would have commenced as it did, and spread as it has, if the spell which held men in its embrace had not been broken by some sudden and violent convulsion. It came; and the rushing throngs of fortune-seekers stood still in amazement. Wall-street was shattered and tottering from one end to the other. Every shock threatened wider ruin, and where could the merchant princes and bankers find a place of refuge? Their millions were gone or going, and they had laid up no better portion. A thickening gloom hung over all the cities, and spread over all the country. While the earth reeled, the heavens were shut up.

It was just then that God put it into the heart of a humble individual to propose a daily prayer-meeting in the lower part of the city of New York, at such a time as would best suit the convenience of business men. At first but few attended, in a little room on the third floor of the consistory of the Reformed Dutch church in Fulton-street. But "behold how great a matter a little fire kindleth;" soon, to the astonishment of everybody, thronging multitudes filled all the three rooms of that building to their utmost capacity. It was a vast daily prayer-meeting of an hour at twelve o'clock, attended by those of all classes and conditions, and included great numbers of business men who had never been seen in a prayer-meeting before. It was the Lord's doing, and marvellous in all eyes. Nor could it long be confined within such narrow limits.

The fire from heaven that kindled the flame there, spread rapidly in all directions. The call to prayer became louder throughout the city than it ever was before. It daily filled some of the largest churches; it gathered thousands into one of the vast theatres; it reached the free academy; the fire and the police departments opened their doors for daily prayer. Rooms were opened by merchants in their stores, in which their clerks met for prayer, and the waiters in one of the large hotels had their daily prayer-meeting. Even Jews participated in the great revival movement, and attended the meetings in various parts of the city. Such in brief was the commencement of this marvellous work of the Spirit. The oldest Christians stood still and exclaimed, "We never saw it on this fashion;" and may I not ask, who ever did? Of such a simultaneous movement we have no recorded example.

2. They were *union* prayer-meetings, attended by all who chose, without respect to denominational differences. This was a new feature in the revival. The middle walls of partition had never before been so thoroughly broken down. Evangelical Christians of every name found they could come together and pray for the outpouring of the Spirit without any sacrifice of church order, and were astonished that they had not sooner found out "how good, and how pleasant it is for brethren to dwell together in unity" at the throne of grace. Oh, how it liberalized the sectarian spirit; how it enlarged the heart; how it tended

to unite the whole household of faith in one common brotherhood. Let it be our united prayer that Satan may never more get an advantage of us, by rebuilding the walls which have so long kept us apart to our mutual discredit and loss. Have we not all one Lord, one faith, one God and Father, who is above all, through all, and in us all? and shall we ever hesitate to unite in praying for the descent of the Holy Spirit, whenever and wherever we can enjoy the privilege?

3. Another remarkable feature in this revival, is the *rapidity* with which the spirit of united prayer spread from city to city, and from state to state, gathering the vast multitudes who in a few weeks were everywhere seen crowding the meetings, giving unmistakable evidence that God was in the midst of them. His presence and power were manifest as never before, in making New York, Philadelphia, Cincinnati, and almost all our large cities centres of this great movement, radiating the spiritual light and warmth which they were the first to enjoy, upon all the regions round about. Thus the united prayer-meetings and the revivals spread with wonderful rapidity to hundreds of places, from the centre to the circumference. It has been variously estimated that there were within one year, between three and five hundred thousand converts.

4. *The earth came in and helped the woman* as never before, since she fled from the great red dragon into the wilderness. Thirty years ago, it was difficult to get even a short paragraph of religious intelligence into a secular city paper. Such a thing as a notice

of a revival, we may almost say, was never heard of through such a channel. The best that could be done was chiefly accomplished with singular tact and perseverence by a minister, well and widely known at that time, as bent on doing good in every possible way.* At first it was a volunteer and gratuitous service, collecting and writing out short articles, handing them to the editors, and getting them inserted more as special favors to the man, than to their readers and patrons. Finding how much good he was doing in this way, a number of religious men contributed moderate sums to sustain him; and this was all that could be done to reach the masses of newspaper readers. I believe I might say it took a whole year to get the amount of two columns into any secular city paper, when revivals in almost every part of the country were going on with mighty power.

But how astonishing the change! Scarcely had the *union* prayer-meetings been set up in New York, Philadelphia, Boston, and other cities, when the same papers, of their own accord, devoted whole closely crowded columns, weekly and daily, to this new religious phenomenon; vying with each other who should most minutely chronicle the progress of these meetings, and spread the news widest. In fact, for some time they took the lead of the religious papers in this department of general intelligence. The change was so sudden and so surprising, that we could hardly believe our own eyes in reading the dailies. This was a great advance upon what had ever before been witnessed.

* The late Rev. Austin Dickinson.

5. I believe there have been more public *prayers* offered up by request for individuals, and more remarkable answers, than in any former revival. This is a step in advance, and a great encouragement for the future.

At the same time I cannot help thinking that proclamations of sudden and surprising conversions have been too many, and too confident in some of the great daily prayer-meetings. Some of the individuals who are spoken of without qualification as brands from the burning, will not hold out. It cannot be known at the time who they are, but some will fall away and bring distrust upon the conversion of others, and upon the genuineness of the great work. Indeed, if I have read the reports right, there is a much greater degree of confidence expressed, as soon as awakened sinners get a hope, that they are truly converted, than there was in the earlier revivals of this century.

The fathers used to speak and write with caution. They did not say without qualification, "We have twenty, fifty, or a hundred converts;" but that "so many have obtained a hope; that most of them have been received into the church, and that so far they appear well." They thought this the safest way. They were accustomed to say, after the example of Peter in his recommendation of Sylvanus, "a faithful brother, *as I suppose.*" And I confess that if the *suppose* were retained in a great many cases where it is left out, and if there were not so many hasty admissions, I think the revivals would bring in a larger number of true converts, and with them more strength to the churches. Still, the work is glorious, and has brought a rich revenue of praise to the Redeemer. Perhaps the number of the truly regenerated has been larger in the last, than in any former year. That the work may continue and spread, and bring still greater numbers to the cross, will be the devout petition of all who love the cause, to God with whom is the residue of the Spirit.

And just here let me say, there are some dangers to be guarded against, growing out of the very remarkable rise and progress of this general revival. As it began outside of the church, as it were; as there had not been seasons of special prayer for the outpouring of the Spirit; as no such mighty works as he has wrought were expected by anybody; as few ministers took an active part at first, and the great union prayer-meetings have been chiefly conducted by laymen, there is danger that the churches will hope for future revivals without much prayer; that they will rely too much upon the prayer offered up for them at the union meetings; and that they will think too lightly of ministers and their preaching, and thus displease the great Head of the church who has appointed "the ministry of reconciliation," without whose labors his cause has never been advanced. However a revival may commence, and seem to prosper for a time, it needs the guidance and teachings of a pious and faithful pastor to guard against irregularities; to go before the flock and lead them safely to the fold of the good Shepherd.

Every revival makes a great deal of work for the minister. This is especially the case when, as in this revival, many are suddenly arrested and hopefully converted, who before had never given serious attention to the subject of religion; and of course, have yet to receive all needful instruction with regard to its nature and evidences. The time allowed in these daily prayer-meetings leaves little room for instruction into the things of the kingdom; and as many of the converts are attached to no Christian denomination, they are to be looked up and taught and encouraged, and led along in the way where, till now, they have been almost as much strangers as if they had been born in a heathen land.

I have said it is yet too early to speak with confidence of the fruits of this revival. We cannot yet compare it with former spiritual harvests. We hope it will continue a great while. But it is easy to see that our hopes may be disappointed. The great adversary is no indifferent spectator. It is certain he will in some way get the advantage of us, and stop it if he can. There was never greater need of watching and praying against his devices. If he can break up the union prayer-meetings, or cause them to be indiscreetly conducted; if he can induce the churches of our several denominations to depend more upon the prayers offered up in these meetings, than upon the ministry of the word and other divinely appointed means; if he can any way "sow discord among brethren," and lead them to scramble for the sheaves in the harvest, he will certainly do it. If he can induce those who are now so happily united to separate, saying, "I am of Paul, and I of Apollos," so as to leave as few as possible for "Christ," he will avail himself of the advantage to the utmost; or if he can induce the awakened to substitute dreams and visions and other fanatical delusions for true conviction and conversion, he will make the most of it to corrupt and put an end to the good work. Our only protection is in the guardianship of Him who is infinitely powerful to protect his church, and for his protection let us now and ever devoutly pray.

ENGLAND AND SCOTLAND.

In dwelling so fully on the glorious work of God in our own land, in the revival epoch which began with the going out of the last and the coming in of the present century, God forbid that I should overlook or undervalue the *simultaneous* work He so wonderfully wrought in the mother country. The terror justly awakened by the rapid spread of French infidelity not only across the channel, but across the Atlantic, stealthily entering the minds of millions, and sapping the very foundations of piety and hope in God, was felt as deeply by Hannah More, and Bishop Porteus, and John Newton, and Dr. Bogue, and George Burder, and Andrew Fuller, and Rowland Hill, and others of kindred spirit, as by any in our land. To roll back this flood, Hannah More for years devoted her gifted pen in issuing millions of her cheap Repository Tracts, so fascinating that they could not but be read, and yet effectually tearing off the mask by which infidelity presented herself as an angel of light. This led directly to the formation of those noble parent institutions in London, the Religious Tract Society, and through that, the British and Foreign Bible Society. The organization and efficiency of these institutions, of the Baptist Foreign Missionary Society, the London Missionary Society, the Church Missionary Society, and the kindred evangelical movements in the mother country for spreading the gospel, which have been so successfully imitated and coöperated with on this side of the waters—all are fruits of this blessed work of the Spirit graciously poured out about 1792, in a period of darkness when the hearts of Christians were failing them for fear; and through the same hallowed influence, their efficient labors have been continued and blessed till the present hour.

And not only did these servants of God devise and carry into effect these great evangelizing organizations, but many of them labored personally in the spirit and power of Whitefield and the Wesleys, full of faith and of the Holy Ghost, to preach the gospel to perishing thousands in the moral wastes around them, under whose labors precious harvests of souls were gathered.

Among the foremost of these were those two remarkable men, the brothers Robert and James Alexander Haldane of Scotland, who will be had in everlasting remembrance for their burning zeal and untiring labors in the service of Christ, and for the cheerfulness with which they consecrated their wealth and talents to Christ in building churches—tabernacles they were called—for the poor, and providing in every practicable way for their religious instruction.

As an example of it, Robert sold his princely estate for *seventy thousand guineas*, and bought into the funds for the purpose of being ready to appropriate his money for promoting the interests of religion. Out of the income of six thousand pounds a year, he limited his family to *five hundred pounds—two* thousand dollars for himself, and *twenty-eight* thousand annually for Christ and the church. He aided no less than three hundred young men in preparation for the ministry, and in his own personal visits to Geneva was blessed in giving an evangelical character to the theological seminary now under the care of Dr. Merle D'Aubigné and men of kindred spirit. The memoir of those noble Christian brothers, an edition of which the American Tract Society have just issued, is a religious biography of great interest, showing how eminently God blessed their preaching and other labors by the outpouring of his Spirit. I might enrich these revival sketches with more copious extracts, but only select a few striking passages.

"In May, 1801, James Haldane proceeded on a preaching tour in the south of Scotland, and for four months preached every Lord's day to large congregations in the open air, and under a tent, and every day in the neighboring towns and villages. Of the good effects of these labors there was abundant evidence. Nor did he, in 1802, seek repose, but again went forth burning with zeal for Christ. Many interesting circumstances were connected with his labors in Buxton, Macclesfield, Matlock, and other places, where he proclaimed the message of salvation in the towns, villages, hamlets, and green hill-sides of Derbyshire and Stratfordshire. Everywhere his preaching was acceptable, and often was it seen that the word was with power. A few years before this period, Messrs. Simeon and Haldane had visited Moulin, and as the result of their labors the conversion of *eighty* persons was reported; in the neighborhood of Dunkeld a minister reported *one hundred and forty-five* persons whom he had ascertained to be the fruits of these itinerating labors, and in Aberfeldie *fifty-seven* attributed their conversion under God to the labors of Robert Haldane's missionaries.

"But the most remarkable revival of religion of this period occurred at Breadalbane, by means of a Mr. Farquharson, a catechist of lowly origin, who had been recommended to Robert Haldane's class of students for the ministry, on account of his earnest piety and zeal. So great was the opposition to this devoted catechist when he entered upon his labors, that in a circle of thirty-two miles round Lochsay, there were only three families who would receive him, and every public-house was shut against him. In spite of opposition and neglect, he went during the whole winter from village to village, reading the Bible and speaking the words of salvation to all who would listen to him. In the early part of 1802, so extraordinary a revival had been gradually brought about, that *one hundred persons* previously ignorant of the gospel, seemed to be converted.

"The accounts of success in Caithness were even more delightful. While the missionaries were sending home the intelligence from Breadalbane and elsewhere, Mr. Cleghorn, the excellent pastor of Wick, wrote of *one hundred and twenty* as giving evidence of the power of truth; and adds, that at Thurso the gospel had been at least equally successful.

"In the spring of 1805, James Haldane, accompanied by Mr. Campbell, made a tour by way of Perth and Dunkeld into Breadalbane, and the people came to hear the gospel by thousands. Mr. Peter Grant, a pious preacher, says, 'The novelty of a field preacher, especially a gentleman, attracted great multitudes. In a short time the whole country was in a stir, and many said that we were all in a lost condition; others endeavored by argument and ridicule to banish their fears, but the gospel kindled a flame at that time, which I hope is not yet extinguished.'

"In reference to the work which had been performed, the late Dr. Russel has left this testimony: 'By means of the movement which took place at that period, there was awakened a spirit of greater religious zeal in various religious bodies; a more pointed manner of preaching was adopted by many. There came to be more discrimination of character. The empty flourish of the instrument gave place to the well-defined tones and melodies which awaken all the sympathies of the soul. The unfettered freeness of the gospel was more fully proclaimed, while its practical influence was more distinctly unfolded. In the course of time there appeared an increasing number of evangelical ministers in the Establishment, and a beneficial influence was found to operate upon other denominations.'"

The foregoing is a mere glance, chiefly at the labors and success of James Haldane in the earlier part of his long ministry. He lived to see his *fiftieth* anniversary, and died not long after, in 1851. He was for half a century a revival preacher in the best sense of the term, and almost wherever he went his labors were richly blessed. He counted it his greatest privilege to spend and be spent in the service, and witnessed many scenes of awakening which we should call, and which truly were, genuine revivals.

Thus all along from 1800 down to the middle of the century, was God here and there reviving his work in Scotland, and England also, under the labors of the Haldanes and other zealous evangelical preachers; and the signs of the times, I think, now give promise of approaching rich and glorious spiritual harvests in those lands.

GENERAL SUMMARY REVIEW.

Here, lifting up our hearts in devout thanksgiving to God, let us pause and review the ground which we have gone over. We have seen that seasons of special religious awakening and reformation, bearing all the essential features of genuine modern revivals, date as far back as the time of Joshua. We have seen that when that generation had passed off from the stage, after ages of national degeneracy, there was a great awakening, though of short continuance, in the days of Josiah; and another soon after the return of the Jews from the Babylonish captivity, in the days of Ezra and Nehemiah. After that, there was another great falling away, down to the close of that dispensation when Shiloh came.

Coming down to the New Testament, we have seen that there was a remarkable awakening under the preaching of John the Baptist, when many were turned to the Lord. We have seen that there was a marvellous outpouring of the Spirit on the day of

Pentecost, followed by a wonderful series of revivals in the apostolic age. We have seen how fast Christianity spread over the pagan Roman empire, during the second and third centuries, and went on from conquest to conquest, till, in the person of Constantine, it ascended the throne of the Cæsars.

Scarcely had he descended to his marble tomb, when the "*Man of sin* exalted himself," and reigned in his stead; and thence, entering the shadows of spiritual death, we groped our way as well as we could through the midnight of a thousand years, by far the longest captivity that the Christian church ever endured—illumined, indeed, by here and there a star of the first magnitude, but scarcely more than to make the darkness visible. It was then that the blood of the martyrs flowed to the horse-bridles, and the devil no doubt congratulated himself that he should be thwarted by no more revivals.

But we have seen how the glorious Reformation in the sixteenth century disappointed and baffled him; spreading rapidly on every hand, and carrying dismay to the pontifical throne itself. Marvellous resurrection, from the slumbers of so many ages!

Then, again, we have seen how God, in the next century, poured out his Spirit upon the north of Ireland and the churches of Scotland and England, and scattered a righteous seed across the ocean to people this western land.

Coming down another hundred years, we have met the "Great Awakening," which turned back the captivity of Zion in England, Scotland, Wales, and America. It was the most remarkable and wide spread revival since the first promulgation of the gospel.

We have next seen how, from various causes, there were grievous backslidings during our revolutionary war, the invasion of French infidelity, and the unsettled state of the country, till near the close of the last century; and how God then once more interposed by "reviving his work in the midst of the years," and visiting his American heritage with an almost unbroken series of revivals, down to the present time.

Thus unmistakably has it been God's method, under different dispensations, and all along through the ages, to carry on his work by successive outpourings of his Spirit.

From this history of the past, we may derive instruction and encouragement for the future. We cannot perhaps confidently predict, in this case, that "that which hath been, shall be." But how, in view of the past, can any church rest contented with only such gradual additions as are ordinarily made where for long years there are no revivals? Does not experience prove that such churches, even if their numbers are not diminished by death and removals, lose much of the life and power of religion? However it may be elsewhere, I am quite sure it has been and is so in this country. The exceptions, if any, are very few indeed. If a church that has been running down, or standing still in cold formalism, could not hope for a revival, how gloomy would be its prospects for coming years and generations. But with the records of the past, in Bible and church history, and in view of what God is now doing, how great the encouragement that, in answer to prayer, He will revive his work even where to human appearance the prospects are darkest.

As God waits to be inquired of before he pours out his Spirit, how earnestly ought every church to pray and labor for the blessing. Yes, to *labor* as well as to *pray;* for there is much work to be done, as well as much prayer to be offered. The fallow ground must be broken up; the backsliding church must rise and shake herself from the dust. She must do works meet for repentance. She must carry her Master's gracious invitation to all within her reach. She must go out into the highways and hedges, and compel them to come in, that his table may be filled with guests. No church that is settled down on her lees has any warrant to expect a revival. "Go, work to-day in my vineyard," is the command. Soul-harvests are to be secured by interceding for them, to the Lord of the harvest, and by coöperating with the Holy Spirit, in humble subordination, as laborers together with him. It was the servant who went into the vineyard who received the reward, and not he who stayed behind, saying, I go, sir, but went not.

To crown the whole, we have seen that, beginning with the apostles, all the prominent laborers in the revivals for eighteen hundred years, have, in every thing essential, *seen eye to eye, and minded the same things;* as much so, as if they had all lived in the same age, and labored together in the same glorious cause. Though differing somewhat in the external means employed, they preached the same doctrines, urged the same motives to faith and repentance, and looked for success to one and the same infinite source of all wisdom and efficiency. In coming along down through the centuries, it is delighful to see how they agreed together, how the same Spirit was in the revivals, awakening sinners, raising them by his quickening and almighty power from spiritual death to a new life, and working in them "to will and to do according to his own good pleasure." Oh, they are all divinely illuminated chapters in the history of Redemption. What would the world have been without them? How could the gospel have been spread in the first ages as it was, without revivals? And so in every age they have been as life from the dead to the church.

In our own country what would have become of the churches, but for the "Great Awakening" and the Revivals of 1800, and those by which they have since been so often refreshed? From what other sources could they have obtained an adequate supply of faithful and godly ministers? What, without them, would have been our religious condition at this hour; aye, and our *temporal* condition too? Who will say, or believe, that there would now have been three or four millions of professors, or half that number, in the evangelical churches of this land? Great as are our obligations of praise and thanksgiving to God for giving us rain from heaven and fruitful seasons, filling our hearts with food and gladness, who can say that they are less due to him for raining down righteousness upon us, as he has done in these times of refreshing.

All evangelical Christians agree that *God pours*

out his Spirit in answer to believing prayer, and that the more earnest and specific the prayer, the greater the encouragement that the very thing asked for will be granted. In his infinite wisdom and sovereignty, God may sometimes depart from his general method in carrying forward the work of redemption. We have no right to say that he never pours down his Spirit upon a church and congregation, till it is specifically and earnestly prayed for; but if there be any such exceptions, I am persuaded they are very few. I very much doubt whether, if we could see the connection between prayer and the glorious revivals that have blessed this land, we should find one that was not definitely prayed for by some earnest wrestlers, or wrestler, at the throne of grace. God loves to hear the petitions of his children for the blessing of the Spirit, and in this richest of his gifts to grant the very thing asked for, just as parents do when they give bread to their children.

Now we cannot *ask* our heavenly Father to revive his work in any place, unless we truly *desire* it. If for any reason we are afraid that it would not be a blessing, it would be scarcely less than mockery to ask for it. No truly pious person could understandingly do it. To pray aright, we must from the bottom of our hearts desire the things we ask for. Nothing seems plainer to me, than that this is essential to true prayer.

If a church can be found in this land, or any other land, where the minister and the members of it are afraid of such genuine revivals as distinguish the religious history of this country, they cannot honestly pray for them; and would it be strange if such a church and congregation were passed by, when other places around were visited? Would it not, on the contrary, be strange if it received the blessing? Is there evidence that God ever revives his work where it is not wished for? If I knew that anywhere revivals were not desired, but rather dreaded, I should want no other explanation of the fact that they are not enjoyed. This seems to me to be reason enough. There may be individual conversions and gradual additions to the churches in answer to prayer, and because they are desired; but can such glorious harvests as many of our churches have from time to time been reaping be expected, if not desired, or prayed or labored for?

When I was abroad more than twenty years ago, and when many powerful revivals were in progress here at home, I was often inquired of by ministers, whether the accounts which they had heard were true; and what was the character, and what were the fruits of these revivals. In answering these questions as well as I could, I magnified the grace of God in what I had myself witnessed. The impression upon some minds was obviously very favorable. They desired to share in the same blessing, and doubtless prayed for it not in vain. There was soon after what we should call a genuine revival in Dr. Reed's church in London, who had travelled extensively in this country the year before, and witnessed what God was doing among us. And other such revivals I believe there have since been in England, though not so much spoken of under that name as they would have been with us.

Within the last year, our brethren in England and Scotland have been remarkably stirred up to the establishment of church and union prayer-meetings for the outpouring of the Spirit, and from the latest accounts it would seem the Lord has heard and answered. It looks very much as if revivals were now springing up in various parts of the kingdom. May they be increased a thousand-fold, not only there, but in all the fatherlands as well as our own. Oh, how delightful it will be to hear songs, "Glory to the righteous," borne across the ocean on every breeze! "Though the vision tarry, let us wait for it; because it will surely come, it will not tarry."

God will work all things according to his own holy and righteous will, but who can conceive that all the dark and besotted millions of heathen and nominally Christian lands will be brought to Christ solely by the slow process of individual conversions through the long succession of years and centuries? As the revival which has just occurred in our own land, in some of its features, differs from, and I think is in advance of any former revival era, so God may speedily bring up the churches to a still higher standard, and multiply conversions both at home and abroad, beyond any thing that has yet been witnessed. Every one will admit that this is possible.

I can conceive that multitudes more of the hopeless classes of the wicked may be plucked from the burning, than in any former revival. I can conceive that far greater numbers of *the young* may be born again, than ever before, where God has poured out his Spirit. I can conceive that where whole classes have sometimes been converted in our Sabbath and other schools, all the classes may be taken in a single year, or month. I can conceive that the next revival may spread over the whole land; that not a single church may be passed by; that it may find its way into both houses of Congress, and pervade all the halls of legislation, and bring our great men with all their influence into the churches. I can conceive that God may give his ministers higher qualifications for their work, endowing them all with a double portion of his Spirit, that he may convert all our merchant-ships, and all the navy, like the ship-of-war "North Carolina," into Bethels to bear the songs of salvation with our stripes and stars round the world, and that all the officers and soldiers in our army may become soldiers of the cross.

The Spirit is not bound. Nothing is too hard for the Lord. I can conceive that in one or more of these respects the next revival may be far in advance of the present, and that in as many of them as may precede the millennium and bring it on, the last may be the most glorious of all. Then there will be no more room nor need of what we now mean by revivals, for the churches will always remain in a revived state; but I am afraid not before. Then, in the thousand years promised and sure to come, all shall know the Lord, from the least to the greatest.

How the successive generations will be gathered into the fold of the true Shepherd and Bishop of their souls, we cannot tell. Children will then be "by nature children of wrath" as they are now, and will just as much need to be born again by the Spirit.

Whether they will be sanctified from the womb, we do not know; but if not, we have reason to think it will be in very early childhood. I cannot believe they will be left for years to grow up enemies to God, when with infinite ease he can convert them before they begin to harden themselves in rebellion against him. It seems to me it could not be the millennium which the Scriptures promise. *All* would not know the Lord, from the least to the greatest.

But I make no pretensions to be wise above what is written. In his own time and way, the whole "earth shall be filled with the knowledge and glory of the Lord."

And now, in closing these imperfect sketches, I feel specially called upon to lift up my heart in devout thanksgivings to God, that he has permitted me to live in this eventful age of the world's religious history; that for more than fifty years, I have had such advantages for studying the character and marking the progress of revivals, and laboring in them as God has given me strength for the service, during a pastorate of sixteen years in two rural parishes, twenty-two years as a pastor and teacher in a public seminary, and as a helper to my brethren in such times of refreshing from the presence of the Lord. Oh, to have been allowed to witness the triumphs of Zion's King, travelling in the greatness of his strength, since I came upon the stage; to have been spared* to go back into the ages past, and trace the footsteps of the Angel of the covenant down through so many

* Dr. Humphrey, in writing this, had reached the age of fourscore years.

centuries, and to bear this testimony in favor of ancient and modern revivals; what a privilege! It is at best, but a rapid, imperfect sketch that I have given. Others I am sure could have done it better, What a history will that be, when some one competent to the task shall collect and arrange the materials which are already so ample for a great work, and which will be increased by every future revival. That day will come; and then, how much will such a history, recording the triumphs of the Captain of salvation over the prince of darkness, surpass all the conquests of all the Alexanders, Cæsars, and Napoleons of the world!

PART SECOND.

REVIVAL MANUAL.

CHAPTER VIII.

"PREPARE YE THE WAY OF THE LORD."

Having in the preceding sketches traced the progress of true religion down through the ages for more than three thousand years, and established, as I think, the great fact, that the church has been restored from her many backslidings mainly by successive reformations or revivals, in other words, by special outpourings of the Spirit, the way is now prepared to inquire, with devout supplications for divine guidance, how such revivals are to be sought for, and by what means they may be promoted. These are vital practical questions.

I am far from supposing that there are any exclusive methods of promoting revivals, suited to all cases and circumstances. Whatever instrumentalities may be employed, there are two conditions which must never be lost sight of:

That there can never be any true revival without the outpouring of the Spirit, and that it can proceed no further than it is carried forward by that divine influence; and

That a revival is never to be expected but in answer to prayer.

But beyond these two conditions there is room for different administrations, as there are divers operations by the same Spirit. Guided by the teachings of the word and Spirit of God, there is room for the exercise of a sound discretion, aided by the best experience which the history of revivals furnishes; and this is what, seeking divine assistance, I have attempted in this humble manual. It is the result of my own experience and observation, with the best helps which I have been able to derive from other sources.

"O LORD, REVIVE THY WORK."

This prayer was offered by the prophet in a time of great religious declension. The people had "slidden back by a perpetual backsliding," and he felt that nothing short of a revival could save them from utter apostasy. It was the greatest and most urgent of all their needs.

As it was then so it is now, wherever a church is in a cold backsliding state, and sinners are slumbering on the verge of the pit. That the need is not felt, that the danger is not apprehended, is so far from proving that no special revival is needed, that this state of things in any church and congregation makes a revival more necessary; the more profound the indifference, the greater the necessity.

Is this the case, dear brethren, with you? You either need a revival, or you do not. Perhaps your church and congregation are large, strong, and united. You have a good minister and support him well, and your congregation rather increases from year to year, than diminishes. You are ready to say with the church of Laodicea, "We are rich and increased with goods, and have need of nothing." Is this your condition? are these your contented feelings? Then, like that church, are you not spiritually "wretched and miserable and poor and blind and naked;" and except you repent, what will all your harmony and outward prosperity avail?

How long is it that you have been thus settled down upon your lees, sowing pillows under all armholes? How many years since you have had a revival? How is it with the rising generation? Are they converted, or likely to be, without a revival? The older members of your church are passing off, and who are to fill their places, if others are not "baptized for the dead?" And what are you doing? Are you on your knees, praying with the prophet, "O Lord, revive thy work in the midst of the years;" or are you waiting for one another, hoping that the whole church will wake up, and call upon God for the blessing? If waiting for this, your expectations will never be realized. That time will never come. We have no reason to think that all the members of any church are themselves truly converted; and if not, how can all the church be expected to unite in prevailing prayer?

Other churches around may be as languid as you are, or they may not. If they are, is that any reason why you should remain so? Ought it not to awaken your fears that God has forsaken the whole region, saying, "They are joined to their idols; let them alone." If, on the other hand, your neighbors are rejoicing in the midst of revivals, why should you not be excited and encouraged to strive for the blessing?

How, dear brethren, would it be with you, in another case somewhat analogous, though infinitely less urgent. Suppose there was a great drought in your town, consuming all your crops and threatening you with famine when what you have on hand shall all be eaten up; and suppose the same were the case with all the region around, would it give you any comfort to know that you were no worse off than your neighbors? Or if the showers were refreshing their parched fields, would it not awaken and increase your anxiety for equally copious rains? Oh, with what eagerness would you watch the rising clouds, and how it would distress you to see them from day to day passing by upon the mountains, and leaving your farms to become "powder and dust," under a brazen and burning sky.

And how can you remain indifferent while a more parching spiritual drought is consuming you? Will you not rise as one man, and call upon God to pour down the rain from the upper heavens, to revive his work in the midst of the years?

"LORD, INCREASE OUR FAITH."

The disciples had faith, but on the occasion in which this prayer is recorded, they seem not to have had the faith necessary to work miracles in Christ's name. They now felt their deficiency, and prayed their Master to help them—to *increase* their faith, so that they might be able to make full proof of its power. They were brought to feel their absolute dependence on Christ for the increase which they needed, at the same time that they felt they deserved his rebuke for their unbelief.

In like manner, Christians are absolutely dependent on Christ to enable them to pray in faith for a revival, or when it is in progress, that it may be continued. How often have we heard the exhortation, "Pray, pray in faith, and God will certainly hear and answer you." This is very true. It shall not be said that such praying breath was ever spent in vain. But faith is the gift of God; and how can you pray in faith, till you receive the gift? The Christian, whether in a revival or out of a revival, is dependent on Christ for a spirit of prayer.

Every true Christian has some faith, however weak and wavering, as the disciples had, and can therefore pray as they did, "Lord, increase my faith;" but that faith, though less than "a grain of mustard seed," would be as much the gift of God as was the strong faith of Abraham or Moses.

If this be so, what is one of the first duties of the members of a church, when their graces are languishing, and stupidity reigns throughout the whole community? Is it not *prayer for themselves?* "Lord, stir us up, give us a spirit of prayer for those who are perishing around us. Lord, we believe thy promises; help thou our unbelief. Increase our faith." This is beginning at the beginning, and if you are in a cold, backsliding state, what can you do? What will your prayers for a revival avail, till you have a revival spirit of prayer? And will you not earnestly ask for that, as the first and essential thing? See what David's penitential prayer after his fall was: "Restore unto me the joy of thy salvation, and uphold me by thy free Spirit; then will I teach transgressors thy ways, and sinners shall be converted unto thee."

So, dear friends, when iniquity abounds, and your love waxes cold, should you say, "Lord, increase our faith," then will we pray earnestly and prevailingly for the revival of thy work in the midst of us. Oh, how much prayer for the conversion of sinners is lost, for want of faith in the hearts of Christians.

HINDERANCES TO REVIVALS.

Are there any; and if so, what are they? That there are no *insuperable* obstacles in the way we know, for revivals have often taken place where, to human view, they were least to be expected. And yet there are hinderances everywhere, which nothing short of divine power can overcome. These are *the world, the flesh, and the devil.* I know of none but may be classed under one or the other of these three obstacles.

1. *The world,* by which I mean its inbred hostility to all spiritual religion, whether in individuals or communities: its direct hostility, its maxims, its al-

lurements, its temptations in their wily and protean forms, stand directly in the way of a revival. There never would be one if the world, thus understood, could prevent it. In enlightened Christian communities, unconverted men may profess to be the friends of true religion, and to wish to see it prosper; but as in their hearts they are opposed to it, they will, in one way or another, discourage that interest and concern in which a true revival consists. They want to have things continue as they are. "We are now at peace among ourselves," they say, "and why should it be broken in upon? Why not let well enough alone? Religion is a good thing," it may be added, "but all public excitements are dangerous. These revivals, as they are called, lead to enthusiasm and fanaticism. They often divide churches and families, and are rather to be dreaded than desired." Thus do the opposers of revivals reason in their hearts, if they do not think it polite to speak it openly. All their influence is directly or indirectly against them. This, in many places, is a very great hinderance.

And the world, ever wise to do evil, knows how to set the lust of the flesh, the lust of the eyes, and the pride of life against the intrusion of revivals. It holds up so many dazzling fascinations, it keeps men so busy, so eager in the pursuit of pleasure, riches, and display, that they have no time for any thing better. It spreads out all these allurements, and hangs them up in their most tempting attractions along the broad way; and alas, with what success—drowning thoughtless multitudes "in destruction and perdition." How many revivals have been kept out by these hostile influences, will not be known till the day of judgment; but they are certainly great hinderances. In fine, whatever the world can do to hedge up the way against revivals, we may rest assured will be done in one way or another. But,

2. *The flesh* is a still more insidious and dangerous foe to revivals. There is more danger within, than without. The hinderances are greater from the church itself, than from the world. It is reasonably expected, that those who profess religion will do more to honor and promote it by their example, by their consistent lives, and by their active influence than any, or than all others out of the pale of the church. Hindcrances from this quarter are often many and exceedingly grievous. Sometimes there are bitter internal dissensions, which would disgrace any mere worldly association. "Brother goeth to law with brother." The personal friends of the parties take sides with their respective favorites, and thus the breach is widened, "as when one letteth out water." The house is divided against itself. Criminations and recriminations are engendered and multiplied. The world looks on jeeringly, and exclaims, "Behold how these Christians *hate* one another! If this is religion, we want none of it. If these are some of the fruits of revivals, the fewer the better."

Sometimes reproaches come from open and indulged immorality. Members of the church become intemperate, dishonest in their dealings, or fall into other habitual transgressions of the second table of the law, bringing great scandal upon their profession, and are not called to account by the church. They are allowed to retain their standing, and come to the Lord's table, year after year. The world looks on and perhaps says, "Here you see some of the fruits of a great revival, as it was called, years ago. These were some of the converts. See what they have come to, and see how the church winks at such scandalous violations of their covenant, when they are known and read of all men. We don't wish to see any more such revivals."

Or if the church-members become so conformed to the world, to its feverish passion for money getting and show, for doubtful, if not positively sinful amusements; if they strive to outshine the gay and thoughtless in dress, in furniture, in parties, in equipage; if instead of "striving against sin," they fall in with the loose maxims of mere worldly men, it cannot but be noticed by those who make no pretensions to piety, and thus prejudice many, not only against real religion, but against all revivals, since in many cases it is understood that the majority of the church-members have been brought in during such seasons of religious interest.

These are "works of the flesh," yielding to biases within and temptations without, which are among the greatest hinderances to revivals. Such churches are in no condition to receive the blessing. The wonder is, not that they are passed by for years and years, but that they are ever visited.

3. There are still other hinderances from a greater foe than either the world or the flesh, "*the wiles of the devil*," who is sure to guard the entrance to a revival by throwing every obstacle in the way, that

his vast capacity and malignity can invent. Against these the church cannot too vigilantly work, or too earnestly pray. His devices to keep out revivals, and to oppose and corrupt them in their progress, are inexhaustible. If he could prevent it, there never would be another. Blessed assurance, that "for this purpose the Son of God was manifested, that he might destroy the works of the devil;" and He will do it. He *is* doing it, by various instrumentalities in the heathen world, and by revivals there, as well as in Christian lands.

All these three, the world, the flesh, and the devil, are positive hinderances, and if God does not interpose, either of them is sufficient to prevent a revival.

"TAKE UP THE STUMBLING-BLOCKS OUT OF THE WAY."

Having pointed out some of the main hinderances and obstacles which lie in the way of revivals, I feel bound to show, if I can, what is to be done to remove the stumbling-blocks—how the way of the Lord may be prepared, that he may come into his vineyard and water it. Where great obstacles lie in the way of any thing, they must be removed. This is the first step. It may or may not be all that is required in any given case, but it is the first thing to be done. The stone that blocks the wheels must be removed. Obstacles which by accident or design forbid the advance of the railcars must be taken away, the track must be cleared; then they can proceed, but not before. So with all physical impediments; they must be removed, or in some way overcome.

The same is true in morals and religion, within their legitimate spheres. Whatever hinderances are found to lie in the path, must be taken out of the way. These hinderances to revivals, as we have seen, are the world, the flesh, and the devil. We cannot prepare the way by gaining "the friendship of the world," which "is enmity with God;" but by his help, we can counteract its hostile influences upon ourselves and others. Neither individuals nor churches can secure themselves from those outward temptations which war against the soul; but by the grace of God, they can resist them. They can let their own light so shine before men, that there shall be no occasion to inquire, "What do ye more than others?" They can so withdraw from conformity to the world, and so carefully shun all appearance of evil, as to shut the mouths of gainsayers, and constrain them to admit, that there must be a reality in religion, and that revivals which produce such fruits cannot be of men, but must come from a higher power. A church that has let down its watch, and ceased to discipline its members when they fall away and bring reproach upon the cause of Christ, can repent, and purge out the old leaven, and take away the reproach. A backsliding church can rise and shake herself from the dust, in spite of all the opiates that the world has power to administer. She can betake herself in earnest to invite a revival, by taking up the stumbling-blocks which impede the chariot of salvation.

There is no preventing our adversary the devil from employing all his temptations and stratagems to keep out revivals. There is nothing that he hates and fears so much as the opening of the heavens to pour down righteousness upon a languishing church, and a dying congregation. With his consent, as I have said, there would never be another "awakening," great or small, to the end of the world. But we "are not ignorant of his devices," and he can be resisted. When the proper means are used to obtain the blessing, he can no more prevent a spiritual shower from descending upon the most parched enclosure of the vineyard, than he can stay the bottles of heaven when the dust groweth into hardness, and the clouds cleave fast together.

There are no hinderances to revivals from without or within, but may be removed or overcome. It is not in wicked men or devils to fence out these visitations from on high, to throw such stumbling-blocks in the way that they cannot enter. Every temptation, every opposing influence, whether open or secret, may be successfully resisted; "not by might, nor by power, but by my Spirit, saith the Lord of hosts."

THE SAVIOUR'S RETURN.

" When Jesus returned, the people gladly received him; for they were all waiting for him." Christ had crossed over the lake of Galilee to Gadara, where he found a raving maniac among the tombs possessed with many devils, and cast them out. How long he staid there, we are not informed; but when he came back, he found the people gathered on the shore and waiting for him. They had enjoyed his presence and instructions and seen his miracles, and they were so anxious for his return, that they resolved to be at the place of landing in season to welcome him; and when he came, they received him with rejoicing.

This incident is full of instruction and encouragement, and was doubtless recorded for our learning on whom the ends of the world are come. Let us inquire then what is meant by *waiting* for Christ's return, when he has been for a longer or shorter time absent.

1. It implies *desire.* When we wait for an absent friend, it is not in a state of indifference. It is because we want to see him, and want to enjoy the pleasure of his society. So it was with that waiting company on the shore of the lake. They would not have gathered there, much less would they have waited, if they had not wished for his return. Neither can a church, that once enjoyed the special presence of Christ in a revival, be said to be waiting for a like blessing, if they do not earnestly desire his return. Time passes. Years perhaps roll away. They sometimes talk about him, and profess, it may be, to lament his long absence. But they are not waiting for him, till they desire his return so earnestly as to pray for it. Any thing short of this is not waiting for him.

2. Waiting for Christ implies *hope and expectation.* Thus when you are waiting for a valued friend who has been some time absent, you have some expectation at least that he will come, though you do not certainly know when; else you would not wait for him: you could not; you would have no motive to wait any longer, however anxious you might be to meet and welcome him. Neither could a church in a time of general declension be said to wait for the Saviour's

return, if they had no encouragement to expect it. It is not in the constitution of the human mind, sanctified or unsanctified, to wait for any thing without hope or expectation. The multitude would not have stood on the shore of Galilee, anxiously looking across the water to catch the first glimpse of the boat, if they had not expected it. They would have gone away, or rather, they would not have come.

3. Waiting for Christ to come and revive his work, implies *a preparation* in the church to receive him. When he came back from his mission across the lake, the people "gladly received him." They were ready to listen to his instruction, and witness his wonderful works. This was what they came together for. They did not remain at home till they heard that he had landed, but went down to meet and welcome him. This was their preparation. This was the proof that they were anxiously waiting for him.

And how do you do when you are expecting a visit from a dear friend, or when you are looking for some distinguished guest, and do not know at what time he will come, whether to-day or to-morrow? You don't put off your preparations till the coach drives up to the door. You consider beforehand what kind of reception he will reasonably expect, and do your best to prepare for it. You would not, when you met him, say, "I am very glad to see you, I have been expecting and waiting for you a long time," when you had got nothing ready to make him welcome and comfortable. There may be delay, but there is no real *waiting* like that which we are now considering, which does not include these three things at least—*desire, expectation*, and some good degree of *preparation* for the desired visit or blessing.

And now, dear brethren, how is it with you? How is it with your church? Much as we read and hear of revivals, and however so many of them there may be in the land, hundreds, yea, thousands of churches remain unvisited, and yours may be one of the number. How long is it then since the Saviour made you his last visit? How many years since he was with you, calling sinners to repentance, and making them "willing in the day of his power?" How long has he been gone, and you mourned his absence? Are you waiting for him to return, as the people were at the lake of Galilee? Do you earnestly desire him to come to you speedily? Does this desire ascend up to his mercy-seat in earnest, persevering prayer? Do you expect him? You may, if you ask aright; for his ear is always open, and he has bound himself by great and precious promises. Have you not been long in a state so cold and indifferent as almost, if not quite, to give up the hope that he will ever return; and have you not very much given over asking him?

The people of Galilee received him joyfully, because they were waiting for him, and prepared for his return. Are you, I ask again, looking anxiously out for him? If he were to return, are you prepared to welcome him into your houses, and into your hearts? Would he find you waking, and looking out for his return; or would he find you saying, "A little more sleep, a little more slumber, a little more folding of the hands to sleep?"

Oh, brethren, brethren, this will not do! "It is high time to wake out of sleep." Souls are perishing, and you are answerable. Christ would ere this have been with you, reviving his work, if you had been waiting for him. Whose urgent voice is it but his, that I seem to hear at your very threshold, "Behold, I stand at the door, and knock. If any man hear my voice, and open the door, I will come in unto him, and sup with him, and he with me." And if he will come to one who is waiting for him, how much more if he finds all his friends waiting as he did on the shore of Galilee?

"COME DOWN ERE MY CHILD DIE."

Jesus Christ was a great physician. He was so regarded by the Jews at Nazareth, where he was brought up. "Ye will surely say unto me this proverb, Physician, heal thyself." They had heard of the wonderful cures which he wrought in Capernaum, and reproached him for not doing the same among them, when they were so far from receiving and listening to him even with common civility, that they thrust him out of the city, and sought to cast him down headlong from the brow of the hill on which it was built. Why should he heal their sick when they would not even allow him to remain another day or hour among them?

He was a physician of the bodies as well as the souls of men. Of this we have the most abundant testimony in the gospels. We have reason to believe he wrought more bodily cures than any other physician ever did, or ever will. Take the following as examples: "At even, when the sun did set, they brought unto him all that were diseased, and them that were possessed with devils; and all the city was gathered at the door. And he healed many that were sick of divers diseases, and cast out many devils." This was done at Capernaum. Mark 1 : 32–34. "And Jesus went up into a mountain, and sat down there," near the sea of Galilee, "and great multitudes came unto him, having with them those that were lame, blind, dumb, maimed, and many others, and cast them down at Jesus' feet, and he healed them." Matt. 15 : 29. "And Jesus went about all Galilee, teaching in their synagogues, and preaching the gospel of the kingdom, and healing all manner of sickness, and all manner of disease among the people." Matt. 4 : 23, 24. He was not the physician of any one city or place merely. He *went about* doing good. He travelled all over the land. He visited and healed the sick wherever he was sent for, and he never lost a patient. Nor did he confine his cures to the sick of his own country: "His fame went throughout all Syria, and they brought unto him all sick people, that were taken with divers diseases and torments; and those which were possessed with devils, and those which were lunatic, and those that had the palsy, and he healed them." What multitudes must he have cured of all sorts of diseases, during the three and a half years of his public ministry, wherever he went. A number of affecting incidents are recorded, of which this is one: "A certain nobleman's son was sick at Capernaum. When he heard that Jesus was come out of Judea into Galilee, he went unto him, and besought him that he would come down and heal his son, for he was at the point of death. Then said Jesus unto him, Except ye see signs and wonders, ye will not believe. The nobleman saith unto him, Come down ere my child die." And Jesus would doubtless have gone down at once, had not the nobleman's faith prevented. "Go thy way," saith he, "thy son liveth." The man believed the word and went his way, and that very hour the child began to amend.

Jesus no longer visits the sick, or cures diseases by his visible bodily presence; but there are now, as there were then, diseases of the soul far more malignant and alarming, and we have, if possible, still greater encouragement to apply to him for healing.

Suppose there was now a terrible epidemic raging all over the land, and sweeping off thousands every week, and so malignant as thus far to baffle all the skill of the best physicians. And suppose that in this state of universal gloom and despair, we should learn that a physician had just come from afar into the very next town, and had already effected many wonderful cures in cases of the greatest extremity; in fact, curing all as soon and as fast as they applied to him, and that he was just as much needed with us as with them; what would you do? Would you not send for him at once, urging him by every possible motive to come, and give you too the benefits of his skill? If the first application did not prevail, would you not dispatch messenger after messenger, urging him with increasing importunity, "Come down ere we all die?" I am sure you would, and so would all in like circumstances, who should hear of his wonderful success. You would give him no rest as long as there was a possibility of persuading him to come. You could not stand and see your children die, till the last effort to save them had failed. And if it became known that he had already visited many other places, with unfailing success, and had never given a refusal when suitably applied to—if by any unaccountable infatuation you had delayed sending for him till he was gone, leaving the pestilence still to sweep on, would not all who should hear of it say, "They have no one to blame but themselves. They are perishing by their own neglect. The physician was near and ready to come, but he was not invited." I know that such a case can never happen. But it strikingly suggests a familiar analogy, which must be still more astonishing to the angels than that would be.

Jesus Christ, the great Physician, is present by his Spirit, wherever there is a revival of religion. Many such gracious visits he is now making, in almost every part of the land. He is doing his mighty works in healing multitudes who were ready to perish. But the number of places yet unvisited is far greater—places where there are no revivals. Yours may be one of them, and the great Physician may have come into your immediate neighborhood, where souls were perishing, and where he is now plucking them as brands from the burning. Certainly he is not so far off, but that you can apply to him without the least delay. Some of you hope, that in some former visit, years ago, when he found you at the point of death, he applied the balm of Gilead and saved you. But in looking round over your families and neighborhoods, you see that hundreds, it may be thousands, are in the same danger that you were in, and you know that they must perish for ever, if not healed in like manner. It is a case of life and death with every one of them—not of *temporal,* but of *eternal* death.

And what are you doing? You cannot save them. None of your physicians can reach their case. It is desperate beyond all human help. But there is the almighty Physician, perhaps within an hour's ride, multiplying his spiritual cures, and waiting to be invited by you with the same earnestness which brought him there. You "stand between the living and the dead;" and let me affectionately ask, What are you doing? Why are you not enjoying the blessings of a revival, as well as your neighbors—as well as any other church and congregation in the land? God is no respecter of persons, or of places. It cannot be owing to any reluctance to come, on the part of the great Physician, that he has passed you by. Nothing is wanting but preparation of heart, and earnest, believing prayer, to bring him to you. He wants to come. He is only waiting for you to ask aright, and he will come. As he never refused when he was personally going about doing good to the bodies and souls of men, so now it shall never be said to those who seek him, that they seek in vain. If there was a mortal sickness threatening to sweep off not more than one-tenth of your population, and you heard of a physician anywhere within reach, who was performing more cures of the same disease than all others to whom you could apply, though he might have lost some patients, you would lose no time, you would spare no expense to bring him to the bedside of your sick friends. And now, will you, can you do less, when the great majority are infected with the heart-plague, which no medicine can arrest; when there is One of infinitely more than mortal skill, who stands ready to come and cure all, without money and without price? If you have no revival and they perish, consider, O ye professed friends of Christ, in whose skirts their blood will be found. Dare you slumber on and meet the answer in the great day? Can you give one blameless reason why you are not now enjoying a revival as well as other churches and congregations?

PREACHING.

Preaching is the chief instrumentality by which the way of the Lord is prepared, when religion has sunk to a low ebb, and he is about to revive his work. The first thing is that the church be awakened from its slumbers. Till this is done, there is very little hope that sinners will be awakened; and it requires an earnestness in the pulpit, a directness of appeal, a sounding of alarm to professors, which shall make their ears tingle. They must be dealt with plainly, as standing in the way of a revival, as stumbling-blocks lying in the path, instead of living witnesses for Christ before the world. The guilt as well as the danger of their backslidings must be faithfully pointed out. They must be earnestly exhorted to "repent and do their first works;" to examine themselves whether they are in the faith, whether their own hopes are well founded, whether remaining as they are, they *can* have any good evidence that they are not yet in their sins. They must be told plainly that there are false professors in the churches, and they must be exhorted to wake and rise from the dead, that Christ may give them life. They must be shown that they are in a fearful degree answerable for the reigning worldliness and spiritual death around them. In dealing with them, the preacher must use the word of God, which is sharper than a two-edged sword, as the surgeon uses his knife, though it cut deep into the quick. It may lead some real Christians for a time to distrust and renounce their hope. It probably will, but it will do them good in the end, by making them more watchful and prayerful and faithful to their covenant vows. Under such a course of preaching, it may be hoped that the wise virgins will be startled from their slumber, and that 'fearfulness will surprise the hypocrites.' It may require more than one sermon, or two. It probably will. How many, no minister can tell till he has made the trial and witnessed the effect. Let him not give over till he has made full proof—"line upon line, precept upon precept." He must expect that many of his hearers will wonder why he should dwell so much upon one topic, and it will not be strange if some of his best members should feel that he bears too hard upon them, though they may not tell him so. But if his searching appeals sink down in their hearts and rouse them to prayer and action, and God pours out his Spirit, they will be thankful that the preacher did not let them alone till, by the grace of God, they were constrained to rise and shake themselves from the dust.

Said one of the most pious deacons of my church, after a glorious revival which brought in nearly all the most influential men in the place, "I wondered, before the work commenced, why you preached so long and pointedly to the church. I knew we were in a cold state, and needed to be waked up, but at the time it seemed almost cruel in you to lay the blame of our never having had a general revival so heavily upon the church; I now see that we needed it, and bless God, that he moved you to deal so faithfully with us, both in the pulpit and out of it." Some others had the same hard thoughts, and were led to change their minds in the same way, after they had seen and rejoiced in the salvation of God. If we had all the facts, I believe it would be found that nearly all of the most powerful revivals have been immediately preceded by a loud and earnest sounding of alarm in the ears of the churches. How can any pastor of a dead church, who "travails in birth" for souls, rest satisfied till, relying on Divine aid, he has faithfully made the attempt? Nor should it be confined to the pulpit. The subject should be kept before the mind of the church at weekly lectures and prayer-meetings, and in private exhortations, till it shall be evident that she is in some good degree prepared to receive a blessing. As soon as that shall be the case, the prayer will go up from many lips, Lord, what wilt thou have us to do?

When a church is brought to this point, there is every reason to hope that God is about to revive his work in the congregation. And then the way is prepared for a series of pointed and rousing discourses to the impenitent. Then is the time for the preacher to wield "the sword of the Spirit," to lift up his voice like a trumpet, to cry aloud and not spare. Just here, the first thing to be aimed at is to gain the sinner's attention. Failing in this, though an angel were to come down from heaven and occupy the pulpit, his preaching would avail nothing. It would do no more good than speaking into the cold ear of death. The careless sinner must somehow be influenced to "think on his ways," to consider what his actual condition is, what his relations to God are, what the law requires, what the gospel offers, and what must be the inevitable consequences of his living as he has done, and dying in his present state. I say you must first gain his serious attention, before you can hope that your preaching will do him good. And how is he to be awakened? "Not by might, nor by power, but by my Spirit, saith the Lord." Nevertheless, it hath "pleased God by the foolishness of preaching," as the Greeks stigmatized it, to *awaken* sinners as well as to *save* them.

And in such a state of things, when a cloud of mercy has come over a place, what kind of preaching is wanted? What texts and subjects are best adapted to wake the slumbering, and constrain them to flee from the wrath to come? Not such preaching as a backsliding church needs, not such as young converts want, but a series of discourses upon such topics as these: the entire sinfulness of the human heart in the sight of a holy God; the strictness and righteous penalty of his law; the certainty that it will be inflicted in the awful and endless punishment of all who die impenitent—leading sinners to despair of obtaining salvation by the merit of their own works, or by their own unaided strivings, be they ever so earnest; stripping them of all their vain excuses, driving them from all their refuges of lies, and pointing them to the cross of Christ as their only refuge.

Many of the most successful preachers in winning souls to Christ have dwelt much and earnestly upon these preparatory topics, as I venture to call them, in the commencement of revivals. They are needed, they come at the right time. This is the proper place for them in the use of the means which God has appointed, and I see not how any minister can hope for a thorough work of the Lord in the conversion of sinners, who does not thus begin at the beginning, who does not show them the desperate wickedness of their hearts, who does not make the law thunder in their ears, and uncover the pit of destruction before them. This is what Whitefield did; this is what Wesley did; this is what Edwards did; this is what Bellamy, and the Tennent's did; this is what all the most successful laborers in revivals have done since their day; and I hazard nothing in saying, that the work has been deep and thorough in proportion to the thoroughness of the preaching in its earlier stages. Sinners must be "shut up to the faith" by the flaming sword turning every way, before they will despair of help from any but an almighty arm. No man, however critical his case may be, will send for a physician till he believes he is sick, and then the more critical he regards his condition, the more ready will he be to use the remedies which the best medical skill can prescribe. So with the sinner; he is sick unto death, but he will never apply to the great Physician till he feels that the case is desperate. The first thing is to bring him to feel this, and to cry out for help. There must be no palliations. His heart must be probed to the bottom, and its corruption laid bare, so that he may loathe himself in his own sight, and smite upon his breast and cry out with the publican, "God be merciful to me a sinner."

In laying so much stress as I have done upon holding up the terrors of the law in the beginning of a revival, and dwelling mostly for some time upon the guilt and danger of impenitence, I do not mean that the way of escape from the wrath to come should be kept out of sight even then. The voice of mercy from Calvary should be heard in the midst of the loudest threatenings from Sinai. But Sinai must utter its thunders. The careless multitude must be alarmed, so as to cry out for help, before they will be ready to receive it. While here and there the Lord opens the heart of a Lydia at once to receive with joy the good news of salvation, this has not been his ordinary method. In the language of the old divines, there must be "law work" to bring sinners to Christ. The experience of Paul in this regard, has been the experience of multitudes who have been converted in revivals: "I was alive without the law once; but when the commandment came, sin revived, and I died."

THE PASTOR IN A REVIVAL.

These things being premised, I will suppose, my young brother in the ministry, that you and your church are now in the midst of a revival. Some are asking what they must do to be saved, and others are beginning to rejoice in hope. It is a critical time with them, and under God much may depend upon the means employed. The revival may pervade the congregation and bring many into the kingdom of Christ, or it may be checked at once. Perhaps there never was a revival so powerful, but that, to all human view, the Spirit might have been quenched, as many have been suddenly brought to a stand by unwise and indiscreet proceedings.

I do not profess to have had very large experience. Many have oftener seen the salvation of God in these blessed times of refreshing than I have, and are more capable of giving advice to the inexperienced; but it has pleased God to afford me a good many precious opportunities of witnessing the presence and power of the Holy Spirit, in the conviction and conversion of sinners.

In the thoughts which I have to throw out, and the advice which I have to offer, I shall give the results of my own observation and inquiries, without claiming any right to mark out a course for others. God has not shut up his ministers and churches to any one method. A considerable range is left for the choice of means according to times and circumstances. In reading a hundred narratives, we might not find the same features and stages of progress in any two of them. As there are diversities of operation by the same Spirit, so there are diversities of means and agencies, which God is pleased to own and bless in reviving his work. Our part is to pray, Lord, what wilt thou have us to do? and then to follow the leadings of his providence and Spirit.

It will sometimes be found, before the work has advanced far, that something lies in the way of its progress. It seems to stand still. Those who have been awakened, remain for days just about where they were; and there are no new inquirers. This ought to alarm the whole church. What is the matter? What hinders the chariot of salvation from rolling on? There should be great searchings of heart; and if we could see the hearts of those who have been waiting for the salvation of God as he sees them, it would probably be found that there is less fervent prayer than there was. Christians are in danger of taking it for granted, as it were, that when God has begun to pour out his Spirit in answer to prayer, he will continue to carry on the good work, though they should neglect this great duty and privilege. But for this they have no warrant. *Continuance* in prayer, if I may so express it, is the motive power, and without which it must come to a stand. But however this may be, there is some cause, some letting down, some neglect of duty on the part of the church, which must be searched out and repented of.

So, again, in the midst of a powerful revival, when Christians have been long on their knees with their faces bowed in the dust, the impression may be stronger than ever, that God not only can, but will carry on his work and glorify himself, though their prayers should cease; or that their supplications might now give place to thanksgivings. When this, or something like this feeling appears, the church should be called together, not to discourage their thanksgivings for what God hath wrought, but to exhort them at the same time, instead of relaxing, to wrestle more earnestly with the Angel of the covenant. Indeed, judging from what I have witnessed in revivals, the church needs to be often called together by the pastor, to keep them constantly advised of the progress of the work, and of the hinderances which threaten to retard it. Without some watch like this, suited to the flowing and ebbing of the waters of salvation, I see not how the church can be expected to preserve a healthful tone of prayer, and a vigorous state of action.

Again, when a revival has lasted for months perhaps, and a great harvest is already in the sheaf, Christians are apt to feel that it is as large as can be expected in one season, and in this way to limit, as it were, the Holy One of Israel. From what I have seen in revivals, I am satisfied that this is a common case. The impression on many minds is something like this: The blessing has already been larger than we could have hoped for, considering our infinite unworthiness, and we regard it as a rich earnest of what God will do for us, when he shall be pleased to come and revive us again; but we must wait. This may never be uttered, but such is the feeling—"We must wait God's time for the conversion of the many who are left." In this way I fear

Satan often gets an advantage of the church, which he could not gain in any other. I look upon it as one of *his* stratagems, because I believe he is never so busy as in revivals, and because I find nothing in the Bible to warrant the impression that the work in progress must needs cease, so long as there are sinners to be brought in, but that, "contrarywise," there is much encouragement to pray and work on.

When the prophet Elisha directed the king of Israel to take arrows and smite upon the ground, he smote thrice and stayed. Whereupon the prophet was angry, and sharply chided him: "Thou shouldest have smitten five or six times; then hadst thou smitten Syria till thou hadst consumed it; whereas thou shalt now smite Syria but thrice." Final deliverance from the invasions of that powerful enemy of Israel was forfeited by stopping short when there was nothing to hinder. So in a revival, what is there but the want of faith and perseverance, to hinder the conversion of all who are brought under its influence? A hundred, perhaps, have been born again. It is certainly a great and glorious work; but why should it cease, when hundreds are still impenitent and ready to perish? Is the Lord's hand shortened, that it cannot save any more? Is his ear heavy, that he cannot any longer hear? Dear brethren, are you straitened in him? Is it not wholly in your own bowels? You say you desire the salvation of every soul; and if so, why not still use the means that have been so signally blessed? Why wait for another revival? If you forfeit your privilege in this, are you sure that you shall ever see another? And if another should be enjoyed in a few years, will all who are yet unconverted live till that time?

You will say, perhaps, that in no place has the whole impenitent population ever been converted in a single revival. And what then? Does it prove that this never can be? that it never will be? As the millennium approaches, we may expect to see greater things than have yet been witnessed. If we are warranted to pray for the outpouring of the Spirit at all, we have the same warrant to pray for the conversion of many as for few. As there is no respect of persons with God, so there is no limitation to the promises, "Ask, and ye shall receive;" "Open your mouth wide, and I will fill it;" "If ye shall ask any thing in my name, I will do it"—"*any thing.*"

"How large the promise, how divine!"

It would certainly be very remarkable if God were to convert *all* in a great revival. But that he can, if he pleases, no praying person can doubt. There seems to have been something very much like it, in the apostolic age. Thus we read, that when Peter passed throughout all quarters, "all that dwelt in Lydda and Saron turned unto the Lord." And in our own times, we have heard of revivals, if we have not witnessed them, in some of our higher seminaries, of the same comprehensiveness. So it is not very uncommon for whole families to be taken at once. Dear brethren, "be not faithless, but believing." Pray without ceasing. Do not let the Angel of the covenant go till you have prevailed for the largest blessings which he has to bestow. The fact that you have already seen the salvation of God beyond all that you dared to hope for, that greater numbers, it may be, have been converted than in any former revival, is so far from affording any reason for relaxing in prayer and efforts for the immediate conversion of those who are left, that the larger the gift received, the greater the encouragement to ask for more.

It were easy to bring many illustrations bearing on the point that the church ought never to be satisfied so long as any remain outside of the ark, hourly exposed to be swallowed up by the rising deluge.

If your neighbor's house was on fire, and the family were all fast asleep, or if they had been waked in time to escape, and some of them had been already rescued from the flames while others were still left, what would you do? Would you say, we have already saved more than we expected, and so relax your efforts to save the rest? No. You would if possible increase them, and never give over till the last child was snatched from the devouring element. And will you cease to pray for those who are still exposed to everlasting fire, because so many have been plucked as brands from the burning?

In a terrible storm, such as often happens on our seaboard, a vessel is driven upon the breakers, and becomes a hopeless wreck. The crew and the passengers are seen from the shore clinging to the shrouds, and ready to be swallowed up. What is to be done? The life-boat is launched. Struggling through the roaring surf, and almost swamped, she reaches the wreck. There are a hundred to be saved, and she can take only ten. Again and again she returns, till more than half the number are landed safe on the shore. But what is to become of the rest? Will the hardy boatmen say, "We have saved many more than we expected when we saw the danger. The winds and waves are more and more appalling. It is night-fall, which increases the danger of further efforts. We will go home, thankful for what we have been able to do, and return early in the morning, hoping to find the sea calmer, and then we will bring the rest ashore." Impossible! It would not be safe for any man to hint such inhumanity to the most hardened sailor. And can you, dear Christian friends, sit down and rest satisfied for the present with the rescue of less than half of your friends and neighbors who were ready to perish, when, by your own acknowledgment, those who are left are in equal danger?

But I have not room for enlargement here. I am not so vain as to feel sure that the course of preaching which I have sketched and recommended before a revival, and in the early stages of it, is better than some other, when there is so much room for consulting times and circumstances. What I have said is chiefly drawn from my own experience and observation in revivals. It may or may not accord with the larger experience of others. Let it stand upon its own merits, nothing more.

It can hardly be necessary to add, that no wise master-builder will indulge the idea that by laboring for a revival in season and out of season, and bringing many converts into the church, they and the older members will need little more of his help to "build them up as lively stones, a spiritual house, a holy priesthood, to offer up spiritual sacrifices, acceptable to God by Jesus Christ." It is just here, if I mistake not, that some excellent pastors are in danger of losing half the fruits of their labors in sowing and reaping, and shouting the harvest home. Believing that all who are born again will be kept by the power of God through faith unto salvation, they seem to forget that all who have lately been converted, however well instructed and established in other things, are but babes in Christ, and need the sincere milk of the word, that they may grow thereby till they become strong in the Lord and in the power of his might.

Those more especially who, till the revival, and perhaps till it was far advanced, had paid no attention to religion, and are brought in suddenly, as in these days many are, have almost every thing to learn of its doctrines, of its evidences, and of its claims. Being just brought into the school of Christ, now is the time to teach them, till they are rooted and grounded in the faith. Now they will learn faster than at any other period of their discipleship, and to this end they will require more teaching.

Some ministers, in their great zeal for the immediate conversion of sinners, think it their duty to preach and exhort at all times just as they do in the midst of a revival, and feel as if they were doing very little good, if they do not see the immediate fruit of their labors in bringing sinners to Christ. Doubtless they cannot be too anxious to have them brought in. But they have work to do in the church, as well as out of it. By pressing too hard after a glorious revival, and without giving the church any time to recover from the physical and mental exhaustion which is likely to supervene, they are in danger not only of increasing the exhaustion, but wearing out their own remaining strength and religious susceptibilities with little or no profit. Mr. Nettleton used to say, that if he was a settled pastor, he would not always be preaching what would be distinctly regarded as revival sermons, as it might disgust and harden sinners, rather than convert them; and I believe he was right.

Suppose there should be an interval of even four or five years between two revivals, would the pastor have reason to mourn that he was all that time laboring in vain, and spending his strength for naught? By no means. If he is doing the work of the Lord faithfully during that interval, he may be eminently useful. The husbandman is not always employed in gathering in his harvests. When one is over, he prepares his grounds for another. He sows for a new crop, though he may not expect it to take root and spring up at once. So the spiritual husbandman, who "goeth forth and weepeth, bearing precious seed, shall doubtless come again with rejoicing, bringing his sheaves with him."

The interval is preëminently the time for study, for imparting solid instruction, for preaching all the fundamental doctrines, for convincing and confounding gainsayers, and for building up a stable, thoroughly educated church, upon "the foundation of the apostles and prophets, Jesus Christ himself being the chief corner-stone." It is just here that some ardent and excellent ministers mistake. They exhort more and better than they teach. When there is no revival, they do so little to prepare for one by raising the standard of piety and training up prominent members for active service, that they derive not half the assistance from them in prayer-meetings, Sabbath-schools, and by other lay helpfulness, that they might have done by thorough training. And owing to this neglect, when trouble arises they have not half so many strong men to lean upon as they might have had.

I am persuaded that a pastor will be most and oftenest blessed with genuine revivals, who, relying upon divine aid, does most to prepare his church for them by thorough doctrinal and practical preaching in the intervals. He will have a stronger and purer church than it is possible to build up without a great deal of teaching, as well after the converts are received into the church as before.

WHERE A REVIVAL HAS JUST COMMENCED.

"And he did not many mighty works there, because of their unbelief." Jesus Christ had come to Nazareth, and showed the deep interest which he felt in their highest welfare by teaching in their synagogues, and healing a few of their sick. From what they saw and heard, they could not dispute that his motives were kind, that he had both the will and the power to do them good. But they were not ready to receive him. He had been brought up among them as the son of a poor carpenter, one of their neighbors. Whence then, they said, hath this man this wisdom, and these mighty works? and they were offended in him. He was to them as "a root out of a dry ground;" he had "no form nor comeliness" in their eyes; "when they saw him, there was no beauty that they should desire him." He had already by his miraculous power healed some of their sick, and was ready to heal them all; but no, he was the *carpenter's son*, and who gave him this power? As Jesus Christ never staid where he was not wanted, he left them, and it does not appear that he ever returned. It was not their unworthiness that cut off his kindred from the blessings which he had to bestow without money and without price; it was their rejection of him. "He did not many mighty works there, because of their unbelief." He departed out of their coasts. If any whom he would have healed were mortally sick, he left them to die.

So it is now in times and places of special revival. Jesus Christ by his Spirit comes into a church and congregation, and shows his presence and power by healing here and there a sin-sick soul; or in other words, awakening and converting a few individuals. In this beginning of miracles of grace, he manifests his readiness to heal all who apply to him, trusting in his ability and readiness to save.

Are the churches whom he thus condescends to visit, always ready to welcome him, and urge him to remain with them as long as he can? If so, what is the reason that sometimes, when a revival has commenced and there have been a few conversions, he departs and the work ceases? Such cases, alas, are but too frequent. Ah, he does not do many mighty works there, "because of their unbelief." This is the sole reason.

What then is this unbelief, that cuts them off? It must be a criminal distrust of his power, or his promises. Nothing is wanting but that faith which takes hold of the promises by earnest persevering prayer to retain him. It can never be true, that any incipient revival ceases after a very few have been awakened and brought in, where the church is on her knees pleading with the Saviour to stay and multiply the trophies of his victorious grace. She must take the blame to herself, if he leaves her families and neighbors unconverted.

And now, dear friends, what is our present condition in this place? After a long absence, in which the ways of Zion have mourned, and all have been ready to die, Jesus of Nazareth has returned, and begun his mighty works among us. Here and there a sinner is asking, What must I do to be saved? A few, we hope, have been born again; but what are they among so many? Scores, hundreds lie in the same perishing condition. What will you do? Will you treat him as his town-people did, and send him away; or will you constrain him by your prayers to remain, and come into your houses and visit all your neighborhoods, and cast out all the evil spirits, and heal all the sick, constraining you to stand still and to exclaim, What hath God wrought!

The state of things with us is beyond expression critical. Now Christ has come, and you see what he can do. He has quickened some who were dead in trespasses and sins. But the work seems to be at a stand, and where is our faith? There are but few, if any new cases of inquiry. Things cannot long remain as they are. It is an awful crisis. The revival must receive a new impulse, or soon cease. Manifestly Christ is ready to depart, and shall we let him go while so much remains to be done; while of all the multitude who are sick unto death, only here and there one has been healed? Shall we let him go? Let us fall down before him, and plead his great and precious promises. Would he have visited us as he has, if he had not more blessings in store, and was not ready to bestow them? When he thus visits any place, and begins to do his mighty works, there is one obstacle to his leaving suddenly which he never breaks over, and that is, "We will not let thee go except thou bless us." Such importunity always prevails. It will with us, if we wrestle as Jacob did. Nothing but unbelief can stop the revival where it is.

O brethren, will you grieve the Holy Spirit to depart; will you send the blessed Saviour away, leaving so many to perish whom he is ready to save? for not to persuade him to prolong his visit, when he is waiting to be gracious, is virtually sending him away. "And he could there do no mighty works, save that he laid his hands on a few sick folk, and healed them. And he marvelled at their unbelief." So here, if he departs, he will leave the great body of the sick, with the most terrible of all diseases, "drawn unto death." How many have we reason to fear have died the second death since he last came among us. As he never went back to Nazareth, who can tell, if he leaves us now, whether he will ever return? And if he should, years hence, how many of those whom he came to cure will then be in their graves, and beyond the reach of salvation.

Mr. Nettleton, writing to a brother in the ministry in 1823, says, "A revival *begun*, is likely to subside without the constant pressure of gospel motives on the consciences of the awakened. It is obvious from experience that God generally blesses far more extensively the means for *extending* his work, than he does for *commencing* it in the midst of surrounding darkness. As the conversion of one sinner is often the means of awakening a whole family, and the impulse is again felt through every kindred branch, and through the village and town, so one town may be the means of revival in another, and that in another. There is as really a season of harvest in the moral, as in the natural world. Neglected a few days, the harvest fully ripe is lost for ever.

"So there is a crisis in the feelings of a people, which, if not improved, the souls of that generation will not be gathered. In the season of a revival, more may be done, more often is done to secure the salvation of souls in a few days or weeks, than in years at other times. One sermon often does more execution in a revival than a hundred out of it. And I verily believe that more good may be lost for the want of that one, than can be done with it, and with a thousand like it, when the crisis is past. 'Say not ye, there are yet four months, and then'—it is now, or never."

With these views, so far as my own observation and experience have gone, I fully concur.

INQUIRY MEETINGS.

Among the means which God has signally blessed in carrying forward revivals of religion, meetings for personal conversation with the awakened are found to hold an important place. These meetings are by common consent called *Inquiry* meetings, in distinction from all others—a better name, I think, could not be given them. And in the progress of a powerful revival, when large numbers are in the several stages of alarm and inquiry, they are so essential, that no pastor who would make the most of his strength, can dispense with them.

When they were first introduced among the means which God has been pleased to own in the glorious "times of refreshing from his presence," I do not know. Where the Lord has poured out his Spirit, good ministers have always encouraged inquirers to come to them for personal conversation and advice, either singly or several together; but where a great many awakened sinners have needed their attention at the same time, they have found it impossible to meet them all, and say even a few words to them at the critical stages of their need of instruction—perhaps the turning-point of their immortal destiny. The question was, Can any thing be done to bring all the inquirers within our reach, so that in a single hour we may learn the state of fifty or a hundred anxious souls, that demand our immediate attention? At this critical point, God put it into the heart of somebody, no matter who or where, to invite all who were anxious to meet their pastor at a given time and place. It was found that in this way the desired object might be accomplished without taking time which could not be spared from other duties that always press hard during a revival. In the great revivals at the beginning of the present century, I neither saw nor heard of such inquiry meetings as we are all now familiar with. Indeed, my first acquaintance with them was about 1817, it might be a little earlier, when Mr. Nettleton was in the midst of his remarkable career, going from place to place in the shining armor of his mission, "the Lord working mightily with him," wherever he went. He held inquiry meetings, (*anxious* meetings as he called them,) and felt that in the midst of a large revival he could not do without them. Other highly favored servants of the Lord, ever since his day, have felt so; and such inquiry meetings as he held are now almost as firmly established, where God pours out his Spirit, as special meetings for prayer.

Rightly conducted, they afford the best possible criterion of the actual stage of the revival, in a large and scattered population. Such a meeting brings inquirers of all classes and from all quarters together, enabling the pastor to feel the pulse, as it were, of the whole vital action, and to judge what instruction from the pulpit and lecture-room is most needed—whether the work is advancing, or at a stand, or declining, that he may "give to every one his portion in due season." In an outpouring of the Spirit, such changes often take place in a few days, that I see not how a pastor can adapt his discourses to the existing state of his flock, without a general inquiry meeting at least once a week, to guide him. In that room, he learns more in half an hour than he could, perhaps, were he to spend his whole time with individuals as he might meet them elsewhere.

It is obvious at the same time, that the helpfulness of inquiry-meetings will depend very much upon how they are commenced, and the manner in which they are conducted. Ministers are sometimes quite at a loss whether there is interest enough in the congregation to respond to such an invitation. If there is not, it might prove a hinderance rather than a quickener towards a revival. If with a vague impression that the way is prepared for such a movement in advance, a pastor were publicly to give out an appointment and nobody should come, the enemy might take advantage of it, and turn it to the prejudice of religion. In pastoral visits the state of individual minds may be so far learned as to guide the pastor aright. Publicly inviting any who may wish for religious conversation to call at the pastor's house or study, is quite a different thing, as it involves no responsibility with regard to the signs of the times.

The next question is, When an inquiry meeting is appointed, who should be invited? Not *all* the congregation of course. It is a meeting for *inquirers*, for those who feel some concern for their souls; not for those who feel no anxiety, whether old or young. I need not say that a great deal depends upon the solemnity of the meeting. If you make the invitation so broad, that those who are in no degree awakened may come in, and they choose to come, it will be likely to affect injuriously the real inquirers, especially if their concern is not very deep; very much as bringing a cold body into near contact with substances but moderately warm, would tend to cool them down to the freezing point, rather than to melt the ice. The careless, in times of revival, are by no means to be neglected; but the inquiry room is not the place to meet them.

I was once invited by a brother, to go into an inquiry meeting and assist him. I went, and found a large room full. There had been a powerful revival in his congregation. In this case, hoping to reach some who had stood aloof, he had made the invitation very broad. I noticed at once the absence of that pervading solemnity which I had been accustomed to witness in such meetings; and when I came to pass along from seat to seat, and converse with individuals, I found nearly as many who gave no evidence of religious concern, as of the anxious; and I was convinced that while the former class were not likely to derive much advantage from being there, their presence was chilling and injurious to the latter. So I think, constituted as the human mind is, it must be in every case. The aphorism, "Old Adam is too strong for young Melancthon," applies here in an important sense. In sympathetic influences which come in conflict, the colder will be almost sure to prevail over the warmer.

The two great objects of an inquiry meeting are, to ascertain the actual state of the revival, and in a very few words, to drop into the ear of the inquirer such advice as seems to be wanted at the moment. Where the number is large, there is no time for extended conversation; but as he passes round, the pastor will ascertain where it is needed, and will reserve such cases for personal interviews elsewhere. The meeting should always be opened with a short prayer, and all should be requested to *kneel*. Some may regard the posture as a matter of very little consequence; but it is "much every way." It brings down stiff knees, that perhaps have never kneeled before; begets a sacred awe and reverence which pertains to no other posture; and no other posture should be encouraged at such a meeting, where there is room to kneel. A few words may or may not follow the prayer. Then it should be understood by the inquirers, that they must have no communication whatever with each other in the meeting; but that they must "commune with their own hearts, and be still." In passing round, the minister may either speak to each individual, in a voice not so low but that those who sit next can hear at least a part of what is said, or lower it down to a whisper, so that the individual alone can hear. I have witnessed both methods in the inquiry room, and am decidedly in favor of the latter. The former diverts the attention of those who sit by, from their own alarming state, and leads to a comparison of feelings, which in my judgment should always and everywhere be discouraged, where the great question is, "What must *I* do to be saved?"

In passing from seat to seat, a few words suggested by the state in which he finds an inquirer, may be usefully addressed by the pastor to all assembled, two or three times perhaps before he gets through, closing the meeting with a short address and short prayer.

Experience proves, I think, that these meetings should not be very protracted; and that they should never be continued to unseasonable hours. Where the congregation is large, some of them may be held in the remote districts; but it is preferable, in general, to hold them in the centre, and to bring the inquirers together from all parts. It makes them acquainted with one another, and helps to bind them together in a common brotherhood. The room should not be much larger than comfortably to seat as many as may be expected to come. However it may be accounted for, the fact is unquestionable, that there will be greater solemnity in a small room well filled, than in a large one where many of the seats are empty.

How *often* such meetings should be held, depends on the state of the revival—as often as once a week, at least, when it is at its height, and generally early in the week, so as to take advantage of whatever impression may have been made by the preaching of the word, and other religious meetings on the Sabbath.

The pastor, when there are a great many inquirers, may feel that he needs help, and if such assistance can be had as dealing with anxious souls requires, let it be called in. Every minister of the gospel ought to be qualified to take part with his brother in this labor of love, but hardly any one is, till he has had some experience himself in revivals. It requires a knowledge of the workings and subterfuges of the human heart, in all the stages of awakening and conviction up to the last struggle, and a quickness of apprehension of the real state of things, which must be acquired before they can be exercised. When ministerial aid of the right kind cannot be had, perhaps some lay brother may be found, and called in and help. But it is not speaking disparagingly of intelligent members of the churches to say, that very few of them are qualified for this kind of service. They have not had the experience which it requires. They can be exceedingly helpful in many ways, but not in this. But I will not enlarge.

The foregoing remarks and suggestions are chiefly the result of my own experience and observation. Others may be better guides when and where inquiry meetings should be held in revivals, and how they should be conducted. If so, I hope they will be followed. So far as I know, these meetings are a step in advance of the aids which pastors had learned how to avail themselves of, half a century ago. If any improvements can be made, or any thing better substituted, I will bless God for putting it into the hearts of his ministers.

CONVERSING WITH THE AWAKENED AND THE UNAWAKENED IN REVIVALS.

There is much to be said by the pastor, and by others outside of the inquiry room; and very much depends upon who shall say it. "A word fitly spoken is like apples of gold in pictures of silver." Every member of the church has something to do to help forward the work. We are all, or should be, laborers together with God. There is no one but can speak a word in season to somebody. The plea so often made, "I can't do any thing, I am not capable of talking with any body," will not hold. You can say *something*. "Out of the abundance of the heart the mouth speaketh;" and God will hold you accountable for what you have, for what you can do and say, whether it be much or little.

It is true, indeed, there may be few members of a church who are capable of conversing with sinners in all the stages of awakening and inquiry. It requires more knowledge, discrimination, and experience than some of the most devoted Christians possess. There are cases where a few words of wrong instruction or advice might "heal the hurt slightly," might quiet the sinner's conscience with a false hope; or on the other hand, drive him almost or quite to despair. But every one is capable of saying something to friends who remain unalarmed in the midst of a revival, or who are not much interested—something which by God's blessing may prove the means of their salvation. If you cannot go abroad, if you cannot exhort your neighbors, you can at least speak to the unawakened in your own households, and urge them to seek the Lord while he may be found, and call upon him while he is near. Talents and learning are not at all essential, so far as this. What is wanted is a warm heart, a yearning of soul which can take no denial. Those who would not dare to talk with inquirers, for fear of doing hurt, can go out into the highways and hedges, where they will find ample room for earnest exhortation, and may perhaps do as much to increase the number of inquirers and converts by bringing in those who would otherwise never come to the gospel feast, as if they could guide inquiring souls to the cross.

It will not be denied, that in the progress of a revival, all impenitent persons belonging to the congregation, or to whom access can be gained, ought to be spoken to and exhorted to avail themselves of the accepted time, and the day of salvation. But there must first be a preparation of heart for this service, before much good influence can be expected from it. No member of the church, however gifted, is in a condition to urge sinners to flee from the wrath to come, till his own heart glows with love and compassion. His conscience may constrain him to attempt the duty while he himself is not awakened, but remains in a cold backsliding state; he may force himself to speak to his neighbors, but they will see at once that it does not come warm from his heart, and may be rather repelled than persuaded by any thing he can say. The Psalmist deeply felt the necessity of a penitent, heart preparation for this duty, when he prayed, "Restore unto me the joy of thy salvation, and uphold me by thy free Spirit; then will I teach transgressors thy ways, and sinners shall be converted unto thee." And no one can be in a right frame to discharge this duty, till the joy of God's salvation is restored to his own soul. But beware, my brother, how you try to excuse yourself by pleading your own coldness and spiritual leanness. It will not do. The Searcher of hearts will not accept it. So far from its being a good excuse, it is your own fault, and you will be held accountable for the neglect. Offer no such plea. You bring yourself in guilty when you say that you are not in a right state of mind to talk with careless sinners, and persuade them to come in. It is pleading a great sin as an excuse for shrinking from an important duty. Every professor of religion ought always to be in such a frame as to converse freely with those who are living without hope and without God in the world; and how much more, when he is pouring out his Spirit, and the kingdom of God is brought so nigh to those who are ready to perish.

I have already said that it requires much judgment and experience to converse with awakened sinners, and lead them to Christ. But few, compared with the whole number in a church, are likely to possess these qualifications. So that while all the members may try to alarm the stupid, and ought to do it to the extent of their ability, the majority cannot be safely advised to go much further in the time of a revival. When they find cases of real awakening, they should report them at once to the pastor, or to some one of his efficient helpers, that they may receive such instruction and guidance as they need. A judicious pastor will generally know who can be trusted to talk with persons asking what they must do to be saved, and he will feel it his duty to discourage others from venturing beyond their depth as guides, where mistakes might be fatal.

In all ordinary cases, the most competent members of the church, in dealing with souls during the critical period between their being awakened and converted, ought to act under the advice and direction of the pastor, and to keep him fully informed, from day to day, of the progress of the work as it falls under this vigilant observation; and to report all difficult cases to him, that they may be promptly attended to. And to aid them in the discharge of their personal duties in laboring to win souls to Christ, a pastor experienced in revivals will call them together as occasion may require, to hear their reports, and in free conversation give them the results of his experience to aid them in the work.

If any one should ask how often the awakened ought to be conversed with, no definite answer can be given. It must depend upon constantly shifting circumstances. It should be often enough to mark their progress step by step, and to sound the alarm at once if they show signs of drawing back. But there is such a thing as saying too much to an awakened sinner, especially when he has come to the turning-point—when his vain excuses have all been taken from him, and he sees clearly that he ought to hold out no longer. Then it is better to stand out of the way, and leave him to settle the controversy with God, than to say much more to him. He may come to you in great distress, asking what he shall do to be saved, and keep coming after you have told him a great many times, till you see he is leaning upon you when he ought to cast himself at once upon the mercy of God in Christ. I have known such cases. I believe they occur in almost every revival. And then, "I can't help you. You have been lingering much too long; I have nothing more to say. You must go to the cross at once; there is no help for you till you get there," is more likely to bring him to a decision, than any thing more you could say. A young man who had been religiously educated, whose attention was called up in a powerful revival in college, and with whom I had often conversed, sent for me late one evening, urging me to come and see him, for he was on the very borders of despair. I had conversed with him that very day, and knew that he was in great distress. It seemed cruel to refuse. But I sent him word, "I can do you no good. In the stubbornness of your heart you are holding out against God. There is but one hope left for you, which you know just as well as I could tell you. You must yield yourself to God, or you are lost for ever." It was hoped he gave himself to Christ before morning, which it is very doubtful whether he would have done, had I gone to see him. It is far more likely that I should have stood in the way. And so I believe it often happens. The convicted sinner often lingers, or rather holds out, as long as he can find anybody to lean upon. It is sometimes as much our duty to be silent and stand out of the way, as at others to warn the same persons to flee from the wrath to come. "He that winneth souls is wise."

And here let me add, those who are active in a revival should have a mutual understanding, so that too many shall not converse with the same person on the same day. While the impenitent ought by no means to be neglected when God is pouring out his Spirit, there is some danger of repelling them by the importunity of too many brethren following in quick succession. It is better to agree upon a division of labor, so that while none shall be neglected, none shall have reason to complain that when they are willing to be conversed with, too many come at once.

One thing further. In looking over any church and congregation, it will be found that wisdom is profitable to direct who can approach this and that individual to the best advantage. This depends on a great variety of relations and circumstances. There should be a consultation something like this: There are many in the congregation who are not much if at all interested, who ought to be conversed with and brought in if possible; and who shall do it? Such a man is prejudiced against me, but he is your friend. I cannot approach him, but you can. To another, A has been your intimate companion. He has confidence in you, he will hear you when he might repulse anybody else. To another, B can be approached better by you than by any of us; you see him every day, and your personal relations are such that you can talk with him and be more likely to influence him; and so on down to the end of the alphabet.

In how many things are the children of this world wiser than the children of light. When they have a favorite object to accomplish, requiring widely extended coöperation, with what skill do they avail themselves of the social principle, and with what success. Let all the members of a church be as much in earnest, and act as wisely; let them consider, in every stage of a revival, what there is to be done to win souls to Christ, and who can do it best; let there be no shrinking, after due consultation, from any assigned duty towards those who are yet to be reached and brought in; and who can doubt that God would own and bless such a judicious division of labor?

INSTRUCTION TO CANDIDATES FOR MEMBERSHIP.

It is commonly the case that sooner or later, in the progress of a revival, or after its close, most of the converts are received into the church together. They are of different ages and classes, and do not all need the same amount of religious instruction to prepare them for membership. Some understand the scriptural qualifications for membership much better than others; but none who offer themselves as candidates, are so well prepared as not to be profited by still further instruction, if judiciously given and rightly received. Next in importance, after giving the heart to God, is an intelligent public profession; and no one can safely take this step without knowing what are the evidences of a saving change, and bringing his hope to the test of these evidences, as laid down in the word of God. A good deal of this teaching, I take it for granted, will be given to individuals in the pastor's study, and from the pulpit; but something more is wanted, which can better be given in meetings of the candidates, called for the express purpose. Such meetings save a great deal of the pastor's time, for so far as the instruction is concerned, he can as well give it to twenty or fifty, assembled for that express purpose, as to an individual; and it is even more likely to be remembered. Such topics as the following might naturally be suggested at these meetings.

The evidences of true saving conversion, what are they? In answering this question, it is necessary to go into the subject largely, guided solely by the Scriptures; to point out these "signs," as President Edwards calls them, distinctly, and then to exhort the candidates to examine themselves by these signs, whether they are in the faith. Have you comfortable evidence that Christ is formed in you the hope of glory? If not, wait, search the Scriptures, and give yourselves to prayer, till you have such evidence. Christ welcomes none but true disciples to his table. "Eat, O *friends;* drink abundantly, O *beloved.*"

It is well also to take up the *confession of faith,* and explain it to the candidates in the most familiar way, so that they may understand what is the doctrinal standard of the church to which they must give their assent. Neglect here has often occasioned much future trouble and perplexity. No member of a church should ever have it in his power to say, "The confession of faith was never explained to me before I joined the church. There are some things in it which I do not believe; and if I had known how they were understood by the church, I should not have come in. I should have offered myself elsewhere, and unless they can be altered, I must leave the church."

Now, if in such meetings as I am recommending, the meaning of every article as understood by the church, had been taken up and clearly explained, no such plea could have been offered; or if it had been, the answer would be, "If you misunderstood our creed it was your own fault, not ours. Great pains were taken to explain it, in meeting after meeting, held for that very purpose. Then was the time to object if ever. There was no compulsion or constraint. After hearing a full explanation of our doctrinal platform, it was left entirely at your option whether to join our church or not. Every one ought to know what he believes, before he puts his hand to any confession of faith. We have done all we could to aid you."

It is desirable fully to explain the *covenant engagements* which are assumed. It is to be feared, that a great many persons stand up before God, angels, and men, without any just sense of the solemn obligations which they take upon themselves. It has often been found useful, in meetings held for the purpose, to take up and distinctly present these obligations; and let all be warned not to proceed without a full and deliberate intention, trusting in God's help, to "stand to the covenant."

How many meetings with the converts it may require to go over all the ground embraced in these recommendations, cannot beforehand be determined. Let time enough be taken to do them ample justice. Besides the duty of helping the candidates to make a good and well-considered profession of their faith in Christ, they are in a better state of mind to receive and be profited by such a course of instruction and advice, than they will be at any future time. Too much pains cannot be taken to have them "rooted and grounded" in the truth, that they may adorn their profession in all holy conversation and godliness. With any thing short of such a course as above indicated, I have not been able to satisfy myself at the close of revivals, where the responsibility rested upon me, and I am persuaded that in letting such favorable opportunities pass unimproved, some ministers forego advantages for building up their churches in the faith and order of the gospel, which with so little labor they hardly ever enjoy.

If the converts follow on to know the Lord, and add strength as well as numbers to the church by an active and blameless Christian life, it is the best evidence of the genuineness of their conversion. But if, on the other hand, in a few weeks or months after the work has ceased, those who were counted as converts relapse into their former state, and bring forth no fruit, it will be an evidence that the work was superficial and not genuine, however it may have been regarded at the time. By faithful instruction, as above indicated, let the pastor and the officers of the church clear themselves from blame, if any should come to the supper without the wedding garment.

TO PERSONS ABOUT TO JOIN THE CHURCH AFTER A REVIVAL.

MY DEAR FRIENDS—You have expressed a desire to make a public profession of your faith in Christ, and to be received into his church. It is well. It is an unspeakable privilege. It is the duty of every true disciple to put on the badge of discipleship, to avail himself of all church privileges, and to witness a good profession before the world. It is a great step which should not be hastily taken, and yet it ought not to be very long delayed by any who have a comfortable hope that they have been born again.

But "let a man examine himself, and so let him eat of that bread and drink of that cup." You have been examined and approved by the pastor and officers of the church. From your own lips they have sought to obtain evidence that you have passed from death unto life. In this they have gone as far as they can. But they cannot search your hearts. The responsibility must rest upon yourselves.

The apostolic injunction is, "Examine yourselves whether ye be in the faith: prove your own selves." And again, "Let a man examine *himself*, and so let him eat of that bread and drink of that cup. For he that eateth and drinketh unworthily, eateth and drinketh damnation (judgment) to himself, not discerning the Lord's body." What better proof could we have, that none but true believers have a right to come to the Lord's table? What then, dear friends, are your evidences that you have cast off the works of darkness, and put on the Lord Jesus Christ? You were once alienated from God. You did not desire the knowledge of his ways. You were carnally minded. Like the poor man in the gospel, you were blind from your birth, only in a different and far more incurable sense. You saw no form nor comeliness in Christ, whereby you should desire him. On the contrary, whether you were conscious of it or not, you said in your hearts, and in your life, by walking according to the course of this world, "Depart from us, we desire not the knowledge of thy ways." In a word, you were by nature "children of wrath," "children of disobedience;" yea, "dead in trespasses and sins."

This was once your deplorable and guilty state. You lay helpless under the condemning sentence of God's holy law, and under that condemnation you might have been justly left to perish. In these most alarming circumstances, you have been called to wake and rise from the dead, that Christ might give you life.

Now, dear brethren, what evidence have you that you have passed from death unto life? I do not ask, whether you can all relate the same experience. "There are diversities of operation, but the same Spirit." In the exercises which go before regeneration, there are striking differences between individuals. Some are much more distressed than others, and for a longer time before they find deliverance. Upon the minds of some, the light breaks in suddenly, so that they can tell the very day and hour when they were brought out of darkness into marvellous light. In others, it is a faint beam at first, which shines more and more unto the perfect day. You will never get any satisfactory evidence of your good estate—I mean, any evidence that can be safely relied upon—by "comparing yourselves among yourselves." You must go to the Bible and compare your exercises with that divine standard. There is no other. "The wind bloweth where it listeth, and thou hearest the sound thereof, but canst not tell whence it cometh, nor whither it goeth. So is every one who is born of the Spirit." All the truly converted are not brought to Christ in the same way, or by the same means.

But the *change* is the same in all, and is wrought

by the same almighty power. They "are born, not of blood, nor of the will of the flesh, nor of the will of man, but of God." By fervent prayer for divine illumination, and by searching the Scriptures, you may know in whom you have believed. You may have the witness in yourselves, more or less clear according to the earnestness of your seeking in reliance upon the aid of the Holy Spirit, who alone can "take of the things of Christ, and show them unto you." What then do you say for yourself? You know where you were once, sinking in the horrible pit and the miry clay. Where do you now stand? Has Christ brought you up, and placed your feet upon a rock? Do you begin to feel its firmness, and rest upon it? Can you say, "One thing I know, that whereas I was blind, now I see?" Have you seen the plague of your own hearts, and do you heartily repent of all your sins? Do you approve of the law of God, which is holy, just, and good? Have you been brought to see the impossibility of saving yourselves, and have you by the grace of God fled for refuge to lay hold on the hope set before you in the gospel? Has your mind within these few weeks passed through a great moral revolution? Do you love that which you before hated, and hate that which you loved? Do you love the Bible; do you love the prayer-meeting; do you love the house of God; do you love the brethren? Time was when you saw no beauty in the Saviour, that you should desire him. How is it now? Is he no longer as a root out of a dry ground, but all your salvation, and all your desire? Have you received him by faith as your Saviour? Renouncing all other dependences, do you really trust in him, lean upon him, love him, cleave to him as your divine Teacher, your atoning Sacrifice, your Lord, and your King? In asking to be admitted into his church, have you counted the cost? Have you considered that a public profession of religion requires nothing less than an entire consecration of body and soul, of all your faculties, of all you have, of all you are, to the service of Christ; and as far as you know your own hearts, are you ready to covenant with him, relying on his grace to help your infirmities?

These, dear friends, are some of the tests by which you ought to try yourselves before you enter the church. Nor will your unaided self-scrutiny be sufficient. Let this be your constant prayer, "Search me, O God, and know my heart; try me and know my thoughts, and see if there be any wicked way in me, and lead me in the way everlasting."

You are all invited to come to the feast. No sense of unworthiness should keep you away. The sacramental table will be spread in a few days, and "whosoever will, let him come." You have no fitting garment of your own in which to come, but the wardrobe is hard by; the guest-chamber is full. An essential condition of the invitation is, that each of the invited shall appear in one of the robes taken from that royal depository; and Oh, fail not when the King comes in to see the guests, to have on a wedding garment. Without it you will be speechless when he shall inquire why this intrusion, and turn you out.

TO THE CONVERTS IN A REVIVAL WHEN THEY JOIN THE CHURCH.

My dear Friends—You have stood up in the presence of God, of angels, and men, and taken upon yourselves the vows of the covenant. You have voluntarily and publicly renounced the world, the flesh, and the devil. You have been received into the church of Christ, which is "the pillar and ground of the truth." You are "no more strangers and foreigners, but fellow-citizens with the saints and of the household of faith." You have come to your first communion with the church at the table of Christ. You have not by constraint, but willingly, enlisted under his banner, and your enlistment is for life. You have put your hands to the plough; you have opened your mouths unto the Lord, and cannot go back. You think you would not for the world go back, if you might. We pray that you may every one of you be "kept by the power of God, through faith unto salvation." A profession of religion is no sinecure. If Christ in the abounding riches of his grace has called you into his kingdom, it is that you at once enter into his service; and your first inquiry should be, *Lord, what wilt thou have me to do?* Christ wants no idlers among his professed followers: "*Follow me,*" is the word of command, by the Captain of your salvation; and who ever set such an example of activity, of entire devotedness to the great objects of his mission, as he did? "Wot ye not that I must be about my Father's business?" was his reply to those who would have diverted him from the great objects of his mission. "It is enough for the disciple that he be as his Master, and the servant as his Lord."

You are now just entering upon a religious life, and as you begin you will be very apt to proceed. If you set your mark high, remembering that "ye are not your own," but "bought with a price," even the precious blood of Christ, you will, by the aid of the Holy Spirit, "witness a good profession before many witnesses," and they will take knowledge of you, that you have been with Jesus. If on the contrary, having got into the church, you take a low stand at first, instead of rising you will invariably decline, till your brethren will be constrained to stand in doubt of you, and the world will ask, What do ye more than others? If a soldier of an earthly prince, upon his first enlistment, by going into winter quarters instead of performing the services of the campaign, would disgrace his profession, how much more would a soldier of Jesus Christ, who should consult his own ease, and shrink away into his cold winter quarters, when he ought to be in the field.

You will not all be called to the same services in the church, or the world. Tho duties of the Christian life are many and various, and there are diversities of gifts. But before I proceed to enumerate them, I must say something about your putting on the armor of God, as you can do nothing without it. We may not forget that you are new recruits, and have a great deal to learn, as well as a great deal to do. Some of you are quite young, and you all want a sure Guide. Till this revival, you scarcely thought of it, perhaps. The broad way was wide, and you had room enough without any guide. Now, the case is different. You have entered a new and untrodden path. Since you began to inquire the way to heaven, your pastor and other pious friends have instructed and directed you, as God has enabled them, and they will continue to do so. But you want an infallible Guide, one that will go with you all the journey through. Can you have such a guide and teacher? You can. Such a one has always been at your right hand, though till lately most of you felt very little need of any special direction.

God might have inspired a prophet like Moses to lead you through the wilderness. He might have sent his angel to go before and guard you. He might have given the Shekinah to shine upon every step of the way to the promised land. But he has done more; O how much more! He has given you "Moses and the Prophets." He sent his Son, "the brightness of his glory and the express image of his person," to lead you in the way everlasting. And when he left the world, he inspired his apostles to be your infallible teachers and guides. And here are all their teachings in this one book, THE BIBLE, just as if they were personally to return to the earth, and you could hear their voices and follow them. Christ is now, as it were, putting you to school, not under the law to bring you to Christ, but under the Gospel, that you may be trained up for his service. And the Bible is your text-book. There is no such teaching in the wide world as you will find here. It is put into your hands now, at your setting out, to be the man of your counsel and the guide of your life. Take it along with you, dear friends, as "a light to your feet and a lamp to your path." It is a book to be read, and studied, and learned by heart. In one sense, it is not new, perhaps, to any of you; but in another sense it is. The *letter* of some portions of it may be quite familiar, but to the *spiritual* meaning your eyes are only now beginning to be opened. You need the sincere milk of the word, that you may grow thereby and gradually reach the stature of perfect men.

Do the younger of you ask how you can study the scriptures to the best advantage—where to begin, and how to proceed? I answer, There is light in every portion of the word, and whatever interests you is profitable. If you would begin with the simpler portions, take the Gospels and the Psalms; pray over every psalm, chapter, and portion as you read; meditate, and thus prepare your minds to grasp the more difficult portions. The Bible is its own best interpreter. By comparing Scripture with Scripture, you will be surprised to find how many difficult passages are cleared up, and the light will shine more and more upon the "things hard to be understood," if you then follow on to know the Lord.

Let me advise you, in reading the Scriptures, not to confine yourselves to a single chapter at a time. The divisions, as we have them, are entirely arbitrary. They often break off abruptly in the middle of the argument or narrative, so that if you leave off at the end of the chapter, you lose the connection, and may forget it before the next reading. In the original, there are no chapters. Many of the books are not so long but that they can be read at a single sitting. Read them sometimes through, as you do other small books that interest you, before you close the book; while at other times, you will find it more profitable to read and meditate upon short portions. Still further, it will take but a moment or two to commit a text to memory every morning, which may be kept in mind through the day. Do this, and you will have treasured up three hundred and sixty-five at the end of the year. How many in ten years? No less than three thousand six hundred and fifty! Dear friends, will you not do it, or rather a great deal more than this? I advise you to commit whole psalms and chapters of the gospels to memory. It will be garnering the richest of all treasures to aid you in prayer. It will give a copiousness to your supplications, confessions, and thanksgivings, which no other language can supply. It was in this way that the Psalmist got his mind and heart so richly stored with divine truth, that he could say, "I have more understanding than all my teachers, for thy testimonies are my meditation."

And now, dear young converts, with your armor on and the Bible in your hands, and the promised aid of the Holy Spirit, what should hinder you from growing in grace and divine knowledge? What other help can you need, to adorn the doctrine of God our Saviour in the discharge of your religious duties? The field of Christian progress and service which you are just entering, is a very wide field. Your whole future lives, from this hour, should be filled up in pressing toward the mark for the prize of the high calling of God in Christ Jesus, and doing all the good you can on the way. Let me exhort you to be faithful unto death, that you may receive the crown. It is only those who endure to the end, that shall be saved.

I can only glance at a few of the obligations which your Christian profession lays upon you. Be careful to recommend religion by your consistent example. Without this, your profession will amount to but very little. Be sure, wherever your lot may be cast, that you do your part in support of the gospel, and just as much more as your ability will allow, to supply the lack of those who penuriously withhold their part.

Fail not punctually and devoutly to worship God in his house on the Sabbath. Let nothing short of some providential hinderance ever keep you away. Never absent yourselves, if you can help it, from the weekly prayer-meetings of the church. On this point, let me be very earnest. Every Christian needs the quickening of such a meeting, at least once a week, between the Sabbaths. So far as I can recollect, I never knew an instance of apparent growth in grace, by a professor who voluntarily staid away from the prayer-meetings; and I very much doubt whether one in a thousand could be found. In the first place, it shows a low state of religion in the soul of such a church-member, and in the next place forfeits the strengthening of his faith which he might have received in the precious visits of the Saviour. You all remember the case of Thomas—how he fell into a sad state of unbelief, by being absent from the prayer-meetings of his brethren, when Jesus met them and comforted their desponding hearts. O what a cutting rebuke, when at the next meeting he said to Thomas,

"Reach hither thy finger, and behold my hands; and reach hither thy hand, and thrust it into my side; and be not faithless, but believing." Beware that you do not thus expose yourselves by absence from the stated prayer-meeting. One such unnecessary absence may cost you the hidings of your Master's face, through many a long month of doubt and declension.

Never excuse yourselves by saying, the meetings are so dull and uninteresting that I derive no profit from them. Are they cold and dull, whose fault is it? You ought to be there with warm hearts, to make them interesting. When called on to pray, never excuse yourselves, though at first you should not be able to offer more than a few short petitions; if offered in sincerity, depending on the Holy Spirit for help, he will ere long put thoughts into your hearts and words into your mouths, with a fulness and freedom of utterance which you now hardly dare to hope for.

While you foster all the moral and religious interests of the local communities where God may appoint the bounds of your habitations, and set your faces as a flint against vice in every form, cast your eyes abroad over the wide world lying in wickedness, and ask the Lord what he will have you to do for its enlightenment. Pray without ceasing for the spread of the gospel, and contribute according to your largest ability to Bible, Missionary, and other societies, organised for the purpose of turning men from darkness to light, and from the power of Satan unto God.

And so, dear friends, I might go on to specify many more of the imperative duties of the Christian life; but what need of proceeding further, when you have your instructions so clearly written out in the word of God, which he has put into your hands as the man of your counsel to guide you into all truth?

Christ has brought you into his church at an eventful period of its history. It will not do for you to rest where you find us in our low attainments. You have more light and greater privileges than most of us had when we came into the church. "Go forward," is the command of your great and glorious Leader. He requires, he expects much of you, as his representatives in a sinful and gainsaying world. Ye are a chosen, a highly favored generation, that ye should "show forth the praises of Him who hath called you out of darkness into his marvellous light." If the true children of God, ye are "heirs of the righteousness which is by faith." Therefore, "giving all diligence, add to your faith virtue, and to virtue knowledge, and to knowledge temperance, and to temperance patience, and to patience godliness, and to godliness brotherly kindness, and to brotherly kindness charity; for if these things be in you and abound, ye shall neither be barren nor unfruitful in the knowledge of our Lord Jesus Christ."

CHAPTER IX.

BRIEF APPEALS.

Having glanced at the obstacles which lie in the way of revivals, and what should be done to "prepare the way of the Lord," and noticed some of the means which by God's blessing have been successfully employed in promoting them, I add brief sketches of Appeals, which I have found useful in successive stages of these outpourings of the Spirit. I do not offer them as models to my younger brethren, much less as comprehending all the topics to be introduced in a revival, but as casting a little into the Lord's treasury for the advancement of his blessed cause. Let others contribute more largely from the richer stores of their experience, and let Christ have all the glory. He knows infinitely better than we do, what should be done to secure the choicest and most abundant spiritual harvests, and I doubt not those who shall come after us, have yet much to learn under his infallible teaching.

"SIRS, WHAT MUST I DO TO BE SAVED?"

Never was this question more earnestly asked, than by the Phillipian jailor. Who he was, or what had been his antecedents, we are not informed, and his remarkable conversion is the last we hear of him. It is not at all likely that he had ever troubled himself much about religion, and least of all about the new religion, which was everywhere spoken against.

He needed a great deal more instruction than could be given in one night. And when he asked the all-important question, "What must I do to be saved?" why did not Paul and Silas direct him to take up the subject in earnest, to study the prophecies which had been fulfilled in the advent, sufferings, death, and resurrection of Christ, through whose blood and righteousness alone he could be saved? Why did they not point out something which he must do preparatory to a saving act of faith in Christ? Why did they not allow him some little time at least for serious reflection and prayer? Simply because they had no authority for any such indulgence, and no delay was necessary. The jailor had nothing else to do, but to *repent and believe on the Lord Jesus Christ.* Then and there was "the accepted time." He might die before morning. By one hour's delay he might lose his soul.

And so, anxious inquiring sinner, it may be with you. You ask just as the jailor did, what you must do to be saved; and no other answer can safely be given, but that which he received, "Believe on the Lord Jesus Christ, and thou shalt be saved." As he closed in at once, both with the condition and assurance, so may you. There is nothing more in your way than there was in his—less indeed, for you are far better instructed into the things of the kingdom, than we have any reason to suppose he was. You have had much greater advantages for knowing your Master's will, than he had ever enjoyed. Why do you linger? Why do some of you come day after day to your religious teachers, asking the same question? They "cannot go beyond the word of the Lord, to say less or more." I mean, they cannot give you any other answer. They cannot mention any duty which you must perform before coming to Christ. The Christian life embraces a very long catalogue of duties. But you must first become a Christian, before you can perform any of them in an acceptable manner. "Whatsoever is not of faith is sin." It may be good in the *letter*, but utterly wanting in *spirit*. You are "shut up to the faith."

God *now* commands you to repent—this hour, this moment—not to-morrow. There is infinite danger in the shortest delay. You are anxious. The Holy Spirit is striving with you. By this one precious hour's resistance, he may be grieved and depart for ever. What is your life but the breath in your nostrils, which may be stopped before you leave the room. Your reason too, how slight a jar may shake it from its throne. "Now," anxious inquirer, "is the accepted time; behold, *now* is the day of salvation." If some important duty were required of you, demanding time for its accomplishment, you might delay. If there was any room to doubt whether Christ will accept you just as you are, you might with some show of reason ask for some delay to make yourself better. If you were not perfectly assured that Christ will accept you on the terms propounded to the trembling jailor, the case would be different. As it is, there is not the shadow of an excuse for delay.

You would not treat an earthly benefactor as you treat the greatest and best Friend you have in the universe. Were you in critical circumstances, in momentary danger of some fatal temporal calamity, and a friend were to step in and say, do this or do that, requiring ever so much effort, you would not hesitate a moment, although he might possibly change his mind, or be unable to fulfil his promise. But here you are with the question on your lips, "What must I do to be saved?" and the answer sounding in your ears, "Believe on the Lord Jesus Christ, and thou shalt be saved;" infinite truth and almighty power stand pledged to make the promise instantly good, upon its cordial acceptance; and do you yet want more time? Christ is now knocking at your door, and instead of hastening to let him in, are you leaving him to stand without till his head is filled with the dew, and his locks with the drops of the night. You ask what you shall do to be saved. We tell you, in the very words of Scripture; and do you still remain in impenitence and unbelief? We cannot leave you here. Oh, when will you close in with the condition and the promise? To-day, even to-day, after so long a time, if you will hear his voice, harden not your heart.

"COME UNTO ME, AND I WILL GIVE YOU REST."

What a blessed invitation; and to whom was it addressed? Not to the self-righteous scribes and Pharisees. They would have rejected it with scorn. Not to the thoughtless multitude who followed Christ for the loaves and fishes. It was addressed to those only, and there were probably very few, who were awakened to a sense of their guilt and danger, who felt the burden of their sins, and knew not where to look for relief. The invitation was not confined to them, but was intended for the encouragement of all sin-burdened souls, not only while Christ was here in the flesh, but in all coming ages. Here then we have the persons addressed; the thing to be done; and the promise annexed, with the certainty of its fulfilment.

1. *The persons addressed:* Come unto me, "all ye that *labor and are heavy-laden*"—you, careless and stupid sinner, are not included! You are in no condition to value the blessing. You feel no burden; and till you do, how can you apply for relief? "They that be whole need not a physician, but they that are sick." And they must *believe*, they must *feel* that they are sick. Go to your neighbor, and with an anxious tone and look tell him that a very distinguished physician has just arrived in town, and advise him to send for him at once. He will stare at you, and ask you what you mean. "I am not sick. I feel perfectly well; and why should I send for him, or any other doctor? Let those who need his prescriptions send for him. It will be time enough for me when I am sick." Or suppose your neighbor to be really diseased, and in a critical state, but entirely unconscious of it; will he take your advice? He may thank you for the neighborly kindness, but he will say, "I feel as well as ever." He must first be convinced that he needs the physician, before he will apply to him.

Just so with the careless sinner: he is not "heavy-laden;" he feels no burden; he wants no help; he has "need of nothing." He must feel that he is a sinner, that he needs help; he must be anxious to know what he must do to be saved. Till then, he excludes himself from the invitation. But, dear friend, if you "labor and are heavy-laden," if you feel that you are "poor and wretched, and blind and naked, and in want of all things," the invitation is meant for you. It is meant for all who feel their need. You may be ready to say, "I am so great a sinner, I have so long turned a deaf ear to the Saviour's call, that I dare not come. How can he accept me at this late hour?" It is a sad and extreme case, to be sure. It is a wonder that God has not cut you off with all your sins upon your head; but you need not despair even now. The gracious invitation is, " Come unto me, *all* ye that labor and are heavy-laden;" " Come now, and let us reason together, saith the Lord: though your sins be as scarlet, they shall be white as snow; though they be red like crimsom, they shall be as wool."

2. There must be *an acceptance* of the invitation, or it can avail nothing. You must come to Christ, not bodily as those who needed healing did when he was here in the flesh. This you cannot do, because, after his resurrection, he ascended up above all heavens. But you can do more; for many who came to him personally did not believe on him, received no spiritual healing by it. Sinners have this great advantage now, that he is spiritually present in every place, especially wherever there is a true revival. In the sense of the invitation, you can come to him at any moment.

And what is it to come? It is to come empty-handed and broken-hearted, casting away all other dependencies, throwing yourself into his outstretched arms, and trusting in his righteousness and atonement alone for pardon, justification, and eternal life. This is the acceptance, and nothing short of this entire surrender can be of any avail. You must come to Christ just in this way, just as you are, or you will be lost.

3. Come thus to Christ, and *the promise, "I will give you rest," is sure,* for he is not slack concerning any of his promises. He will lift off the burden from your troubled conscience. He will relieve your anxious laboring mind. He will say, Son, daughter, be of good cheer; thy sins are forgiven thee. Oh, how many can testify that they have experienced the fulfilment of the promise: that they could find no relief till, with Bunyan's toiling pilgrim, they came to the cross, and there it fell off.

And now, burdened sinner, what can we more say? What need we say more? "The Spirit and the bride say, Come;" and will you come? Every obstacle is removed. There is nothing in the way but your own obstinate and impenitent heart. Will you come? will you, or will you stay away and perish?

"Come, ye weary, heavy-laden,
Lost and ruined by the fall;
If you tarry till you 're better,
You will never come at all.
Not the righteous—
Sinners Jesus came to call."

"THE CARNAL MIND IS ENMITY AGAINST GOD."

What is meant here by "the carnal mind?" The true answer to this question is vital; and is too plain to be mistaken by any candid reader of this chapter.

The *carnal* mind is directly the opposite of the *spiritual* mind, as in the sixth verse: "To be carnally minded is death, but to be spiritually minded is life and peace." The difference in a religious sense is as great as that between life and death in a natural sense. It is the heart, every heart, in its natural, unregenerate state. There is no life in it. Nay, more, as the state of the body after death is in its decay loathsome, and as it were opposed to life, so the carnal mind is *enmity* against God—not only entirely destitute of love to God, but in a state of actual and habitual hostility to him, to his holy character, to his law and his government. You see the language of the apostle is in the superlative degree, *intensitive*. If he had said, the carnal mind is opposed to God, is inimical to him, that would have been very strong; but it is enmity itself, all enmity.

This being settled, it follows as a matter of course, that it is not subject to his law, and remaining in this state, cannot be. It is impossible in the nature of things, just as impossible as that a man can live and move so long as he is dead. An enemy may be reconciled and become a friend. The most inveterate hatred may be subdued, and give place to love; but till that radical change in the affections takes place, it remains enmity, and nothing else. It is not subject to the law of God, which demands the heart, "neither indeed can be."

And the conclusion in the next verse irresistibly follows: "So then they that are in the flesh," in this carnal state of enmity, "cannot please God." They can be subdued, they can be changed, they can be brought into the opposite state, for with God all things are possible; but till then, whatever they may do, whatever profession of attachment to him they may make, he can have no pleasure in them. He can look upon them only as enemies, who are not subject to his law, neither indeed can be.

This, my impenitent friends, is your guilty and alarming condition—every one of you. There are different degrees of depravity, different degrees of enmity in the natural heart; but it is depravity, it is enmity and nothing else. There is no true love to God till the heart is changed. Some of you have been awakened during this revival; some of you have been more or less anxious for a good while, and in your unregenerate state you can do many things. You can read your Bible, you can use the words of prayer, you can attend all the meetings; you can break off from your easily besetting sins, and lead a blameless life in the sight of men; you may be more exact in all the external duties of religion than some professors are; you may persuade yourselves that you are growing better; but whatever you may do in your present carnal state, you cannot please God. "My son, give me thy heart," is the first of his requirements; he will accept of nothing short; and why should he? How can he? You are in a state of rebellion. You must lay down your arms. You must come to the point of unconditional submission. You must feel that God is right, and you are wrong; you must close in with his offers of pardon on his own terms, which are nothing short of repentance, of godly sorrow for sin, and faith in the Lord Jesus Christ.

This, dear friends, is the true state of the case; how can you help seeing it? Do what else you will, how can a holy, sin-hating God be pleased, so long as you withhold your hearts, your affections from him? Reading the Bible is a duty, prayer is a duty, attending public worship and other religious meetings is a duty, outward reformation is a duty—all that you have done, and more, it was your duty to do. All these externals are a part of true religion, and accepted as such when the heart is right. Then they please God. You could not please him without them. Though you could multiply them a hundred-fold, without faith and repentance it would avail nothing. "Whatsoever is not of faith, is sin." Will you say, "If this is so, all my prayer and striving, whatever I do, is sin, and I may just as well leave off praying and striving—nay, better, as it is only making my condition worse?" Do such thoughts come into your mind? Reject them at once. They are not from above, but from beneath. Do you think that neglecting all these means of grace would please God? You cannot believe it. You know it would displease him and aggravate your guilt. The truth is, you are shut up. You cannot go back without infinite peril to your soul. And you cannot stay where you are without adding sin to sin. You cannot please God either way. Your carnal mind is enmity against him, is not subject to his law, neither indeed can be. You must repent. You must cast yourself upon the mercy of God, as a lost sinner. Your case admits of no delay.

Only one word more. Were it possible for you to go to heaven, carrying with you the carnal mind which is enmity against God, what would be your condition? Could you be happy there? Would it be heaven to *you?* Impossible. Perfect love to God is heaven; perfect enmity is hell; and must be every where, and for ever and ever.

"STRIVE TO ENTER IN AT THE STRAIT GATE."

This is a very urgent and alarming exhortation. By the strait or narrow gate, is meant the entrance into the kingdom of heaven, in contrast with the wide gate and broad way that lead to destruction. That those who make no efforts to enter, should fail, is a matter of course, and they comprise the whole body of careless, delaying sinners. But it is startling to hear Christ say, that even many who "*seek* to enter in, shall not be able"—shall fall short and perish, after all their seeking. Why shall they not be able? What hinders? Though the gate is narrow, it always stands open till the day of grace is past. There must be some strange reason or reasons, why they cannot enter in and be saved. I can think of four, at least. There may be others.

Our Saviour, here, does not mean to discourage seeking. Far from it. In another place he says, "*Seek*, and ye shall find; knock, and it shall be opened unto you." Without seeking, no one ever entered, nor ever can. It must then depend upon the *kind* of seeking, or the *time*, or both.

The first reason why some who seek to enter in shall not be able, is, that they *trust in their own good works and good resolutions* to save them. If their lives have not been blameless, they reform. They break off from sinful habits. They "do many things." They want to be saved, and they strive to work out their own salvation by the strict performance of external duties, till they are ready to ask, with the young ruler, "What lack I yet?" Like the Pharisees of old, they "go about to establish their own righteousness, and do not submit themselves to the righteousness of God," to the plan of salvation which he has ordained and proposed for their acceptance. This is reason enough why they cannot enter. The gate is not wide enough to admit them, thickly clad with their own righteousness; the thicker, the greater the difficulty of entering. They must strip their rags all off. That is, they must utterly renounce all dependence upon their own righteousness as the ground of justification, that they may be clothed with the robe of Christ's righteousness. This way of seeking sets aside the gospel plan altogether. It is seeking salvation by the door of the law, by which "there shall be no flesh justified."

A second reason why some who seek salvation cannot enter the kingdom of God, is, that they *do not seek in earnest.* They are awakened. There is a dreadful sound in their ears. They feel that they are in danger of being lost, and must do something. So they break away from their careless associates, and betake themselves to the external duties of religion. They read the Bible, they punctually attend public worship and listen to preaching, as they never did before. They pray in secret every day perhaps, and sometimes oftener. They attend prayer-meetings, and perhaps go to inquiry meetings. They are *seekers,* and willing to have it known by their impenitent associates, from whose companionship they have withdrawn. They seem to be so much engaged for a time, that their pious friends entertain strong hopes that they will not only seek, but find—that they will press into the kingdom of God. Still they do not "*strive* to enter in at the strait gate." They are not half so much in earnest as they would be if some great temporal good was to be gained, and could not be secured without their utmost efforts. Then you would see them in earnest; they would not turn aside, or permit themselves to be diverted by any minor interest, till the desired object was obtained. And how can they expect to win the heavenly crown, while they are so much less in earnest? "The kingdom of heaven suffereth violence, and the violent take it by force."

A third reason why many who seek to enter fall short is that they do not *persevere*. For a while they seem to be all engaged to obtain the prize. You would think their entrance almost certain. They seem to be already at the gate, and just ready to go in. But they are not so near as we supposed. They vacillate. They hear the word with joy, but the good seed falls upon stony ground, where, though it springs up and looks green, it takes no root. In the sense in which Christ addressed the young ruler, they are "not far from the kingdom of heaven," but they never reach it, because they do not persevere. They find it so much harder than they expected to get in at the narrow gate, that they give it up, gradually leave off seeking, and finally sink down into deeper stupidity than ever.

A fourth reason why many who seek to enter in

shall not be able is that they seek *too late.* I know impenitent sinners flatter themselves that it can never be too late as long as life lasts, and they point us to the thief on the cross, who repented in the last agonies of crucifixion. So he did, and we do not deny the possibility of any sinner's conversion at the last hour, on his death-bed; but that it is then too late for thousands who rely upon some such miracle of grace, does not admit of doubt. Though we may not know the hour when the day of grace ends, it may end days and weeks, if not years, before the sinner dies. There is such a thing as the unpardonable sin, and it may be committed we know not how long before death. It was too late for Judas to seek forgiveness, after he had betrayed his Master. He could cast down the thirty pieces of silver, exclaiming in an agony of remorse, "I have betrayed the innocent blood," but it was the remorseful repentance of despair. He went away and hanged himself.

So that awful denunciation in the first chapter of Proverbs: "Because I have called and ye refused, I have stretched out my hand and no man regarded," therefore "I will laugh at your calamity, I will mock when your fear cometh. Then shall they call upon me, but I will not answer; they shall seek me early, but they shall not find me." It was too late; the divine forbearance was exhausted.

So it may be, and so we have reason to fear it is, with many hardened sinners under the gospel. The time comes when it is too late to call. The die is cast. Nothing remaineth but a fearful looking for of judgment and fiery indignation.

But aside from all this, that with many who seek it will be too late, is settled by our Saviour himself in the words immediately following those upon which I have been speaking. Let us take them in their connection. "Strive to enter in at the strait gate; for many, I say unto you, will seek to enter in, and shall not be able. When once the master of the house is risen up and hath shut to the door, and ye begin to stand without and to knock at the door, saying, Lord, Lord, open unto us; and he shall answer, and say unto you, I know you not whence ye are: then he shall say, Depart from me, all ye workers of iniquity." Ah, it was too late. However long they might have been seeking, the day of grace was past—the door was shut. Heaven was lost. So it will be with many, we have reason to fear, among us; their seeking will be too late.

You will not wonder, my friends, that I so address you at this time. I could think of nothing more appropriate to the present crisis. God is pouring out his Spirit. Some, we trust, have entered in at the strait gate, and are rejoicing in hope. But do not others of you belong to the class of seekers whose case I have described? You are not indifferent spectators of what the Lord is doing among us. You feel that you as well as your friends have a personal interest to secure. You want to be saved. You feel that you are in danger of being lost, and you are seeking to enter in at the strait gate. But how? What is the reason that you have not succeeded, as well as others? If you are trying to establish a righteousness of your own, if you expect in the least degree to merit salvation by your good works, that is reason enough. Though you could multiply them ever so much, though you could pile them up to the skies, and live a thousand years to do it in, it would not aid you at all. The righteousness of Christ is the only ground of justification before God. Good works follow as the fruits—they never go before a saving change as the procuring cause, or reason. "The bed is shorter than that a man can stretch himself on it; and the covering narrower than that he can wrap himself in it."

Do you belong to another class of seekers, who have given up the hope of being saved by their works, but are not more than half in earnest? Is this your state, dear friend? Then you are in an evil case indeed. With all your half-hearted seeking, you are nothing better, but rather grow worse; for you are commanded to "strive" to enter in at the strait gate, which you are not doing at all. Your own conscience testifies that you are not half so much in earnest as you have sometimes been to secure worldly interests of no comparative value. Perchance you have risen early and sat up late, and ate the bread of carefulness, and deprived yourself of sleep, for fear of not gaining your object. You left no stone unturned, you would not rest day or night, so long as you was in danger of losing your property by delay, or for lack of any possible effort to secure the title. But here you are seeking indeed—reading your Bible, attending meetings, and using other means of grace, hoping you shall feel more, and then seek more earnestly, and so at last obtain. Alas, you are deceiving yourself. Oh, when will you be in *real* earnest? When will you seek the Lord so as to find him? Now he is near, and waiting to be gracious. Call upon him to help you; *strive* to enter in, or you will as certainly perish, as if you had remained utterly indifferent to this hour.

Have any of you been seeking without finding, and are you tempted to give it up? Are you already beginning to relax, to say in your heart, It is of no use to seek any longer; I have tried and tried to become a Christian, and it does no good. "Why should I wait for the Lord any longer?" Yes, you have tried, but it has been in your own strength. You have been seeking, but not so as to find; and you never will find, so long as you rest in mere seeking; and never, if you give over. You must seek salvation, but it must be with an earnestness which you have not yet felt. You must "*strive*" to enter in at the strait gate. The original here is a great deal stronger than the translation. The word is *agonize* to enter in. Summon all the energies of your awakened soul; let them be concentrated in the anguish of the sharpest pangs of an awakened conscience. Strive with all the agony of a broken and contrite heart. Cast yourself at once upon the mere mercy of God, through Jesus Christ, and he will save you. His blood cleanseth from all sin. His arm is mighty to save. O perishing sinner, why do you linger, grieving the Holy Spirit more and more every hour? Oh, to perish, after all, with those who seek to enter in and shall not be able. What an infinite loss! Infinite; infinite!

"SHE WAS NOTHING BETTER, BUT RATHER GREW WORSE."

This was the pitiable condition of a woman in a crowd of people on the west side of the lake of Galilee, where they were waiting for the return of Jesus from Gadara, lying on the opposite shore. She had long been afflicted with a wasting disease; had spent all her living upon many physicians; had gone from one to another, still hoping for a cure, till their skill was exhausted; and "she was nothing better, but rather grew worse." Despairing of any relief from the physicians, she in her great extremity pressed through the throng till she could touch the hem of Christ's outer garment; for she said, If I may touch but his clothes, I shall be whole.

Here was a case of strong faith under the most discouraging circumstances. Though she had no promise of a cure, and it does not appear that Christ had ever seen or spoken to her before, she believed not only that he had power to heal her, but that in some mysterious way that power would be communicated through a mere touch of the hem of his garment. Great indeed was her faith, and she was not disappointed. Straightway the fountain of her blood was dried up, and she felt in her body that she was healed of that plague; and how was it? "Jesus immediately knowing in himself that virtue had gone out of him, turned about in the press, and said, Who touched my clothes? Then the woman, fearing and trembling, fell down before him, and told him all the truth." She doubtless expected to be rebuked for her temerity. But no; He smiled upon her, and said, not woman, but, "*Daughter*, thy faith hath made thee whole; go in peace, and be whole of thy plague."

This remarkable incident in the life and miracles of our Saviour strikingly represents the case of an awakened sinner who, instead of coming directly to Christ to be healed, applies first to *many other physicians* for relief; who, in other words, resorts to all the expedients, uses all the means he can think of to obtain peace and pardon. He has such a sense of his danger that he cannot rest. He must be doing something to make himself better, and conciliate the favor of God. He begins to break off his sinful habits; withdraws from his wicked companions; reads his Bible; attends public worship, and listens as he never did before to the preaching of the word; but he gets no relief: he cannot rest here; he begins to call upon God, he attends the prayer-meetings, he makes his feelings known to some pious friend, and is resolved to do as well as he can, hoping thereby to make some amends for the past, and render himself more worthy of the divine favor. But neither will this do. He finds no rest. Rather, his distress increases; and what more can he do? He is more and more afraid he shall be lost; and if the Spirit of God continues to strive with him, he repeats and redoubles his efforts, reads his Bible more, prays oftener, attends more meetings, and resolves to be more exact in the performance of every religious duty. In this way he flatters himself that he is making some progress towards securing the favor of God. He is sure he is a great deal better than he used to be, and cannot think that God will cast him off after doing so many things. He says he has done all he can, and tries to persuade himself that it would be unjust; especially as, if he has not done enough, he is ready to do more, to make any sacrifice however great, to secure the salvation of his soul.

Thus, instead of submitting himself to God, he has all along been trying to build up a righteousness of his own. He has been trusting in his outward reformation, in his prayers, in his religious observances. Or in other cases, like the young man in the gospel, he is ready to say, "All these things have I kept from my youth up; what lack I yet?"

Now I do not say that the process which I have been describing is the only way in which sinners are led to Christ, or are left to quench the Holy Spirit. I know it is not. Such cases, however, are not uncommon in revivals of religion. There may be at least one such person present in this meeting; and, dear friend, what shall I say to you? You have "done many things." When one has failed, you have tried another, and then another. You have, so to speak, applied to many physicians, and you have flattered yourself that you were growing better. You probably do still; but you are not healed. You think yourself nearer the kingdom of heaven than you was months or weeks ago; and so you are nearer in one sense, if you ever get there—not that you are better prepared for heaven. On the contrary, you are nothing better, but rather growing worse. You are more guilty, in the sight of God, than you was when first awakened; and instead of growing better, you are growing worse every day. Does this startle you? I wish it might. Do you ask how it can be, when you have broken off from bad habits, and are reading the Bible and praying every day, and attending all the meetings, and striving to do better, and be better? Are you ready to say, "If all I have done is to go for nothing, I don't see how I can ever be saved?" Oh, my friend, you never can be saved in this way. A thousand times as many prayers and tythings would not save you. The fatal mistake is, that you have been "going about to establish your own righteousness." You have been building upon your own works and good resolutions.

Now, I do not say that you have been growing worse faster since your attention was called up, than you would have done, had you remained indifferent to this hour, under all the privileges that you have enjoyed. I do not know. It is not for me to strike the balance between the guilt of utter indifference at such a time as this, and the guilt of resting where you now are. But I am afraid that even a sorer condemnation awaits you, if you fall short of heaven; for the Spirit of God has been striving with you; you have not submitted to his righteousness; and must not the guilt of sinning on from week to week, or from day to day under these strivings, be more aggravated? May not this be your case? Instead of growing better with all your doings, may you not have been growing worse faster than ever? I do not see how it can be otherwise. Can you see?

But suppose that, in the sight of God, there is no such aggravation. Let us look at your case in the most favorable light possible. You will not for a moment claim that you have committed no sin since your attention was first arrested. You will admit, that you have sinned more or less, in thought, word or deed, every day; and if so, then you are no better than when you began, but worse. It must be so; for all your sins, up to that time, stand charged against you just as they were. Not one of them has been truly repented of; not one of them has been pardoned; and now there is this addition to the long black catalogue. You are therefore nothing better, but have rather been growing worse all the time. There is no escaping from this conclusion, alarming as it is.

And now, dear friend, what will you do next? How much more time will you waste in trying to build up a righteousness of your own? And suppose you could build it ever so high on your sandy foundation, what would it avail when the floods come, and the winds blow and beat upon it?

Of all diseases, that of the heart is the most alarming and fatal. The most skilful physician can do nothing with it. He cannot reach it. This is your disease. Your heart is corrupt to the very core. No human skill can stay the plague. Yet, blessed be God, you need not despair. There is ONE PHYSICIAN who can cure you, and would have done it long ago, had you felt that your case was desperate, and applied to him. It is a wonder that you are not dead; but still his infinite compassion yearns over you. And will you not follow the example of that poor woman, who had spent all her living upon many physicians, and was nothing better, but rather grew worse? This is exactly your case. Will you not, as it were, press through the crowd this very evening, and in the exercise of like faith touch the hem of Christ's garment, that you may be healed? Do this, and virtue will instantly go out of him, and he will say, Son, or daughter, thy faith hath made thee whole.

"And is this all?" methinks I hear you tremblingly ask. "Casting away all my dependences, may I come to Christ the great Physician, and be healed at once?" Yes, this is all. Strange, incredible as it may seem, nothing else is required. No worthiness, no fitness to come. Simply "believe on the Lord Jesus Christ, and thou shalt be saved." Embrace him as a divine and almighty Saviour. Receive him by faith as all your salvation and all your desire, and your sins shall be blotted out, in room of the filthy rags cast for ever away. You shall be clothed with the robe of his righteousness, be justified through the merits of Christ, and have a new song put into your mouth, even praise to our God.

And now, dear friend, what do you say to all this? Do you believe that the way to be saved is so clear, so simple, and can you remain any longer outside of the crowd that is pressing upon Jesus to be healed—merely looking on and wondering, while your spiritual disease is making steady progress towards a fatal termination? It must not be. Your life, your soul is too precious to be thus thrown away. You must press your way through the throng, that you too may touch the hem of Christ's garment and be healed. Will you; will you do it now, this very hour, this very moment?

"GO THY WAY FOR THIS TIME: WHEN I HAVE A CONVENIENT SEASON, I WILL CALL FOR THEE."

This, you know, was the promise extorted from Felix, the Roman governor of Judea, under a sermon delivered by Paul, the prisoner of Jesus Christ, brought to his bar by the Jews, not to preach, but to be judged and condemned. It was an extraordinary spectacle. There sat the judge in his purple, and there stood his prisoner in bonds, and under the fierce accusations of his enemies thirsting for his blood.

At the first hearing, Paul's masterly defence made such an impression upon the mind of Felix, that he adjourned the trial, that he might inquire into the case more perfectly for a new hearing, and this was the day fixed upon. He sent for Paul, and strange to say, instead of going on with the trial, as the Jews expected, he heard his prisoner concerning the faith in Christ. It must have been a Divine impulse upon the mind of this heathen judge, which gave so unexpected a turn to the hearing. And as Paul, taking advantage of it, reasoned of righteousness, temperance, and judgment, Felix trembled, and answered, "Go thy way for this time: when I have a convenient season, I will call for thee."

And why did Felix tremble before his prisoner, as if he himself had been suddenly arraigned before an infinitely higher bar? It cannot be doubted that he was awakened by the Spirit of God to an awful sense of his guilt and danger; nothing else could have made him tremble, especially in such a public presence. He trembled because he could not help it. The appeal roused his conscience, and overmastered his pride of office and self-control. But alas, it did not bring him to a decision to embrace Christianity, to repent of his sins and put himself at once under the further teaching of the apostle; but so powerful was the impression, that he could not altogether dismiss the subject; and so, to make a compromise, he again adjourned the trial, and turning to Paul, said, "Go thy way for this time: when I have a convenient season, I will call for thee." It is probable that he really intended, at some future time, and when he should be more at leisure, to receive further instruction. But there is no evidence that he ever did—that the convenient season ever arrived. The contrary is evident from the fact, that though he often sent for Paul, it was in some way to get money from him, rather than further instruction; and that, failing in this, when he was superseded in the government by Festus two years after, "willing to show the Jews a pleasure, he left Paul bound." O Felix, Felix, why didst thou quench the Holy Spirit? Hadst thou cherished the convictions which made thee tremble, thou mightest have been saved; but ah, that fatal procrastination! The convenient season never came; and where art thou now?

This melancholy case of Felix strikingly represents that of thousands who sit under the sound of the Gospel; and this is the reason why I have taken it as the basis of an earnest appeal at this time. Hardly any thing is more common, and nothing is more dangerous, during a revival of religion, than this putting off the subject to a more convenient season. I have met with many such cases; and who that has had much experience in revivals, has not? A sinner is alarmed by the Spirit of God, under some powerful appeal from the pulpit, and like Felix, he trembles. The danger of his condition stares him in the face. His guilt has been clearly set before him, and his conscience testifying against him, urges him to immediate repentance. There is a great struggle in his mind. On the one hand, he is not ready to yield, and on the other he dare not dismiss the subject for ever. So he resorts to a compromise. He virtually says to the Spirit, who is striving with him, "I cannot yield now, I am very busy; I will think seriously of it as soon as I am more at leisure. Go thy way for this time: when I have a convenient season, I will call for thee." Thus he grieves away the Holy Spirit. The convenient time never comes, and he dies in his sins.

Fellow-sinner, is not this your case? Has not God awakened you? Have you not been urged to an immediate decision; and instead of yielding, have you not tried to quiet your conscience with the hope that you should find the more convenient season on which Felix fatally rested? Is not this your case now? Are you not saying in your heart, "Go thy way for this time;" and promising yourself that you shall have a better opportunity? If so, let me earnestly expostulate with you. We cannot go our way, we cannot consent to let you alone, upon a future indefinite promise. Nothing can be more delusive, or dangerous. If you are not ready, after so long a time, to give your heart to God, when will you be? If you send us away now, as Felix did the apostle, when shall we call again? Shall it be to-morrow? If that is too soon, shall it be next day? shall it be a week hence? When shall it be? This trusting to a more convenient season will never do. *Appoint the time* when you will not only listen to us, but repent at the foot of the cross—and shall we then go and tell our Master, that though you are not quite ready, you are in a hopeful way; that you are making some progress; that you have done talking about a more convenient time; that we have your promise, that you will repent to-morrow, and ——?

But no; what am I saying? I take it all back. You have no right to set us a future time, and we have no right to ask it. There are many reasons why no such compromise can be allowed. God says, "*Now*"—not to-morrow—"*now* is the day of salvation." If you wait till to-morrow, God may finally withdraw his Holy Spirit, and then it will be all over with you. Every hour's delay is infinitely dangerous. And again, dear friend, what promise have you that you shall live through another night; or that if spared, your reason may not be taken from you by some sudden and mortal sickness? Let that voice ring in your ears, "Boast not thyself of to-morrow; for thou knowest not what a day may bring forth."

And still once more, the longer you delay, the harder will it be to submit to Christ, to break off your sins and make your peace with Him. So far from getting any better prepared by delay, you are a greater sinner to-day than you was yesterday, and if you live, you will be a greater sinner to-morrow than you are to-day. Give your resolutions of becoming a Christian at some future day to the winds. They are good for nothing. They are worse. They quiet and deceive you. There will be no more "convenient season" than the present.

"ALMOST THOU PERSUADEST ME TO BE A CHRISTIAN."

Agrippa was the son of that Herod who beheaded John and imprisoned Peter. With the title of king under the Roman emperors, he administered the provincial government of Cesarea, and several of the annexed districts. Paul having been sent down under arrest from Jerusalem, charged by the Jews with the crimes of apostasy and sedition, was on the first convenient day arraigned for trial; and in so masterly a manner did he defend himself before the king, that when he came to make that bold and remarkable appeal, "King Agrippa, believest thou the prophets? I know that thou believest," Agrippa was so overpowered by it, that he answered Paul, "*Almost thou persuadest me to be a Christian.*"

Here we must carefully distinguish. Agrippa was not even an *almost Christian.* Saving the conviction of the moment, he was as far from it as ever. He was only almost persuaded that he ought to *become* one. We have no reason to think he ever did. The greater probability is, that he gave himself no more concern about the new religion; that he never after came so near as to be "almost persuaded," but perished in his sins.

In this, king Agrippa may be taken as the representative of a very considerable class of persons in religious revivals. From a state of deep indifference, they are awakened by the Spirit of God under the preaching of the word. They find themselves condemned by the divine law, and that they are in danger of perishing, which they had never realized before. They see others pressing into the kingdom of God. They no longer make light of the revival. Their consciences tell them that they are sinners, and need the salvation which the gospel offers. They dare not remain where they are. They resolve to take up the subject of personal religion, and yield to its claims. They are accordingly punctual in their attendance upon public worship. They listen to preaching as they never did before. They brush off the dust from their neglected Bibles, and may be said to "search the Scriptures" with considerable interest. They attend the prayer-meetings, and it may be the inquiry meetings. They are willing to be personally addressed on the great subject, and their impressions of its paramount importance are deepened. The thought of being left, while many of their companions and others are taken, is painful and alarming. They "do many things." It is no pretence. They are sincere as far as they go. It may truly be said of some of this class at least, that they are "almost persuaded" to be Christians, and this persuasion is not a sudden impulse, as in the case of Agrippa, to pass away almost as soon as felt, but abiding, sometimes for days and weeks.

But alas, there they remain. The last and essential step they do not take. They are only *almost* persuaded, not *quite*. In the sense of Christ's address to the young ruler, they are "not far from the kingdom of heaven;" but like him, they remain without till the door is shut.

Are there not some of this class here? I believe there are. You may not in so many words have classed yourselves with Agrippa, but you stand just where he *said* he did. You are almost persuaded to be Christians. At least, you think you are. You have become so far interested in the present revival, as to attend all the meetings and class yourselves with the inquirers, and under the clear exhibition and claims of the gospel you have sometimes been almost persuaded, almost ready to yield your hearts to God. Your pious friends have been waiting and hoping to see you come out of the *almost* to a full decision. And how much longer will you stand halting between two opinions? What do you expect to gain by it? How great the danger that you will lose every thing. You are resisting the Holy Spirit, and how long can you expect he will continue to strive with you? Oh, if he should depart for ever, as he may at any moment, what remains but "a fearful looking for of judgment and fiery indignation?"

You are now "almost persuaded;" but what will that avail in the day when God shall take away the soul? What does this being only "almost persuaded" amount to, in any case? Here is an inebriate "almost persuaded" to leave off drinking. Will that save him from filling a drunkard's grave? Yonder is an habitual profane swearer. Will his being "almost persuaded" to break off from the habit reform him?

Will he not keep on profaning God's holy name, till he is quite persuaded to leave it off? The command of universal obligation is, "Remember the Sabbath-day to keep it holy." Will any one's being "almost persuaded" to keep it, prevent his breaking it? Must he not be *quite* persuaded? Here, again, is a person who has been addicted to stealing. Will he steal no more, because he is "almost persuaded" to leave it off, and become an honest man? Who does not see that such *almosts* fall fatally short of securing a thorough reformation?

How much more in your case, my impenitent friends, remaining as you are only "almost persuaded" to be Christians. You are yet in your sins, and if you go no further, you are just as certain to be shut out of heaven and perish, as if you had never been awakened at all. Nay more, you will have to answer for quenching the Spirit, which would have "sealed you unto the day of redemption." In vain did the man-slayer *only almost* reach the city of refuge, however near he got to it, when the avenger of blood overtook him. He must actually enter the gate, before he could be safe. To escape the scalping-knife of a savage foe in hot pursuit, the border settler must reach the fort. Overtaken anywhere outside, though ever so near, he is cloven down by the tomahawk.

But what can I more say? Here you are, dear friends, lingering upon the "almost" persuasion of Agrippa, and in the greatest danger of perishing as he did. I beseech you not to rest another hour where you stand. To be "almost persuaded" is only to be almost saved, and to be almost saved is to be eternally lost!

"COMMUNE WITH YOUR OWN HEART AND BE STILL."

When sinners are awakened under the striving of the Holy Spirit in a revival, and become thoroughly alarmed, instead of going to their pastor at once, and asking what they must do to be saved, they commonly try something else first. If they are young and have intimate companions, their sympathies sometimes draw them more closely together than ever, long before they are converted, if converted at all. It gives them a sort of relief to sit down together and talk and weep over their danger. And why should they not? It is a danger to which they are both alike exposed, and which is much greater than they imagine. Each needs help, and must have it from some quarter, or perish. If there were any thing to be gained by mutual weeping and condolence under such circumstances, it should be encouraged. But what good can it do? What help or encouragement can either of them give to his friend? They both lie under the same condemnation, and can no more aid each other than if they were condemned prisoners in chains.

Nay, the more they condole together, the greater the danger that they will grieve the Spirit to depart from them. Many awakened sinners have in this manner talked and wept away their concern, and returned to their former careless state.

Rather, O sinner, commune with thine own heart. Be much alone. Your friend, under the same condemnation, cannot help you. Pray God to show you your guilt, as well as your danger. The publican in the parable did not go to his brother publicans, to get their sympathies and ask them to help him. He knew they could not help him. He went out by himself, and when he got in sight of the temple, which he dared not enter, and so burdened that he would not so much as lift up his eyes to heaven, he smote upon his breast and cried, "God be merciful unto me a sinner." "Go thou and do likewise." Weeping with thine impenitent friend ever so long, will do neither thyself nor him any good.

But when two companions are awakened in a revival, and one of them is brought out rejoicing in hope, the case is entirely different. Then he may go to his friend—he cannot help going—and tell him what a Saviour he has found, and try to show him the way to the cross; and with the blessing of God upon their renewed intercourse, he may be brought into the kingdom of Christ.

I go a step further. When two bosom friends are awakened about the same time, they should not talk much with each other on any subject, till they have made their peace with God. The reason is obvious. Whatever the subject may be, though ever so suitable under other circumstances, there is danger of its diverting their minds from the great salvation, not yet secured, which demands all their thoughts. And the same holds true, I think, in all cases. When a sinner is awakened and brought to inquire what he must do, till the great question is settled, till he has submitted and given his heart to God, it is not safe for him to talk much on common subjects with anybody. Then is the time to find and secure "the pearl of great price;" and he must not let any thing hinder him. He will not if he is as much in earnest as he ought to be. "The one thing needful" first, and then other interests in their proper place.

"QUENCH NOT THE SPIRIT."

The Holy Spirit—by whose divine agency sinners are awakened, convicted, regenerated, and sealed to the day of redemption—by which also Christians are sanctified, built up in the most holy faith, and "made meet for the inheritance of the saints in light." To quench, in the ordinary sense of the term, is to extinguish or allay, as water puts out fire, and quenches thirst. In the sense here used, it is to check, to stifle.

As Jesus Christ is the only Redeemer, so the Holy Spirit is the only Renewer and Sanctifier. From the highest degree of holy love, shed abroad in the heart of the established believer, down to the first awakening of the impenitent sinner, it is the same Spirit. And so, all along through every stage of awakening and conviction, up to the new birth; and after that, to the "helping of our infirmities with groanings which cannot be uttered;" it is the selfsame Spirit, that worketh all in all.

At every step, from first to last, the Spirit may be quenched, may be checked, may be stifled, and hence the necessity of the exhortation now before us. Let us then inquire briefly, in what way or ways, by what means the Spirit is often quenched, especially in revivals.

1. The Spirit may be quenched in the earliest stage of awakening *by some trifling cause,* of which the sinner is scarcely conscious at the time. This may be your case, my friend. The Holy Spirit may now be gently moving you to "think on your ways." If any Christian friend, seeing you at the prayer-meetings, were to ask you whether you feel any particular interest in the work that is going on, you would probably, or you *might* answer, that you do not. You hope you shall, but you persuade yourself that as yet the exhortation, "Quench not the Spirit," does not apply to you, as you have not experienced any thing of His special influence. But beware how you give Satan this advantage over you. It is one of his subtle devices, by which he will divert your mind from the subject, if he can. With his consent, you never would have bestowed a serious thought upon your own salvation; and if he can blind you to the fact that the Spirit is beginning to strive with you, he will most certainly do it; for then he counts on being sure of you. Cherish the divine influence, however faint at first, as you would a spark of fire, if you had no assurance that, once extinguished, it would ever be rekindled.

2. The Spirit may be quenched by *the neglect of opportunities.* When God is pouring out his Spirit, preaching is generally more direct and pungent, and religious meetings are more frequent than ordinary. There is no reason to doubt that many have quenched the Spirit and lost their souls by withdrawing from these means of grace, at the turning point. Their attention was arrested, their interest was grad-

ually increased at the prayer-meetings, and had they but held on, they might by striving, have entered in at the strait gate; but for some cause, after a while they withdrew, and in so doing quenched the Spirit, and sank down into deeper stupidity than ever.

I warn you, my friends, against following these fatal examples. "No man having put his hand to the plough, and looking back, is fit for the kingdom of heaven. God, who in his great mercy has called up your attention to the claims of the gospel, does not allow you to hope that you shall be saved, if you turn back and neglect the means which he has appointed. True as it may be—and nothing is more certain—that there is no saving efficacy inherent in the means themselves, that the excellency of the power is all of God, yet he so honors his own appointed means, that those who voluntarily neglect them, grieve the Spirit to leave them, just as truly as if every thing depended on the means alone. Beware then that you do not in this way quench the Spirit.

3. The Spirit is often quenched by *delay*, by putting off the subject to a more "convenient season." Perhaps there is no temptation on which the great adversary depends so much in seasons of revival, as this. Resolving ever so sincerely to repent at some future time, be it ever so near, is not to be depended on for a moment. Every hour that you delay is at your peril. You are in danger of quenching the Spirit, which, if finally withdrawn, will leave you to perish. You may promise every thing for to-morrow; but what will it avail, if your soul should this night

be required of you? Or if not, should the Spirit be grieved by your procrastination to depart for ever, what would then be your condition? It is appalling to think of it. The convenient season would *never* come. Supposing a sinner, thus forsaken, could live a thousand years, and in the enjoyment of the highest religious privileges, he would only be treasuring up wrath against the day of wrath. No sinner ever came to Christ, or ever will, without being drawn by the Holy Spirit. How fearful then the danger of quenching it by any delay. "Behold, *now* is the accepted time." The promise reaches no further. It contains no future time.

4. The Spirit may be quenched by the absorbing demands of *worldly business and cares.* While industry in some lawful occupation is a common duty and necessity, there is always the greatest danger that "the cares of this world, the deceitfulness of riches, and the lusts of other things, will choke the word and make it unfruitful." Especially is this the case in revivals. When the attention of a busy worldly-minded sinner is called up to seek the pearl of priceless value; when he begins to feel that he must have a better portion than this world can give, and the Holy Spirit urges him to seek for it in earnest, he has so much on his mind and on his hands, that he is strongly tempted to put it off a little while, till he can so adjust his affairs as to be more at leisure, and then he will give his time and his heart to the work. The moment he forms this resolution, he grieves the Spirit to forsake him. It is of God's infinite forbearance, if he does not in this way quench it for ever.

It matters not in such cases how lawful in itself the engrossing worldly business may be, it must be entirely given up for the time being, or so arranged as not to interfere with the immediate claims of the gospel. "What shall it profit a man, if he gain the whole world, and lose his own soul?" Lose his own soul he will, if the good seed is choked by the thorns, whose end is to be burned.

5. Nor may we stop here. When a sinner is under awakening, he cannot allow any thing, however proper or innocent it might be under ordinary circumstances, to *divert* his mind from the one great question, "What must I do to be saved?" without running the fearful hazard of quenching the Spirit. The human mind cannot entertain two engrossing subjects at once, however lawful and proper in themselves, and do justice to either. There is a crisis in the case of every awakened sinner, when the least diversion of the mind may quench the Spirit, and prove fatal. It may be nothing more than forming a new partnership in business, or making an honest lucrative bargain, or attending a social party, or going out of town to visit a friend: any thing which comes in between the sinner and the claims of the gospel to his immediate repentance and faith in Christ may quench the Spirit, and thus prove as fatal to the soul as any deliberate rejection would be. And here lies one of the greatest dangers. While the awakened sinner perhaps breaks off from ensnaring company, and is on his guard against the most obvious hinderances, he can hardly be persuaded that trifling, innocent diversions may be equally ruinous. But they

may, and probably they oftener are, than the more obvious worldly attractions.

I might suggest many other cautions against quenching the Spirit; but let these suffice. If God arrested you anywhere in the broad way, if he has awakened you to a sense of your guilt and danger, it may be the last time, and probably will be, if you suffer any thing to hinder you from hastening to the foot of the cross in "the accepted time, the day of salvation."

"THE WILES OF THE DEVIL."

That there is a fallen spirit, malignant and subtle, walking about among men "seeking whom he may devour," is so fully asserted in the Scriptures that I need not stop a moment to prove it. He is called by different names in the Bible—Angel of the bottomless pit, Prince of darkness, Satan, Beelzebub, the Serpent, the Deceiver, a Liar, the Prince of the power of the air, and the god of this world. Frightful names; infernal agencies; awful dangers!

As this great adversary of God and man was active in trying to counteract our blessed Saviour in the great work of saving men, which he came into the world to accomplish, so we may be sure he will redouble his efforts to counteract the Holy Spirit in seasons of special revival. In times of profound stupidity, he need trouble himself but little about those whom he has led captive at his will, for he is in no danger of losing them. But when Jesus Christ comes into a town, and sinners begin to inquire what they must do to be saved, he is sure to be there, and to oppose the work in every possible way. However mysterious it may seem, the Bible abundantly testifies that he has direct access to the minds of men, and knows how to turn and apply his temptations to the greatest advantage.

His first object of course will be to prevent sinners from taking any interest in the revival. To this end, he will do what he can to keep them away from public worship, and especially from extra meetings. If he cannot keep them away, the next step is to prevent them from treasuring up what they hear. "Then cometh Satan immediately, and taketh away the word that was sown in their hearts," lest they should believe, and be saved. This, I doubt not, is just what he is doing here every Sabbath. If he does not succeed in this, he will persuade them that what they witness is a mere temporary excitement, which will soon die away. If under an alarming sermon they begin to tremble, he will tell them not to be frightened; there is no hell to be afraid of: just as he told Eve, "Ye shall not surely die;" for he is a liar from the beginning, and the father of it. If this does not answer, he will persuade them to dismiss the subject for the present, and take it up at a more convenient time. Thousands have yielded to these and other suggestions of the great Deceiver, and have perished in their sins. I have no doubt of it. Nor have I any doubt that there are some—I fear there are many in every revival—under the same diabolical delusion. And the more control Satan has over them, the more stoutly will they deny that there is any thing in it. God may open their eyes before it is too late; but of all classes of impenitent sinners, none are in greater danger; their feet stand on the most slippery places.

Now that some of you are awakened, you must not flatter yourselves that the wily tempter will let you alone. Depend upon it, he will employ all his subtlety to hold you fast in his snare. If he cannot hinder you from asking what you must do to be saved, he will put you upon such a course of "impenitent doings," if he can, as will quiet your fears, without at all losing his hold upon you. He will do his utmost to persuade you that a person so moral and inoffensive as you have been, cannot be in danger of being lost. "God is too merciful. If you have failed in any thing, repent of it. Do the best you can, and dismiss your concern. Be honest and kind and sober and blameless in every way, and all will be well." The Deceiver, I have no doubt, is trying to quiet some of you by suggesting that you are too young to be so anxious. "Wait a few years, till your minds are more mature, and you have had more religious instruction to prepare you for taking up the subject to a great deal better advantage." I am very much afraid he will succeed with some of you just here. Remember, that "he is a liar, and the father of it." If it suits his purpose better, he will tell you that you must "wait God's time" and not be discouraged; or wait till the excitement is over, so that you may take up the subject calmly, and not be deceived. Or that "you are so wicked, and have held out so long, that God will not receive you. You might have come in, but it is too late."

These are some of Satan's "devices," of which we

are not ignorant. He, no doubt, employs a great many others, as occasion serves him, in special seasons of revival; and when all fail, he will in the last resort do his utmost to persuade you to settle down upon a false hope. Then, though it will have given him no little trouble to follow you, step by step, through your alarm and convictions, he will not regret it, as his object is gained at last, by your dismissing all your concern, and settling down "at ease in Zion."

Oh, my friends, this is no bugbear, conjured up to frighten weak women and young children. It is a voice of warning from the Scriptures, against "the wiles of the devil," which should make every impenitent sinner tremble. Evil spirits are not visible to mortal eyes, and they are infinitely more dangerous on that account. Could you see them waiting for you at the door to catch away the sermon when you come out of the church, meeting you in every prayer-meeting, and following you everywhere—could you hear them whispering their temptations in your ears, to dismiss your concern, and have no more to do with the revival, it would doubtless startle you. Be on your guard; the tempter is here. He is in all places of worship at such a time as this. Your only safety lies in giving no place to the devil. Not content with what he and his angels can do to banish your concern, and drive away your convictions, he will stir up his agents, some of your neighbors, your companions perhaps, to ply you with plausible dissuasives, with ridicule, or whatever else may better suit his malignant purpose. It is through such agents that Satan sometimes "is transformed into an angel of light." He may deceive and destroy those, who would be alarmed and resist him were he to show himself in his true colors.

Depend upon it, dear friends, that whoever opposes you, or tries in any way to prevent your becoming Christians, is an emissary of his father the devil, who speaks through human organs, just as the devils did when our Saviour was casting them out. Oh, my dear friends, put your fingers in your ears as Bunyan's Pilgrim did, and go on crying, "Life, eternal life! eternal life!"

"THE WILES OF THE DEVIL"—Continued.

To young Converts.

My dear Friends—On a former occasion, when you were awakened by the Spirit of God, and asking what you must do to be saved, I took occasion from the word of God to warn you against the "wiles of the devil," who is more active in times of revival than ever; and who, I felt sure, would persuade you to turn back if he could. Since then, you humbly trust that God in his great mercy has delivered you, and brought you into "the kingdom of his dear Son." Now, at last, you feel safe. This great deliverance is final, you trust. For why should he hope to get any advantage of you, now that you have renounced him and all his works for ever?

But why should he not hope and even expect to bring you into bondage again, notwithstanding you have joined the church, or are about to join? How does he know that you have got beyond his reach?

How does he know that you have been truly regenerated? Your being received into the church does not prove it. On the contrary, he knows very well that some are self-deceived, and fall away, proving that notwithstanding their fair profession, they belong to the class of stony-ground hearers, who "receive the word with joy, and in time of temptation fall away;" or to that other class, represented by the thorny ground, who hear the word, and the cares of this world, the deceitfulness of riches, and the lusts of other things choke the word, and it bringeth no fruit to perfection. Tares and wheat grow together till the harvest, then to be separated, the one to be garnered, and the other to be cast into the fire. Of the ten virgins, five were foolish, and having no oil in their vessels with their lamps, were shut out when the Bridegroom came. And again, many will say unto me in that day, Lord, Lord, have we not eaten and drunk in thy presence? and thou hast taught in our streets; to whom he will say, I know you not whence ye are. These are very alarming scriptures. There is no reason to suppose that the devil is ignorant that there are a great many false professors in church, and that he has again led them captive at his will. Surely he will not relinquish the hope of leading church-members to apostatize, as long as he has so many trophies, won back by his stratagems.

If he does not know who are really converted, and who have only the form of godliness—and there is no proof that he does—then why should he not tempt every professed disciple to deny his Master, and hope to prevail? And supposing he did know that you have been truly converted, would that infallibly protect you? It did not discourage him from tempting our first parents, though perfectly holy as they came from the Creator's hand; and he succeeded. Nay, he had the amazing audacity to tempt the Lord Jesus Christ himself, and to ply his temptations no less than forty days in succession. What security then would there be, even if he knew that you had all the protection which the most eminent Christian in the world ever enjoyed? God told Satan that his servant Job was a perfect and an upright man. But that did not discourage him. He only wanted permission to put Job to the test, and having obtained it, confidently expected to prove him a hypocrite. Failing the first time, he wanted to subject him to a still severer trial. It was granted to the extent of satanic ingenuity and malice, simply forbiding his taking away Job's life. Who then should he fear to attack?

Now turn to your Bibles, and see how earnestly the churches, and of course all the members of the churches, are warned against the assaults of the devil, and exhorted to put on the only panoply that can protect them. Let me quote two or three passages: "To whom ye forgive any thing, I forgive also—lest Satan should get an advantage of us; for we are not ignorant of his devices." 2 Cor. 2:11. "Be sober, be vigilant; because your adversary the devil, as a roaring lion, walketh about seeking whom he may devour: whom resist, steadfast in the faith, knowing that the same afflictions are accomplished in your brethren that are in the world," that is, in *all* believers. 1 Pet. 5:8. He would devour every one of you if he could. Nothing but prayer and vigilance, relying on the arm of the Lord for protection, can save you.

In the sixth chapter of Ephesians you have the Christian armor described piece by piece, and you will want the whole suit. You cannot be safe without every part of it. For want of a single piece of this heavenly panoply, many soldiers of the cross have been cast down wounded. With it, and under the eye and banner of the Captain of salvation, you will be sure to come off conquerors, and more than conquerors. You need not fear what earth and hell can do to take your crowns. Watch and pray against the wiles of the devil, and with every temptation God will make a way for your escape. The moment you let down your watch you will find yourselves, if not actually on the enemy's ground, so near the lines that some of his fiery darts may reach you. Therefore stand fast in the Lord, and he will be your high tower and strong deliverer.

"HE THAT ENDURETH TO THE END SHALL BE SAVED."

To young Converts.

My dear Friends—We have come here to get our hearts warmed, and to set up our Ebenezer on this spot, so hallowed by the presence and intercession of the Holy Spirit. For many weeks past, this has been our Bethel, the morning family altar of the church, our Bethesda, from whose waters, agitated by the angel, so many have lately come up, praising God for his healing and restoring mercies.

A hasty glance at the few months past would show what reason we have to call upon our souls and all that is within us to praise the Lord for visiting us in our low estate, and putting this new song into our mouths. But while you, my friends, who have just begun to lift up your hearts with your voices, can never praise him enough for this great deliverance, you may not sit down rejoicing, as if you would have but little more to do than to raise your hallelujahs higher and still higher to Him who hath set you free.

You are now very much in the condition of the children of Israel, when, in looking back upon their marvellous deliverance from Egyptian bondage, and the destruction of their cruel masters, they sang that memorable song in the fifteenth chapter of Exodus: "I will sing unto the Lord, for he hath triumphed gloriously: the horse and his rider hath he thrown into the sea. The Lord is my strength and song, and he is become my salvation. Who is like unto thee, O Lord, among the gods? who is like thee, glorious in holiness, fearful in praises, doing wonders? Thou in mercy hast led forth thy people; thou hast guided them in thy strength unto thy holy habitation. Thou shalt bring them in, and plant them in the mountain of thine inheritance, in the place, O Lord, which thou hast made for thee to dwell in."

Thus did the Hebrew tribes rejoice in their deliverance, and such were their anticipations, as if they had already got possession of the promised land. They forgot that they had but commenced their journey, that the wilderness was before them, and that when they had sung out their song, instead of resting where they were, they must go forward, encountering all its hardships and perils. They forgot that there were enemies yet to be met, out of whose hand the Lord alone could deliver them; and that there was no bread and no water there. But for the miraculous supply which awaited them, they must all have perished at the very entrance of the wilderness. They must be sustained by the manna from the skies, and the water from the rock, all the journey through.

So, dear friends, it is with you, rejoicing in your late deliverance from a far more cruel taskmaster than Pharaoh. In the overflowing of your thanksgivings, you are in danger of forgetting that this is not your rest, that you have only entered upon your journey towards the heavenly Canaan, and that you too have to go through the wilderness. While on the journey, you cannot live without the supplies of grace in your hearts, symbolized by the manna and the water that flowed from the smitten rock. The analogy all along is exceedingly striking—the deliverance in the one case from Egyptian servitude, and in the other from the bondage of sin and Satan: the song of triumph, the wilderness, the manna, the water, the enemies to be encountered and vanquished by the arm of the Lord.

Yes, dear friends, you have to pass through the wilderness. There is no other way to the promised land. In looking forward from your present standpoint, it probably does not appear very formidable. The setting out is so delightful, every thing seems so easy, that you cannot understand how there can be much of danger or hinderance, or hunger or thirst, before you—you have safely passed through the Red sea; the cloud and the pillar of fire will lead you on, and what have you to fear? You may persuade yourselves that your spiritual enemies are all dead. Would that they were. But some of us have entered the wilderness before you. By painful experience we have learned something of what you must expect, and it would be unkind and unfaithful in us, not to forewarn and give you the best directions in our power.

First then, as the Israelites could not live without food, and as the wilderness yielded nothing their bread must be rained down from the skies, so it will be with you. You cannot live without spiritual food. You *must receive that Bread which came down from heaven* to give life to the world. In other words, you must receive supplies of grace from the infinite storehouse above. You cannot advance a single stage without them. And as the Israelites must gather the manna every morning, so must you seek supplies every day from your heavenly Father. Just as he supplies your bodily wants, by giving you day by day your daily bread—only one day at a time—so you must ask him, day by day, for the true Bread to nourish your souls. The grace which God bestows upon you to-day, is no more than you need to-day, and can no more be kept over than the manna could. You must, as it were, gather it fresh every morning. You must ask for new supplies every day, thus availing yourselves of the blessed assurance that your heavenly Father is more ready to give the Holy Spirit to those that ask him, than earthly parents are to give bread to their children.

Moreover, you must be *satisfied* with the Bread of heaven all the way through the wilderness, and till you reach the promised land. Just here the children of Israel made a fatal mistake. Angels' food was not good enough for them. They longed for the leeks and onions of Egypt. They loathed the manna. They lusted for flesh, and God in anger sent them the quails, and the plague closely followed. He gave them their request, but sent leanness into their souls. So, dear friends, it will be with you if, at any stage of your progress, you lose your relish for the spiritual manna, and turn back to "the beggarly elements" of the world. If you long for the carnal indulgences, the follies and amusements which you have left behind, "the lust of the flesh, and the lust of the eyes, and the pride of life," God may grant your request, but if he does, he will "send leanness into your souls." You will pine away and die.

Again, as the Israelites would have perished with thirst, if God had not brought water out of the rock for their daily and constant supply, so must you without that *living water* which Christ alone can pour down from the infinite fountain above, and which, if you receive it, "shall be in you a well of water springing up into everlasting life." As the water from the smitten rock flowed along, and accompanied the Israelites in all their marches till they got through the wilderness, so Christ was with his ancient church all the way, as the apostle testifies: "Brethren, I would not that ye should be ignorant how that all our fathers were under the cloud, and all passed through the sea; and were all baptized unto Moses in the cloud and in the sea; and did all eat the same spiritual meat, and did all drink the same spiritual drink; for they drank of that spiritual Rock that followed them, and that Rock was Christ." So, dear friends, that spiritual Rock will follow you, if you cleave to him. He will be to you "as rivers of water in a dry place, and as the shadow of a great rock in a weary land." He will daily refresh your souls with grace and strength, to go on your way rejoicing.

But after all, it is a wilderness which you have to pass through, "and there are many adversaries." You will have fightings without and fears within. The devil, who led Christ himself into the wilderness, will assail you with his temptations. Now is the time for you, as good soldiers of Jesus Christ, to put on the whole armor of God, that you may be able to stand against the wiles of the devil. "For we wrestle not against flesh and blood, but against principalities, against powers, against the rulers of the darkness of this world, against spiritual wickedness in high places. Stand therefore, having your loins girt about with truth, and having on the breastplate of righteousness, and your feet shod with the preparation of the gospel of peace. Above all, taking the shield of faith, wherewith ye shall be able to quench all the fiery darts of the wicked. And take the helmet of salvation, and the sword of the Spirit which is the word of God; praying always with all prayer and supplication in the Spirit, and watching thereunto with all perseverance and supplication for all saints."

Though these things are spoken to us in a figure, they strikingly represent the Christian warfare. You will have occasion for the whole suit of armor, in many a sharp conflict, befôre you reach the fords of Jordan. But if you are faithful unto death, you will come off conquerors and more than conquerors, through Him who hath loved you and given himself for you.

Go forward, not in your own strength, but "strong in the Lord and in the power of his might." Nothing else will stand you in stead a single day, for you have foes within as well as without. They are your in-dwelling sins, which though vanquished are not all slain, and they are in correspondence with the enemy without. Indeed, but for this advantage the grand adversary with all his legions could have no power over you: "Get thee behind me, Satan," would put him to flight in a moment. When constrained to cry out with Paul, "Who shall deliver me from the body of this death?" may you also be able to exult as he did: "Thanks be to God, who giveth us the victory through our Lord Jesus Christ."

And now, dear brethren and friends, what more shall we say? We bid you God speed with all our hearts. May He who dwelt in the bush go with, guide, and protect you all the journey through. The earthly Canaan, flowing with milk and honey, you may never see, but if you "endure to the end," you will at last reach that better country, "even a heavenly," where there are no foes to be driven out—where the river of the water of life flows out from the throne of God and the Lamb, watering all the heavenly plains—where there shall be no more fighting, no more hunger, no more thirst, but where you shall find infinitely sweeter refreshments than the honey of the rock, or the clusters of Eshcol. Press on then towards the mark of your high calling, singing as you go,

Guide me, O thou great Jehovah,
Pilgrim through this barren land;
I am weak, but thou art mighty,
Hold me with thy powerful hand:
Bread of heaven,
Feed me till I want no more.

Open wide the crystal fountain,
Whence the healing waters flow:
Let the fiery, cloudy pillar
Lead me all my journey through:
Strong Deliverer,
Be thou still my strength and shield.

When I tread the verge of Jordan,
Bid my anxious fears subside:
Death of death, and hell's Destruction,
Land me safe on Canaan's side:
Songs of praises
I will ever give to thee.

REVIVAL CONVERSATIONS,

BETWEEN A PASTOR AND INQUIRERS.

CONVERSATION I.

INQUIRER. (In the pastor's study.) Are you at leisure for a little while this evening?

PASTOR. I am, and am happy to see you.

I. My mind has for two or three days been considerably exercised on the subject of religion; and I have called to see if you can help me get over some of my difficulties.

P. Whatever your difficulties may be, I hope they are not insurmountable. Will you have the goodness to state them?

I. My father and mother are both professors, and I have been instructed in religion. They took me with them to public worship earlier than I can remember, and I have regularly attended on the Sabbath ever since. I have been taught to believe in the necessity of regeneration, not only from the pulpit, but at home and in the Sabbath-school; and I have never doubted the reality or the importance of experimental piety. I always intended to become religious, some time or other; and when I was a child I was alarmed more than once, under the preaching of our excellent minister. But these impressions soon wore off. When I came to college, I had a secret hope that I might be converted before I got through; and ever since this revival began I have felt uneasy. Nothing has gone right. I have felt dissatisfied with myself, and with every thing about me. I am not awakened, but I am unhappy. Preaching troubles me; religious conversation troubles me; the prayers that I overhear as I pass through the college entries trouble me. Sometimes I resolve not to attend any of the meetings; but when the time comes, I cannot stay away. I go, but do not feel any thing, and I cannot, except it be an irresistible and unaccountable inclination to find fault with the doctrines which I hear, and with professors of religion: sometimes because they do not live up to their profession; sometimes because they are overmuch righteous; sometimes because they speak to me on the subject, and sometimes because they do not. I am a bundle of contradictions. I cannot analyze my own feelings. I want to be saved, and yet I do not care any thing about it; if I did, I should not remain as I am.

P. Your case is certainly an alarming one; and I am afraid it will never be any better. According to your statement, you have sinned against great light. It is not for want of religious instruction that you have lived so long "without hope and without God in the world." And what do you think is the reason? If I understand you right, you admit the infinite importance of being reconciled to God. Why then do you hesitate? What hinders you from becoming a Christian this very hour?

I. I do not know. I am a wonder to myself. I certainly wish to be saved, but what can I do?

P. What *have* you done? Have you done *any* thing? God has been commanding you every day, for a great many years, to repent of sin and believe in Christ. Have you done this? He has been calling upon you, with all the authority and tenderness of a father, "My son, give me thy heart." Have you given him your heart?

I. Oh, you misunderstand me. I have not got so far. I have told you already that I am not even awakened; and how can I repent? I am somewhat troubled, to be sure, or I should not be here. But my feelings are all indefinite.

P. Do you think your not having *got so far* is any valid excuse for not repenting and giving your heart to God? The question is not how far you have advanced, or how you feel, but how you *ought* to feel.

I. I do not feel any thing. I have no sense of my sins, and how can I have? I wish I could feel as others do, but it is impossible.

P. My dear young friend, do stop and think what you are saying. You do not feel! You have no sense of your sinfulness! Astonishing! A sinner against a holy God, and under condemnation, and liable every moment to drop into a burning, hopeless eternity—and yet you cannot feel, cannot be alarmed, cannot "flee from the wrath to come!" Oh, how dead you must be! "Hear, O heavens; and give ear, O earth!" What a heart you must have! You can feel and act on every other subject but this. What would you think of a man standing still on a wide prairie, while the smoke and flames were rising to heaven around him, were he in reply to your expostulations to say, "I have no *feeling;* I cannot be alarmed at my situation, though I know the fire is all the while approaching?" What would you think of a prisoner under sentence of death, were he to say, "I know that if I am not pardoned, I must soon die; but I cannot feel enough alarmed about it to sue for pardon. I wish I could. I hope I shall, before the day of execution arrives." How would you be shocked and distressed, to hear a friend laboring under a wasting disease say, "I know my danger, but I cannot feel it. I have heard of a physician who has cured thousands under the same circumstances, and has never yet lost a patient; and I have no doubt either of his willingness to hasten to my relief, or of the infallibility of his remedies. But I cannot apply to him, I cannot send for him. I wish I felt interest enough in the preservation of my life to come to a decision; but it is not in my power. I must wait till I can *feel* my danger, and then I will send for the physician."

What would you think of such infatuation? How would you be shocked at it! And yet your own case differs from these only by exhibiting still greater infatuation. It is not your life that depends upon your *feeling* the danger and *fleeing* from it, but your immortal soul; and if you had a thousand lives to lose, it would be nothing in comparison with the everlasting pangs of "the second death."

I. I begin to see the folly and madness of my indecision in a clearer light than I ever did before. I have delayed too long. I ought to be in earnest. I wonder I am not; but still the question returns, how can I see my sins, and feel my danger, and repent? It seems to me impossible.

P. But wherein does the impossibility lie? Is there any thing in the way but *disinclination*, aversion to holiness, and love of sin? Let me now put you to the test. Will you now, without any more delay, take up the subject of religion in earnest, and do what you can to secure the salvation of your soul? Tell me, my dear young friend, are you ready?

I. (After a pause.) I do not like to make any promise, lest I should break it; for that, you know, would be worse than not to promise at all.

P. Just stop and consider into what a maze of contradictions your deceitful heart is leading you. You want to be saved; you believe in the necessity and duty of repentance, and yet you are not willing to engage to do any thing, lest you should break your promise. Your promise to do what? Why, to take up the subject at once, and do what you can. How much does that ship-wrecked sailor want to be saved from drowning, who will make no effort to reach the life-boat which is pulling off from the shore to rescue him? How much does that sick man want to recover, who will neither promise to take the only medicine that can do him any good, nor take it without promising? And how much do you want to be saved from sinking into the blackness of darkness for ever, when you are neither willing to pledge yourself to do any thing, nor to do any thing without a pledge? How much does that prisoner want his liberty, who will not come out, or even try to cast off his fetters, when the door is set wide open?

I. I cannot answer you now. I am bewildered. I want time to think of the subject. I will call again.

P. You want more time! What if you should die in a fit, before you get home? "Behold, *now* is the accepted time; behold, *now* is the day of salvation." "Boast not thyself of to-morrow, for thou knowest not what a day may bring forth."

CONVERSATION II.

PASTOR. (In the inquiry room.) What progress have you made, my young friend, since I last saw you? Have you given your heart to God?

INQUIRER. I cannot say that I have; but I hope I have made some progress. I have taken up the subject with the determination to seek till I find. I used, you know, to indulge in some bad habits. From these I have entirely broken off. I never used to pray, nor hardly ever to read the Bible, nor to attend any sort of religious meetings except on the Sabbath. But now I read the Scriptures regularly, and pray morning and evening, and I do not mean to be absent from a single meeting, if I can help it. In short, I mean to perform every duty, to do all I can, and I hope in this way to conciliate the divine favor.

P. I am glad to hear that you have forsaken your old companions in sin, that you pray and read the word of God, and punctually attend on the means of grace. All this is right and necessary; but according to your own account, it is merely *preparatory* work. You are not yet a Christian, but using means to become one? you are not *in* the ark of safety, but going *towards* it? Now, suppose you should die before you get there, or in other words, while you are taking what you seem to regard as the preparatory steps? What would become of you? Could you go up to the bar of God, and plead, that when arrested by the stroke of death, you was doing "many things," and even *trying* to repent? Would such a plea avail? "God *now* commandeth all men everywhere to repent;" but when and where has he said that all or any of them must *try* to repent? Mere trying falls just as far short of repenting, as trying to speak does of speaking, or trying to walk does of walking. When God requires you to do a certain thing, it is vain to think of putting him off with something else, as either *preparatory* or *collateral*. You must do the *very* thing, or you lose the blessing.

You seem to think, that although you are not yet a Christian, you are in a fair way to become one; you have set out, and are a good deal nearer the kingdom of heaven than you was a month ago. Now, supposing this were really the case, it would be madness to linger as you do, when the brittle thread of life may be cut at any moment. If you should be within one step of repentance when you die, you would as certainly perish as if you had been ever so far off. The drowning mariner who only *almost* reaches the plank that was thrown over to save him, sinks to rise no more. The man-slayer who only *almost* reached the city of refuge before the avenger of blood overtook him, might as well have been cloven down a hundred miles off.

Let me tell you, my young friend, and prove to you, that instead of being better, you are at this moment more sinful in the sight of a holy God, than you was when this revival began. You certainly have made no atonement for the sins which you had committed before that time. They will stand charged against you, just as if you had not bestowed a thought upon the subject of religion. And have you not since committed any sin? You will not, you cannot answer this question in the negative. Your own conscience testifies that you have sinned every day, and every waking hour. These sins are added to the long black catalogue in the book of God's remembrance—so that you are a greater sinner to-day than you was yesterday; and if it were possible for you to live a thousand years and to spend the whole time in reading and prayer without regeneration and without repentance and faith, you would be vastly more sinful, and of course more unworthy of pardon than you are now.

I. (In a desponding tone,) I suppose it is so; but how discouraging! According to this view of the case, I might just as well have remained as I was to this hour. It is all lost labor.

P. Yes, all that you have ever done or can do to weave a robe of self-righteousness, is *lost* labor. "The bed is shorter than that a man can stretch himself on it, and the covering is narrower than that he can wrap himself in it." Salvation is a free *gift*, and not a *reward* bestowed. "Not by works of righteousness which we have done, but according to his *mercy* he saved us by the washing of regeneration and renewing of the Holy Ghost." God has infinite blessings to *give*, but none to *sell*. He has pardons for the penitent and believing, but he makes no compromises. He looks upon no other righteousness, save that of his beloved Son.

CONVERSATION III.

PASTOR. (In the inquiry room.) I am glad to see you here once more, this evening, and hope you have come with a new heart, and a new song in your mouth.

INQUIRER. I wish I could say that I have; but I do not see that I make any progress at all. All my struggling and striving does not bring me a step nearer to the kingdom of heaven.

P. Indeed, I am more and more alarmed for you. You have held out a great while. The Spirit of God will not always continue to strive. Excuse yourself as you may, the sin lieth at your own door. And why, my dear young friend, will you not throw down the weapons of your rebellion, and submit unconditionally to Christ?

I. I have no power to submit, and how can I get the power?

P. Have no *power* to *submit!* What power does it require to *submit*—to leave off contending with God—to cast yourself down at the foot of his throne as a perishing sinner? It is the prerogative of power to *resist*, not to *submit*. What would you think were a garrison, when closely besieged and reduced to the last extremity, to use this plea for not surrendering the fortress—*we have no power to submit?* Thousands have had no power to hold out against a besieging enemy; but who was ever too weak to surrender at discretion? How strangely would it sound in your ears were a perverse and rebellious child, when under chastisement, to plead as an excuse for not confessing his fault and promising amendment, that he has no power to submit!

And yet, when God commands you to repent, to submit at the foot of the cross as a poor sinner, you try to quiet your conscience by pleading that you have no power to *yield.* Why, the difficulty with you is, that you have *too much power,* as you have hitherto used it. You have a power of *resistance* which is perfectly astonishing, and which nothing short of Omnipotence can overcome. You have held out, day after day and week after week, against motives which one would think must be enough to conquer a world—against threatenings and invitations and promises the most urgent and alluring that were ever addressed to rebels under the curse of God's holy law. What you need is, to have this terrible power of resistance overcome. All you want is the right disposition, a "humble and contrite heart;" and that you lack this is your own fault.

I. I cannot answer your arguments; but although I begin to see the subject in a new light, it does still appear to me that I have been honest and sincere in trying to do all I can; and will not a God of infinite compassion pity my weakness, and make up the deficiency?

P. God will never give up his rightful claims. He will never cease to command, however you may refuse to obey; and if you die in your sins, he will justify the reasonableness of your condemnation before the assembled universe. Admitting the validity of your plea, there will be a great wonder in the day of judgment: you, of all the countless millions of the human family, will stand alone, as one that did all he could to comply with the conditions of salvation—and yet was not saved. Every one who perishes will be self-condemned. "Thou hast destroyed thyself," will ring louder and louder in his ears, as he sinks deeper and deeper in "the blackness of darkness for ever."

I. What more, then, can I do? I am sure I am willing to do every thing that God requires, cost what it will.

P. No, my young friend, you are not willing. Here lies the fatal mistake. You deceive yourself. You want to be saved. You shrink back from the bottomless gulf, upon the brink of which you are standing. You would doubtless give the world, if you owned it all, for the ransom of your soul; but you will not give your *heart* to God—you will not repent—"you will not come to Christ, that you might have life." If there is any thing in the way but your own obstinate and wicked heart, do tell me what it is. Does God stand in the way? do I stand in the way? do any of your Christian friends? do your sinful companions? They may try to dissuade, but they cannot hinder you from coming to the cross. The difficulty is within, and not without.

CONVERSATION IV.

Pastor. You will recollect, Mr. A——, that I spoke with you last evening in the inquiry meeting; but not having time to enter into your case fully, I have called this morning to renew the conversation. When I urged upon you the duty of immediate repentance, and entreated you not to delay another hour or moment, I think your answer was, that you had not been under conviction long enough. Did I understand you correctly?

INQUIRER. Yes, sir, you did. That is one of my difficulties. It is scarcely three days since I began to think seriously on the subject; and having been all my life so stupid and wicked, how can I turn right about and repent at once?

P. How long do you think you ought to be under conviction, before you repent?

I. I cannot tell exactly; but it seems as if a sinner must have some time to think, and make up his mind, before he acts.

P. Well, here is the Bible—will you turn to some passage which justifies him in delaying?

I. I have read the Bible so little and so carelessly, that if there were a hundred, I should not be able to find them. But if I was as familiar with the Scriptures as you are, I presume I could find many such passages.

P. No, my friend, not *one*, if you had committed every word of the Bible to memory. There are texts enough on the other side. "God *now* commandeth all men everywhere to repent." "To-day," even to-day, "after so long a time, if you will hear his voice, harden not your heart." This is the current language of the Bible on the subject. It does not allow you a day—no, not a moment—to obtain clearer convictions of your guilt and danger before you yield to Christ. But how much longer indulgence do you want? Will one day satisfy you? will two? will a week?

I. It seems as if I ought to repent and give my heart to God in less than a *week;* but a day or two longer, devoted to serious reflection, cannot be much compared with all my life spent in sin and folly.

P. No; but have you any promise of living a day or two longer? What if God should say, "Thou fool, this night thy soul shall be required of thee?" What will become of you? Will your waiting for more time to think of the subject save you? Besides, it seems as if God was now striving with you. But what if he should in anger withdraw his Spirit the next hour, and say, This man is joined to his idols; he will not forsake them at once, he will not repent of sin: "let him alone!"

I. I see the danger of delay. I *may* die, I know, at any moment, or God may leave me; but what can I do? I am not fit to come to Christ. I want to be better prepared before I come.

P. And when will you be any more fit than you are now? What can you expect to gain by delay? Will holding out against God a day or a week longer make you any better? Are you not adding sin to sin, and growing more and more unworthy to come, every hour you live? Will waiting cancel any of your past transgressions; and is not a new page written against you every day in the book of remembrance? Did the prodigal son, "when he came to himself," wait to strip off his rags and make himself more fit to return to his father; or did he go just as he was, in the last extremity of guilt and famine, and cry, "Father, I have sinned against heaven and before thee, and am no more worthy to be called thy son?" Did the publican wait to make himself more worthy of divine compassion, before he "smote upon his breast and cried, God be merciful to me a sinner?"

O, my friend, if you think that by waiting you can make yourself any more fit or worthy of being saved, you mistake the ground of acceptance altogether. Salvation is wholly of grace. No sinner was ever accepted on account of his own *fitness*, his own *worthiness*, nor ever will be. "The Son of man came to seek and to save that which was *lost*." He does not say, "Come unto me, all ye that are *fit*," but, "all ye that labor and are heavy-laden, and I will give you rest." No, you must come just as you are, poor and wretched and blind and naked and in want of all things, if you come at all. On no other terms can you be received. Christ has thrones and crowns to *give*, but not a morsel of the bread of life or a drop of living water to *sell*. "By grace you are saved through faith; and that not of yourselves: it is the gift of God."

I. Yes; I see, I see at last, that it must be so; but I am such a great sinner, that I dare not come. I am afraid Christ will not receive me.

P. That your sins are more heinous in the sight of God, than you have ever imagined, I have no doubt. But for whom did Christ suffer and die, if not for great sinners—for David and Manasseh and Mary Magdalene and Paul, as well as for Samuel and Josiah and Daniel and John? Are there any little sinners, in the sense which you mean—any with whom God is but a *little* displeased? I am sure I have never met with such a one; and if there were, are the offers of salvation addressed exclusively to any class of sinners? Does Christ say to one, I invite you; and to another, I invite you to the gospel feast; but to a third, You must not come—"you are so unworthy, so great a sinner, that I cannot allow you to taste of my supper?" Does he not say to his servants, "Go out quickly into the streets and lanes of the city, and bring in hither the poor and the maimed, the halt and the blind, that my house may be filled?"

I. (With great emotion.) Still, I have lived so long in sin, and rejected so many offers, I am afraid he will not receive me. What shall I do?

P. What shall you do? Why, my dear sir, your duty is perfectly plain. You say that you are a great sinner; and you ought to repent and trust in Christ immediately. There is a subtle delusion at the bottom of your difficulty, which I fear has ruined thousands of souls. You must have some pledge that Christ will save you, before you come to him; and when you have it, you are not satisfied. To all your other sins, you add the guilt of distrust of his great and precious promises. You virtually charge him with insincerity and falsehood. You do not intend it; but just look at the excuse, and tell me, if you can, what less it amounts to. You are afraid that Christ will not receive you if you do come, when he tells you expressly that he will. You would be glad to come, you wish to comply with his offers, but if you do he will not receive you. This, it seems to me, is your real position. This is the deception which you have been practising upon yourself, on the very brink of destruction. Dare you rest here?

I. No, no, I dare not any longer. Oh, what shall I do?

CONVERSATION V.

Pastor. You see, my young friend, that many are pressing into the kingdom of heaven, and I am anxious to know how you feel.

Inquirer. I feel as if religion was very important, and I hope I shall not be left.

P. I was afraid you did not feel much interest on the subject, as I have rarely seen you at our meetings. You say you hope you shall not be left. Let me ask you what you are doing to obtain "the pearl of great price?"

I. I acknowledge I am not doing much—and how can I? The work is all of God, and I am waiting for the influence of his Spirit. He has awakened and converted a great many, and I hope he will, in his own time, convert me.

P. But what if he should not? Here you are, a sinner, saying with the sluggard, "A little more sleep, a little more slumber, a little more folding of the hands to sleep," and resting upon a vague hope that God will awaken you. What reason have you to expect it? Has he given you any promise to that effect? Is he under any obligation to save you. Will he do you any injustice if he passes you by? And if he should pass you by, what will become of you?

I. If he should, I must be lost, of course; but I hope he will not: I trust he will not. Does not the Bible somewhere say, "Wait patiently for the Lord?" and in another place, "It is good that a man should both hope and quietly wait for the salvation of the Lord?"

P. It does; but you entirely misunderstand these passages, if you suppose they allow you still to continue in sin and unbelief. They imply an act of humble trust in God, and his covenant faithfulness. How did the Psalmist and other holy men of old *wait* for the salvation of God? Did they listlessly fold their arms as you do and hope for the best, and sleep on? No: just take the Bible and read for yourself. They waited on God in fervent and believing prayer for those blessings and deliverances which he has promised to his people.

You are waiting God's time to arrest you and bring you into his kingdom. God's time! My dear young friend, what do you mean by God's time? When is it—to-day, or to-morrow; now, or a week or a month hence? Point me to one solitary text, if you can, which justifies you in delaying one hour for God to awaken you, or which authorizes you to expect that he will come, if you thus delay. What a fatal quietus to your conscience! What a false and ruinous security! What is God's time, in the only proper meaning which can be attached to the inquiry? What does he say in his word? "Behold, *now* is the accepted time; behold, *now* is the day of salvation." "God *now* commandeth all men everywhere to repent." "Boast not thyself of to-morrow; for thou knowest not what a day may bring forth." What liberty or encouragement, my dear A——, do these Scriptures give you to continue in your sinful unbelief?

I. What else can I do? I have no power to awaken myself; much less, to change my own heart.

P. That is, you mean, or ought to mean, that you have at present no *disposition* to make religion the all-important subject of inquiry—that you have no *heart* to break off your sins by righteousness, and your iniquity by turning unto God—that there is in you a wicked disinclination to do what God commands you to do. You have power enough on the other side, in opposition to God, to astonish the universe.

You are *waiting*, you say, for him to come and save you. How are you waiting? In the use of the means of salvation which he has appointed—in reading the Scriptures, in prayer, in devout attendance upon the preaching of his word? No; but in the neglect of all, or nearly all these duties. Is this the way in which the farmer waits for the blessing of the Lord? Does he fold his arms and say, I will wait for the harvest till it pleases God to bring it to me; or does he "break up the fallow ground," and sow the seed? Were you starving, would you wait for God to send the ravens to feed you, or would you make every possible effort to relieve yourself? What did the prodigal son do, when he came to himself? He said, "I will arise and go to my father," and he went. Had he remained among the swine, he would have perished. How was it in the days of John the Baptist? The kingdom of heaven suffered violence, and the violent took it by force. What was the answer of Christ to the question, Are there few that be saved? "Strive to enter in at the strait gate; for many, I say unto you, will seek to enter in, and shall not be able." What were the exhortations of his inspired apostles? "Draw nigh to God, and he will draw nigh to you. Cleanse your hands, ye sinners, and purify your hearts, ye double-minded. Be afflicted, and mourn, and weep. Humble yourselves in the sight of the Lord, and he shall lift you up?" "Awake, thou that sleepest, and arise from the dead, and Christ shall give thee light." And how is it that sinners in this revival, or any other, "make their calling and election sure?" Is it not by fleeing from the wrath to come, and laying hold on eternal life?

Yours, I am sorry to say, is no uncommon case. I am sure it is not too late, if you will now rise and flee to the strong-hold; for you are yet a prisoner of hope. Your case, though alarming, is not desperate; I hear a voice from heaven, "Let the wicked forsake his way, and the unrighteous man his thoughts; and let him return unto the Lord, who will have mercy upon him; and to our God, for he will abundantly pardon."

CONVERSATION VI.

Pastor. (To one in the inquiry meeting who had long been in a state of extreme depression.) Is the great controversy between God and your rebellious heart settled?

Inquirer. O no; and how can it ever be? I am afraid I have committed the unpardonable sin.

P. What makes you think so? Have you openly ridiculed and opposed the revival, and tried to stop it?

I. If I have not, I have done that which is worse. I have resisted the Holy Spirit. God has called, and I have refused. He has said, "Turn you, turn you; why will you die?" and I have virtually answered, "Depart from me; I desire not the knowledge of thy ways."

P. You say you have resisted the Holy Spirit. Have you done it maliciously? Have you spoken against Him, and ascribed your distress to satanic, or some other malignant influence, contrary to the convictions of your own conscience, thus doing "despite to the Spirit of grace?"

I. I desire to be thankful that I have not yet been left to pour out the wickedness of my heart in any such way. The bare thought makes me shudder. But still it seems to me, that for any one to hold out so long as I have done, must be unpardonable—must be to sin beyond forgiveness.

P. Has the Spirit entirely abandoned you? Have you thrown off the subject from your mind, and determined to think no more about it? Have you no concern, no feeling; no longer any desire to be saved in the way which God has appointed?

I. Oh that I could be saved! But my heart, my wicked heart—I am sure there never was one so hard as mine. I am sure it will never yield, and how can I be forgiven?

P. Your condition is indeed very alarming. I have thought so for many weeks. It is certain that if you do not repent and believe on the Lord Jesus Christ, you cannot be saved. But I see no reason to think that you have committed the unpardonable sin; I mean the sin which seals the man over from that hour to certain destruction. I believe that thousands are now in heaven, who were once in the very state that you are this morning. They looked round for help, and none came till they cast themselves unconditionally upon the mercy of God through a Redeemer. Every sin has demerit and malignity enough to destroy the soul, if unrepented of.

Far be it from me to cry, "Peace, peace," when God says, "There is no peace to the wicked." You are in great danger. You cannot resist the Spirit another moment without adding sin to sin, and increasing the danger; and if you hold out against God to the last, you will as certainly perish as if you had committed the sin against the Holy Ghost. All sin is alike unpardonable, after death. But it is a stratagem of the great adversary to persuade sinners that they are given over to final reprobation, when he cannot hinder them from inquiring and striving in any other way; and I think this is the snare in which he has caught you. Full well does the subtle destroyer know, that if he can make you despair of mercy—if he can hinder you from "fleeing from the wrath to come," he is sure of his prey. My fears are, not that you have committed the unpardonable sin, but that you will not accept of pardon on the humiliating terms of the gospel.

I. Do you really believe, then, that there is still any hope for me?

P. Certainly I do. I have no doubt of it. The door of mercy yet stands open. Turn, I beseech you, turn to the strong-hold while you are a prisoner of hope.

CONVERSATION VII.

INQUIRER. (In a desponding tone.) Do you think I shall ever come to Christ?

PASTOR. I do not know. I am afraid you never will. You have held out so long, and your heart is so hard, that the prospect is exceedingly dark. I do not know what more powerful motives can be addressed to you, than you have resisted. You certainly have not grown any better by delay. On the contrary, the habit of sinning gains strength every day that it is indulged, and of course the prospect grows darker and darker.

I. What more can I do?

P. What have you done?

I. I have read the Bible and prayed, and attended all the inquiry meetings, and been hoping every day that my heart would bow, and I should find relief; but it all does no good, and it seems as if I might as well give up first as last.

P. Give up what? Give up your heart to God? or dismiss the subject, and think no more about it? If you mean the former, you are perfectly correct. It is more than time that you had given your heart to God. But if you mean that you may as well give up seeking, and return to your former stupidity first as last, you amaze me. There is too much reason to fear that you have not yet seen "the plague of your own heart." If you dismiss the subject now, it will in all probability settle the question for ever. You may never witness another revival; and if you should, it may be only to "behold, and despise and wonder and perish."

I. I know it; and when I think of it, it makes me tremble. But what shall I do? I am sure I desire to be saved, and would repent if I could.

P. Do you mean, then, to cast the blame upon God?

I. Certainly I do not. How can you think so?

P. Does he not require, does he not *command* you to repent and give yourself to Christ?

I. If I believe the Bible, I must believe that he does.

P. And yet you say you would repent if you could. Is not this shifting the blame off from yourself? And upon whom, if not upon God—either for requiring you to repent, or for not giving you a penitent heart, in spite of your resistance of the Holy Spirit? I know, my dear young friend, what you want. You want to have me encourage you; and I would do it with all my heart, if I could in faithfulness to my Master and to your precious soul. You would be glad to have me say that I think you will by and by repent, if you keep on as you have done; but I dare not say it. I do not see that you are any nearer the kingdom of heaven than you were a month ago; and how can I encourage you? I do not know what God of his infinite mercy may do; but all the encouragement I can give, when you ask me what you must do, is, "Seek the Lord, while he may be found; call upon him while he is near." "Let the wicked forsake his way, and the unrighteous man his thoughts: and let him return unto the Lord, who will have mercy upon him; and to our God, who will abundantly pardon." "The Spirit and the bride say, Come. And let him that heareth say, Come. And let him that is athirst come; and whosoever will, let him take the water of life freely." Indeed, what greater encouragement can you desire, than is found in these and similar passages of Scripture? "I cannot go beyond the word of the Lord, to say less or more." And how can you expect, or even wish to be saved on easier terms than these?

CONVERSATION VIII.

Pastor. (In his study.) Walk in, my young friend; I have been wishing to see you for two or three days, but have not found time to call at your room. When you was here last, you was in great distress. You saw what your duty was, but your will would not bow; and it seemed to you that there was very little, if any hope in your case. Others might be saved, but your heart was so hard that nothing could break or melt it; and you left me with the acknowledgment that it would be perfectly just if God were to cast you off for ever. Is there any change in your feelings?

INQUIRER. There is a change; but I hardly know whether it is for the better or the worse. The burden which bowed me down to the earth, and under which it appeared to me I could not live much longer, is gone. I sometimes fear that it is because I have grieved away the Spirit, and I try to bring back my distress, but cannot. I have been calm for the last twenty-four hours, almost in spite of myself. What to make of it, I do not know.

P. Will you tell me a little more particularly what the exercises of your mind have been, since our last interview?

I. I felt that night as if I was utterly forsaken of heaven and earth. You told me you could not help me; and it did seem as if God's "mercies were clean gone for ever." I went to my room, and tried to pray; but my mouth was shut, and it seemed as if the pit of destruction was opening to receive me. At length I was enabled to say, "God be merciful to me a sinner;" and it seemed all at once as if there was mercy for me. Several texts of Scripture came to my mind, particularly these two: "O Israel, thou hast destroyed thyself, but in me is thy help;" "Believe on the Lord Jesus Christ, and thou shalt be saved." And I cried out, "Lord, I believe; help thou mine unbelief." From that moment, light gradually broke into my mind. I did not then think that my heart was changed, and I am now by no means sure of it, for I have had too much experience of its deceitfulness to trust it. But of one thing I am certain: a great change of some sort has taken place in my views and feelings. I do not seem to be the same man I was before. Every thing appears new. The sun shines brighter, the flowers are more beautiful, the birds sing more sweetly, the mountains lift up their heads in greater majesty, and all nature seems to be praising God.

I thought, when I was fighting against him, that he was a hard master, and wished I could get out of his hands. I was afraid to trust him. How strange. I do not, I cannot feel so now. Every thing with him is just as it should be; his government, his law, his hatred of sin, his threatenings—all, all is right.

The plan of salvation by Christ is so new, that it seems as if I had never heard of it before. How wonderful that God should send his only begotten Son to die for sinners! What a glorious Saviour! And how astonishing that I could have lived under the light of the gospel so many years without seeing any comeliness in him why I should desire him. When I think of my past life, it seems too much to hope he will forgive my sins; but I do not see how I can help loving him.

P. How does the Bible appear to you?

I. O, quite like a new book. I have read it more or less from my childhood; so that in one sense it has been familiar to me, but in another sense it has been a sealed book. Every chapter I read strikes me as it never did before. The words are the same, but the sense is different. The psalms and the gospels, especially, open new fields of contemplation which I never thought of. I used, when my mother required me to read a given number of chapters every Sabbath-day, to be tired of it; but now I should be glad to read it all the time.

P. How is it in respect to prayer? Your parents taught you to pray when you was a child, and have been urging the duty upon you ever since.

I. Yes, but it was always a task. It was mere lip-service. My heart was not in it. And as I did not love to pray myself, neither did I want to hear prayer. Many a time have I hastened off to bed to get rid of the evening devotions of the family. After I was awakened, as

I have told you, I could not pray. I tried again and again; but every word was cold as ice, and my conscience told me it was but solemn mockery. I feel very differently now. Why it is, I cannot say. Whether God has opened my mouth, I do not know. About one thing, however, I cannot be mistaken. Prayer is no longer a task, but a pleasure. I love to spread my wants before God, and to make supplication to him. It may be from selfish motives, or from mere temporary excitement. I fear it is; and I ask your prayers that I may not be deceived.

P. Is there any change in your feelings towards Christians?

I. There is a very great change; and yet the time is so short, that I do not know whether I can place any dependence upon it. I used to respect those whom I thought sincere in their profession, though I confess with shame that I was sometimes censorious, and secretly pleased to find flaws in church-members. I cannot say that I ever took pleasure in their society as Christians; my taste led me to choose associates of a different character. How it will be hereafter, remains to be proved. I have yet had no opportunity to bring myself to the test. It *seems*—and that is all I can say—as if my heart was drawn towards them as it never was till now, and as if I should be more happy in their company than in any other.

P. If God has chosen you to salvation, and called you into the kingdom of his dear Son, is it owing to any worthiness in you, more than in others who are still in the broad way to death?

I. O no, no; certainly not. It is all of grace. There was nothing in me which a holy God could approve—nothing but wickedness and rebellion in my heart. It seems to me that no other heart is so hard, so vile as mine has been. If saved, I am a brand plucked out of the burning.

P. But you have always maintained a good moral character, have you not? How then can you look upon yourself as the chief of sinners?

I. God has indeed kept me back from open and scandalous sins, and I was ready to thank him that I was not as other men are, "extortioners, unjust," and the like; but Oh, this wicked, deceitful heart! This is what God looks at; and who ever had one more deceitful and wicked than mine?

P. I think you take the right view of the matter, and I have been greatly interested in this conversation. If God has "made you willing in the day of his power," it is certainly an act of free and sovereign grace; and let him have all the glory. If he has "begun a good work in you," he will carry it on "until the day of Jesus Christ." But, my dear young friend, it is a great thing to "pass from death unto life;" and the change in your views and feelings is so recent, that it is difficult to say how much reliance is to be placed upon them. You want time for reflection, prayer, reading the Scriptures, and self-examination. You cannot tell how you may feel a few days hence. Time alone can decide the question. It is infinitely more important that you should build upon the right foundation, than that you should be numbered or count yourself at once with the young converts.

CONVERSATION IX.

PASTOR. Understanding from one of your classmates that you have expressed some interest in the revival, I have called this morning to converse with you on the subject.

STUDENT. It is true I have thought more about religion of late than usual, and for two or three days have felt extremely uneasy. There is so much said about it, and so much praying in every college entry, that I have serious thoughts of asking leave of absence for a few days, till the excitement is over.

P. Ask leave of absence! you astonish me. How dare you "flee from the presence of the Lord" at such a time as this? Nothing should induce you to think of it for a moment. It would be turning your back on heaven, and might land you for ever beyond the reach of hope. There cannot be greater madness than for a sinner to run away from a revival, either through fear of being awakened, or to throw off conviction. Many have done it, and thus lost their golden opportunity; and where are they? It argues infinitely greater infatuation for a sinner to withdraw from the midst of a genuine revival, for fear of being brought under its influence, than it would for an inmate of a hospital, with all the livid spots of a malignant plague upon him, to flee from it at the very time when a physician of preëminent skill was going from ward to ward and curing all who would submit to his prescriptions.

S. I do not know that I shall leave at present; but I acknowledge that I am afraid of so much excitement. It seems to me there is great danger that many will get false hopes, who, if they would look at the subject calmly and rationally, might ultimately become Christians.

P. Will you explain yourself? The term *excitement* is so indefinite, that I do not know exactly what you mean. Have you noticed any thing like extravagance or enthusiasm in any of our meetings or elsewhere among the students? Do you hear any vociferous appeals to the passions from our preachers—any thing that is calculated to make fanatics, or to encourage false hopes?

S. You do not quite understand me. I have no fault to find on that score. Perhaps there is as little to object to in this revival as any other. But then, you know, there is a great deal of feeling. Religion is the all-absorbing topic. One half the students can neither talk nor think of any thing else.

P. You are quite mistaken on one point, at least. The recitations are, upon an average, as good as they were before the revival began, and the attention on college exercises is better.

S. Still, my classmates and others all around me are *excited*, and I am getting excited also. The safest way therefore, I think, is to stand still and wait till the agitation subsides. When every thing becomes quiet again in college, and I feel perfectly calm myself, I intend deliberately to take up the subject of religion as a rational thing, and become a Christian.

P. Oh, my young friend, how can you deceive yourself in this manner! You would pronounce any man insane who should reason on secular subjects as you do upon this. You have felt interested, *excited* as you say; and instead of "fleeing from the wrath to come," you are going to "quench the Spirit," and wait till you become perfectly uninterested, perfectly *stupid* again; and after that, when the Holy Spirit is gone, and you have no feeling, and there is a dead calm all around, you intend to do—what? Why, to "think on your ways," to repent of your sins, and flee to the ark of safety. Was any thing ever more preposterous?

CONVERSATION X.

PASTOR. As it is a time of great religious interest, and I do not see you either in the lecture or inquiry room, I have felt it my duty to call and urge you to improve the golden opportunity while it lasts. Soon, I am afraid, your unavailing and bitter cry will be, "The harvest is past, the summer is ended, and I am not saved."

STUDENT. It is very kind in you to visit me. I wish I could become a Christian, but it is impossible.

P. What evidence have you that it is impossible? Many others are pressing into the kingdom of heaven, and why may not you?

S. Mine is a very peculiar case. I have passed through several revivals, and have tried over and over again to repent, but could not. I formed a thousand good resolutions, but they all came to nothing, and each failure left me more callous than I was before. I am sure I want to be saved, but I dare not take up the subject again. I dare not attend the meetings, for fear my distress will return, and I am sure it will do no good.

P. Who has told you that it will do no good? Is God a hard master? Is he insincere when he says, "Let the wicked forsake his way, and the unrighteous man his thoughts, and let him return unto the Lord, who will have mercy upon him?" Is it God that hinders you? Is it Jesus Christ who died for you? Or is it your own wicked heart?

S. Whatever the hinderance may be, I despair of ever overcoming it. Having been baffled so often, I have concluded not to try any more, especially as I have once been deceived and embraced a false hope. If I try again, I shall at best be deceived just as I was before. I know that by sitting down and doing nothing, I shall be lost; and so I shall, do what I will. Let me then enjoy the present as well as I can, and think as little of the future as possible.

P. Oh, my young friend, you do not know how much you alarm and distress me. You talk as if you were absolutely beside yourself. Because you have repeatedly tried to escape from the greatest of all dangers, and have failed, you will make no further efforts. Just think of it. Suppose you was in a burning house, and had tried once, twice, or even ten times to escape, and had been as often driven back by the flames, would you give over? Would you not again and again rush towards the door or window, as long as life and breath remained? I know you would, and so would every other man in like circumstances.

Oh, N——, "madness" is certainly "in your heart." I seem to see you sitting with perfect unconcern upon a sand-bank which a raging torrent is every moment washing from beneath your feet. Alarmed at the danger, I call upon you to make for the shore instantly, and your cool answer is, "I have tried more than once already, and beg you will not disturb me." Others gather anxiously around; a rope is thrown within your reach, and you are earnestly entreated to seize it while you may; but no, you will not put forth a finger. It would be the second or third trial to save yourself, and you will not make it. Nay, I am doing you great injustice by these suppositions. You are not so indifferent to the preservation of your life. I see you straining every nerve up to the hundredth trial.

But when I point you to the ark of safety which is floating by, and urge you to enter the open door, you coolly reply, that having made several attempts and failed, you have resolved to stay where you are and take your chance with the world of the ungodly. When

I warn you to flee from the wrath to come, and assure you that Christ stands with open arms to receive you, your answer is, that having more than once tried to flee, you dare not try again, lest you should be equally unsuccessful. I come to you in the midst of this glorious revival, and entreat you to put yourself in the way of receiving the blessing; but cannot persuade you to do any thing, because when you have been awakened in times past, you have quenched the Spirit, and said unto God, "Depart from me; I desire not the knowledge of thy ways." Your poor body you would do any thing, every thing to save, upon the barest *possibility;* but you will not make one effort more to save your deathless soul. If this is not infatuation, tell me by what other word I can express it.

CONVERSATION XI.

PASTOR. (In the inquiry room.) Are you not almost tired of attending these meetings? If I mistake not, you were present the first evening we met after the revival began, and though three months or more have elapsed, I am not aware that you have ever been absent.

INQUIRER. No, sir; I resolved from the beginning that I would attend all the meetings—that I would seek till I found, if there was any such thing.

P. *How*, my dear young friend, have you sought, and what progress have you made? Is there any change in your feelings since I saw you last?

I. I do not know that there is; I am almost discouraged; still I cannot bear to give it up.

P. I am discouraged too. It seems to me your case is, I will not say hopeless, but it certainly is exceedingly critical. I have conversed with you so much, and gone over the whole ground so often, both in the inquiry room and in more extended interviews elsewhere, that I really do not know what more to say. I cannot advise you to stay away from the meetings; and yet my heart sinks within me every time I see you. You have held out so long against God's most reasonable claims, that I am afraid you will never yield to them. Going on as you have done, if your life were to be protracted a hundred years, and you were to attend some religious meeting every day and every night, you would be no nearer the kingdom of heaven than you are now. I cannot see that you have advanced a single step for the last two months; and I believe you do not yourself think you have; but you *hope* you shall. When? The probability is growing less and less every day.

CONVERSATION XII.

PASTOR. When I saw you last, you expressed a full determination not to linger any longer, but to flee to the ark of safety as soon as possible. Have you kept your resolution?

INQUIRER. I do not know how to answer you. I am sure I was sincere. I did *intend* to repent and give my heart to God, and fixed the time. But alas, when it came, I was not quite ready; and so it has been with me over and over again. What shall I do? My best resolutions vanish like a vapor, and come to nothing.

P. The grand adversary, I fear, understands but too well how to manage you. He does not try to persuade you to give up the subject at once, and think no more about it, for that he knows would alarm you, and you might break the snare and escape. He is too subtle for that. He cares not how many good *resolutions* you form, if you do not keep them. You may, with his full consent, "resolve and reresolve," provided only you "die the same." And let me tell you, that in the very nature of the case, you never will, you never *can* repent, so long as you are resolving to do it at some *future* time. If you resolve ever so sincerely to repent *to-morrow*, it settles the point that you will not repent *to-night*. You will certainly put it off; and when to-morrow comes, you will almost as certainly defer it to a more "convenient season." It is the remark of an old divine, that "hell is paved with good resolutions." The prodigal son could not remain starving upon husks another day or hour, after he came to himself. No sooner was his resolution taken, than it was executed. "I will arise and go to my father," not to-morrow, but immediately; and he went, and was received as a penitent child. You must do as he did; not *resolve* that you will return by and by, but *return* at once. Every moment's delay is a moment of danger and sin.

CONVERSATION XIII.

Pastor. I hope, my young friend, you are no longer "halting between two opinions," as I found you last week. Soon will the "harvest be past, and the summer ended." If you continue to hesitate and linger, and finally "return again to folly," the revival will leave you more callous than it found you; and should you perish after what you have witnessed and felt, your condemnation will be more aggravated than it would have been had you never enjoyed these high privileges.

Inquirer. I am aware of it, and would that I had never enjoyed them.

P. You make me shudder. Have you then no thanks

to render that the "kingdom of God is thus brought nigh unto you?" Does infinite tenderness and mercy deserve such a return from one who is ready to perish?

I. How can I be thankful for that which does me no good, but may sink me in darker despair for ever?

P. Whose fault is it, if, when the bread of life is freely offered, you will not take it—if, when the waters of salvation flow at your feet, you will not stoop down and drink—if, when the blessed Saviour comes to the door and knocks, you will not let him in? It certainly will aggravate your final condemnation, that you have been thus exalted to heaven, if you remain impenitent. "Unto whomsoever much is given, of him shall much be required."

You wish you had never enjoyed such religious privileges. The wish comes too late. You *have* enjoyed them, and can never place yourself back where you was before. You can hereafter, if you choose, throw away your Bible, and forsake the house of God; or if you do not, you can stop your ears and harden your heart under the means of grace; or you can flee away to some remote region of darkness, where there is no Sabbath and no preaching. You can go and live among the heathen, and die with them. But still it will remain true that you was born of Christian parents, that you received a religious education, and that you passed through this great revival. It is all recorded in "the book of remembrance;" and your regrets can no more alter the record, than they can blot out your existence. There is no way for you ever to be placed on the same level with those who never enjoyed the gospel, and never witnessed a revival. If you do not repent of sin and believe in Christ, it will be more tolerable for them in the day of judgment, than for you.

CONVERSATION XIV.

Pastor. I have just been conversing with some of your family, Mr. A——, who feel a lively interest in the present revival; and if you have a few moments to spare, I should esteem it a favor to talk a little with you. I have always regarded you as among the best friends I have in the congregation, and you are one of my constant hearers on the Sabbath; but I am not aware that you have felt any particular interest in the work of the Lord which he is now carrying on, not only in this place, but in all the towns around us. Many of your neighbors are pressing into the kingdom of heaven. "Now is the accepted time, now is the day of salvation," and I am anxious to see you also "striving to enter in at the strait gate."

Parishioner. I am afraid that many of them are too fast. They get their hopes too quick and too easy. They act as if they could do all the work themselves, and repent just when they pleased. The good old doctrine of dependance and divine efficiency under which I was brought up, seems to be going out of fashion. Sinners nowadays change their own hearts, or at least think they do. It was not so when I was young. They were under concern for weeks or months, waiting for God to renew them. I am for giving all the glory to God. He is an absolute Sovereign. His time is the best time, and I know of no other way but to wait and hope for his salvation.

P. While it is impossible to ascribe too much glory to God for his immediate and omnipotent agency in the conversion of sinners, we must beware how we presume upon his mercy while we fold our arms in indifference. Who ever entered in at the strait gate without striving?

While others are asking what they must do to be saved, and a "new song is put into their mouths," you congratulate yourself upon being more deliberate. You are afraid they are too fast, and so you sit perfectly still. You are afraid they are getting false hopes, and so rest contented without any hope at all. When called upon to give yourself to Christ, you take shelter under sovereignty and efficiency, and persuade yourself that you are honoring God by waiting for him to come and do what he has commanded you to do.

Par. How can I do any thing till God gives me strength? Have I not heard you say a hundred times in the pulpit, that regeneration is the work of God, and that he alone changes the heart?

P. I dare say you have; but is this all that I have said? Have I not always urged upon sinners the duty of immediate repentance and faith, and insisted that there is no obstacle in the way but a wicked and impenitent heart, which is so far from constituting a reasonable excuse, that it is the very thing for which the sinner will be condemned?

There is not, my friend, I will venture to say, one solitary text from Genesis to Revelation, which justifies you in resting in impenitence for God to awaken and give you a new heart. Your great error lies in supposing that you honor God by laying so much stress upon the riches of his grace, as to excuse you in your present indifference and unbelief. You are afraid to "flee from the wrath to come, and lay hold on eternal life;" you are afraid to do any thing, lest you should dishonor God by taking the work into your own hands. How strange! You are living in habitual disobedience to every command of God addressed to the impenitent, and you act upon calculation and principle, so that if you are ever converted, the whole universe may acknowledge it to be by the mighty power of God. How preposterous! What amazing presumption!

I tremble for you, my respected friend, as I never did before. Here you are in the midst of a great revival, blessing yourself that you are not carried away by impulses, that you are a firm believer in divine sovereignty and irresistible grace, and all the hard doctrines which many who call themselves Christians reject. And this, my dear sir, is your religion. You have no other, and you do not yourself think it will save you. You hope that God in his own good time will convert you. Oh, how deceitful above all things is the human heart! You have been waiting now thirty or forty years for God to come and save you, and have no doubt for the most part kept your conscience quiet by persuading yourself that you was honoring him by entertaining such high thoughts of his sole prerogative in the work of regeneration. How much longer will it do for you to wait? Like myself you are growing old. Grey hairs are here and there upon you. Death cannot be very far off—it may be very near. And if God should not awaken and regenerate you, wrapt up as you are in false security, will you console yourself at the close of life with the reflection, that you have waited patiently for him all your days, and that it is not your fault if you die impenitent?

CONVERSATION XV.

PASTOR. You must have noticed, Mr. N——, that there is a great change of late in the aspect of our congregation on the Sabbath, and that religion is the leading topic of conversation among the people in their daily intercourse. May I ask what you think of it?

PARISHIONER. I hardly know what to think. I hope

some good will come of it, if it lasts; but there is one great obstacle in the way of my being benefited by it.

P. I am very sorry for that. Will you have the goodness to explain yourself?

PAR. Why, to be perfectly frank, then, I see so much inconsistency in the members of your church, that it stumbles me exceedingly, and I know of others who feel just as I do. If I were a professor, I think I should try to live up to it.

P. Then you believe there is such a thing as true religion?

PAR. Certainly I do, and that all who profess it ought to adorn their profession.

P. Do you look upon yourself as a Christian? We have long been looking for your assistance on the side of religion.

PAR. I do not think I have ever experienced that great change of which you speak so often in your discourses.

P. Do you believe you can go to heaven without it?

PAR. I fear not; and if professors knew what stumbling-blocks they are in the way of sinners, I am sure they would not give the world so much occasion as they often do to suspect their sincerity.

P. I cannot stop to debate the question whether they are sincere or not. But, my dear sir, suppose the worst you can possibly imagine—suppose half the members of our church were rank hypocrites; would that excuse you from the duty of immediate repentance? Do not, I beseech you, live any longer upon the real or supposed faults of professors of religion. It is poor fare for a soul that is famishing, and ready to perish. We read of those in the Bible who "eat up the sins of God's people as they eat bread;" but we never read of their being nourished by it.

God, my dear sir, has not set you to watch his church to see how many "motes," or even "beams," you can find in it. But he has given you a deathless spirit to care for; and if you do not "give all diligence," it will be lost. Many who are in the church may perish; I fear they will, but that is not the question for you to settle. Were the whole world to perish with you, that would not assuage the pangs of the second death. Let who will go down to the pit, be entreated to flee from it, and lay hold of everlasting life.

CONVERSATION XVI.

PASTOR. Good morning, my young friend; how do you do?

INQUIRER. Oh, I am in very deep trouble, and have come to you again as the last resort. I have read the Bible a great deal for the last ten days, but it gives me no light nor relief. I have attended all the meetings, but it does me no good. I have prayed and prayed, and prayed again, but God will not hear me. I have tried to repent and cannot. I have fully resolved to give my heart to God, but it will not yield to him. I would give the world if I could come to Christ and be washed in his atoning blood, but my efforts are all in vain. I cannot move a step further.

P. And so you have come to me, who am but a poor feeble, sinful worm, *as the last resort*. But what can I do? I cannot take you out of God's hands if I would, and I would not if I could. His claims are perfectly just and reasonable. His law, which you have broken, and which condemns you, is a good law. He requires nothing of you but what would be perfectly easy, if your stubborn heart did not stand in the way. This is a great obstacle I admit; but it is voluntary, it is criminal. It is just like the obstacle which hinders a disobedient child from submitting to the authority of his father. He is so stubborn that he will not. And what would you think were he to say, "I wish I could submit, but I cannot bend my obstinate will?" Cannot! you would reply; what sort of *cannot* is this?

You have come to me as the last resort! Then you are a lost man, for I cannot help you. Oh that I could persuade you to go to Him who is mighty to save, and who is as ready as he is able "to save to the uttermost" all who come to him. If you want instruction, I am most happy to give it to the full extent of my ability; but what can I say more than I have said, both in sermons and conversation? The case lies in a very narrow compass. You are a sinner. The law condemns you. You cannot deliver yourself from its awful curse. But Jesus Christ can deliver you. He came down from heaven "to seek and to save that which was lost." In dying on the cross, "he gave himself a ransom for all." He invites you to come just as you are, and receive the rich and free salvation of the gospel. He bids you come and "buy wine and milk without money and without price." You are a prodigal son, and he invites you back with all the tenderness of a father. Will you return—will you come and wash in the fountain which infinite love has opened for sin and for uncleanness—will you accept of salvation at the hand of a bleeding, dying, risen, and glorified Saviour? *Will you; will you?* I can say no more, I can make the terms no easier, I cannot help you. [*Inquirer withdraws in silence and great depression.*]

CONVERSATION XVII.

PASTOR. At our last interview you spoke of a decided change in your feelings, though you could not then determine what it was. You was beginning to indulge what you called a trembling hope. Do you still retain it; and if so, does it grow stronger or weaker?

INQUIRER. I cannot say that my evidences are much, if any, clearer than they were at that time. They certainly are not so clear as I wish they were; but still, I would not give up what little hope I have for the world.

P. I do not know that I understand you. I suppose, when you speak of your hope as weak and trembling, your meaning is, that you are afraid it is not well-grounded—that although your feelings are changed, and at times you have some evidence of having "passed from death unto life," still you have many doubts and fears. Is this your meaning?

I. It is; I feel a great part of the time as if I had very little if any reason to hope.

P. And yet you would not *give up what little hope you have for the world?* Surely, if it is a *false* hope, you ought not to *keep* it for the world. The sooner such a hope is renounced the better. It is infinitely dangerous to cling to it.

I. But what shall I do? I cannot think of going back again into the wilderness, and commencing anew. I should be the most wretched being in the world if I were entirely to give up my present hope.

P. I do not undertake to decide whether your hope is good or bad, sound or unsound. I only say that nothing is so dangerous as a *false* hope, and that you ought not to rest satisfied in your present state of doubt and uncertainty for a single hour. However painful it may be to find by careful self-examination that you have been deceived, it is infinitely worse to settle down upon a sandy foundation.

If a sinner who has embraced a false hope could never by throwing it away obtain a good one, his case would be deplorable indeed. But blessed be God, this is not the alternative. He may still flee to the stronghold. He may build again, and build upon the right foundation. He may repent, he may believe on the Lord Jesus Christ, he may embrace the offers of mercy, and be saved. Many have given up their old hopes as unsound and baseless, and have exchanged them for that good hope, "which is as an anchor to the soul both sure and steadfast."

Do not, I pray you, my friend, cling as it were with a death grasp to a hope which, according to your own acknowledgment, is very unsatisfactory. No man would sit down quietly, if his estate was in like jeopardy. Search the Scriptures. Examine your title. Look well to your foundation. Dig deep. Be thorough and honest in the whole process, and if you find your hope brightened, strengthened, and confirmed, bless God for it. But if it will not bear the test, renounce it, and never rest till you obtain one that will. Many, I fear, have perished in their sins, because *they would not for the world give up what little hope they had.*

CONVERSATION XVIII.

Pastor. Do you think, my young friend, that you have given your heart to God?

Inquirer. I hardly know what to think, and have come to you for instruction and advice. I dread, more than death itself, the thought of settling down upon a false hope.

P. Then you have *some* hope; and it is indeed infinitely important that it should be "a good hope." How did you obtain it? Will you give me a short account of your religious feelings and exercises?

I. For some time after the revival commenced, I was more careless and hardened than ever. I felt a strong aversion to religion, and did not wish to hear any thing on the subject. Strange as it may seem to you, I was unwilling that others should attend to it; and my heart rose against God for passing me by and awakening them, at the same time that I was prepared to resist every influence upon my own heart. At length my attention was arrested; I do not know how. I became anxious; and soon began, in spite of the pride and stoutness of my heart, to feel that I was a sinner.

I tried to shake it off, but in vain. The law of God thundered not only in my ear, but in my conscience. Every sermon that I heard made me feel worse. I saw that it was my duty to repent, to love God, and to consecrate myself to his service. But instead of yielding, my heart grew more and more obstinate. Nothing could move it; neither love nor fear—neither the law nor the gospel. I saw that I was justly condemned, and that Christ was the only deliverer. In this extremity, I tried to make terms with God. I would repent and yield to him, if he would save me. I was ready to buy salvation at any price; but not to accept of it as a free, unmerited gift.

Thus did I struggle like a wild bull in a net, till I had no more strength left. I was in the hands of a holy God, who would not relax his claims; and I saw at last, that it would be just if he were to cast me off for ever. This brought me to the brink of despair. I knew not which way to turn. I could not remain where I was—I dared not go back, and I could not go forward. Here the thought came into my mind, "I will cast myself upon the mercy of God; and if I perish, I perish."

I know not how or why it was; but from that hour I felt calm. I might be lost; it seemed probable that I should be. But God was right; his character was glorious; all nature was praising him; the plan of salvation was wonderful—was full of love and mercy: why had I not seen and embraced it before? Christ was precious. My hard heart seemed to be melted, and my lips were opened in praise. About this time a gleam of hope dawned upon my soul. Could it be all a dream, or a delusion? It did seem to me that if I loved any thing, I loved God, and loved the Saviour, and loved Christians, and loved to pray.

P. You represent your heart as having been very hard and obstinate at the beginning of the revival. Do you think it was totally depraved?

I. I am sure it was, if there is any such thing as total depravity.

P. What, had you no love to God at all?

I. None; not in the least. My heart was full of enmity to Him and his cause.

P. How then came you to take up the subject?

I. It was the Spirit of God that awakened me. I am sure nothing else could have arrested my attention.

P. Do you mean to say that there was a special, divine influence upon your mind, different from what you had ever experienced before?

I. I have no doubt of it. There must have been; for I have heard the same kind of preaching for years without being moved at all. Though the last revival was more general and powerful than this has been, and though I saw and heard more than I have now to excite me, I remained through the whole of it almost as stupid as the beasts that perish.

P. I infer, from your saying your heart was totally depraved, that you believe in the necessity of regeneration.

I. I do.

P. And you hope your own heart has been renewed?

I. I have a gleam of hope, as I remarked in the beginning of our conversation; but my heart is so deceitful that I am afraid to trust it.

P. Then you obeyed the command of God and made yourself a new heart, did you not?

I. No sir; I never obeyed any of his commands, till he made me willing in the day of his power. If I have a new heart, he gave it to me. It seems to me that passage in the thirty-first chapter of Jeremiah, which I was reading this morning, suits my case exactly: "Surely, *after* that I was turned I repented, and after I was instructed I smote upon my thigh." If I have any reason to hope, I ascribe it entirely to the free grace of God, from beginning to end. I was going down the broad way as fast as I could, when he arrested me; and if I am saved, all the glory belongs to him.

P. These are views which it is safe for you to cherish. But you have a great deal yet to learn. Search the Scriptures. Be much in prayer to God for the illumination of his Spirit. If he has given you a new heart, and you consecrate it to his service, He will give you more light, and clearer evidence of your adoption.

CONVERSATION XIX.

PASTOR. I am glad to meet you this morning, Mr. L——. We are going to have a meeting in your neighborhood this evening, and I hope you will attend it.

CAVILLER. What good will it do me, if I should?

P. That will depend in a great measure upon yourself. If you go with a sincere desire to hear the truth, and treasure it up in a good and honest heart, it will do you good.

C. I like your preaching pretty well when I happen

to hear it, which, you know, is not very often, and perhaps, if not otherwise engaged, I may comply with your invitation; but there are some of your doctrines which I do not believe.

P. I am very sorry for that, if they are true, as I think they are or I should not preach them. But will you be so kind as to specify some of them.

C. Why, depravity, for instance. I do n't believe that all mankind are totally depraved.

P. You do n't? I thought you did. I am quite sure I have heard you say very lately, and with a good deal of emphasis too, that all the world is a cheat; that you can trust nobody, and that the longer you live the worse opinion you have of human nature. This is carrying the matter further than I do. I do not think all men would overreach and defraud you, if they had the opportunity. On the contrary, I believe there is a great deal of honesty in the world, though I at the same time believe that all men are by nature entirely destitute of holiness, and that, in the language of Scripture, "the carnal mind is enmity against God; for it is not subject to his law, neither indeed can be." You believe that we are all sinners, that we ought to repent of sin, and that we need pardon through Christ; do you not?

C. Undoubtedly.

P. Will you allow me then tenderly to ask, Have *you* repented; have you obtained the pardon of your sins, so that if you were to die the next hour, it would be well with you? Whether you are totally depraved or not, you are certainly so much depraved that you cannot be saved without repentance and forgiveness. A millstone of a hundred pounds will as certainly sink a man in the depths of the sea as one of a thousand.

C. Well, but you hold to the necessity of *regeneration*, as well as to repentance. You say that our hearts must be changed by the Spirit of God, or we cannot be saved. Now, I do not believe that any such divine agency is necessary. We are not machines to be acted upon. We are free moral agents. Any man can repent and turn to God when he pleases, and this, I hold, is all the change of heart that is necessary. My Bible reads, "Awake, thou that sleepest, and rise from the dead." And again, if I am not mistaken, "Make you a new heart and a new spirit; for why will ye die?"

P. My Bible reads just so too. And by the way, you *do* believe in total depravity as I hold it, after all. For how can a sinner rise from the dead, if he is not dead, but only sick, *very* sick if you please? Or what need can there be of his making himself a *new* heart, if his old heart is not entirely bad? But let this pass. If you will betake yourself to the task in earnest, if you will awake and rise from the dead by your own power, if you will at once make yourself a new heart, as you are certainly bound to do, I certainly shall not object. What I earnestly desire is, to see you a sincere and devoted Christian. Give your heart to God without waiting a moment for him to make you willing. This is what you ought to do. "Repent and be converted, that your sins may be blotted out." This is your immediate duty.

CONVERSATION XX.

INQUIRER. Availing myself of your kind invitation so often given from the pulpit, I have called this evening to ask a few questions, and get your views in regard to several points on which I need instruction.

PASTOR. I am very happy to see you. Will you propose your questions?

I. You have often spoken during the revival of the

distress of awakened sinners under genuine conviction, in view of their guilt and danger. I have for some time been indulging a trembling hope that I have passed from death unto life; but I must relinquish it if none can be converted without such distressing antecedent convictions, for I have never experienced them. Do you think that all who are brought to Christ must pass through these deep waters?

P. I do not. On this point my own observation coincides with what I understand to be the true scriptural view of the subject. "There are diversities of operations, but the same Spirit who worketh all in all." A great many are overwhelmed with a sense of their guilt and danger. Their sins stare them in the face. The law, which "worketh death," thunders so loudly in their ears that they can hear nothing else. This appears to have been the case with the three thousand on the day of Pentecost. They were "pricked in their hearts," and cried out, "Men and brethren, what shall we do?" This was the case with Saul of Tarsus. Being arrested by the Lord Jesus on his journey to Damascus, he continued three days in such extreme mental anguish that he neither ate nor drank. Before this, he "was alive without the law; but when the commandment came, sin revived, and he died." So the astonished and convicted jailor at Philippi "sprang in, and came trembling, and fell down before Paul and Silas, and said, Sirs, what must I do to be saved?" I know it is often said that these were extraordinary cases; but I have myself witnessed many very much like them, as every pastor must have done who has been much conversant with powerful religious revivals.

On the other hand, the Spirit sometimes moves so gently and sweetly on the sinner's heart, that he passes through the new birth with scarcely any consciousness of its pangs. Zaccheus the publican seems to have been of this number. Attracted by curiosity to see the Saviour, he runs before the crowd and climbs a sycamore-tree, that he may get a better view of him than he could from the ground, being "little of stature." "And when Jesus came to the place, he looked up and said, Zaccheus, make haste and come down; for to-day I must abide at thy house. And he made haste and came down, and received him joyfully." A few analogous cases have fallen under my own observation. Individuals becoming interested in the revival, have almost immediately come out "rejoicing in hope;" and some of them have worn well—they have lived like Christians, and died in peace. I have noticed, however, that where "the work of the law" does not precede conversion, it is very apt to follow it. He who does not see much of the plague of his own heart before he passes from death unto life, will ere long find himself constrained to cry out with the apostle, "O wretched man that I am! who shall deliver me from the body of this death?"

My own view of the matter is this. Where the doctrines of the gospel are distinguishingly and faithfully preached, sinners are generally slain by the law, before they find joy and peace in believing. But I do not feel authorized to say that this is always the case. "The wind bloweth where it listeth, and thou canst not tell whence it cometh, nor whither it goeth; so is every one that is born of the Spirit." But whether the degree of conviction and distress be great or comparatively small before conversion, the sinner must see and feel enough of his guilt to repent, and of his need of a Saviour to embrace him.

Your main difficulty, if I understand it, is that you have experienced so little distress in view of your sinfulness and danger.

I. It is. When I converse with others, and hear them tell into what straits they were brought before they found peace; how their hearts rose against God, and how they trembled in view of his power and justice, I am afraid my hope is not well founded, for I am sure I have not had such experience.

P. The question is not how much or how little distress you may have experienced. Many a sinner has been awakened, without being converted. Conviction, however clear or long continued, is not *regeneration.* Some "quench the Spirit," and "draw back unto perdition," after painful and protracted struggles; while others, "drawn by cords of love," "hold on their way, and wax stronger and stronger." Whereas you was once blind, do you now see? The true question is, Are you *in* the ark of safety? not whether you came in just as others do. If you love God; if you delight in his law after the inner man; if you truly and heartily repent of all your sins; if Christ is precious to you, and you believe on him, and trust in him as "all your salvation and all your desire," you need not distrust your hope because you may not have had so much distress as is common, but should rather "give all diligence to make your calling and election sure."

I. There is another thing which sometimes leads me to distrust my hope. Some of the young converts can tell *the hour* when they were brought out; but I cannot tell the day, the week, nor even the month. The light, if it shines in my heart at all, broke in so gradually that I know not when it first began to dawn. If I could give the date and place and circumstances of my conversion, I should feel much more sure than I do now.

P. This is a point on which I lay very little stress, one way or the other, in examining candidates for admission to the church. Some converts are undoubtedly able to specify the time when God "brought them out of darkness into marvellous light." All the circumstances are and for ever will be fresh in their recollection. Zaccheus, the jailor, and most of the "three thousand" were evidently of this number.

But so far as my inquiries have extended, a very large majority of those who adorn the Christian profession cannot tell when they gave their hearts to God. They can say with happy Bartimeus, "Whereas we were blind, now we see;" but cannot be confident as to the precise time when the first ray of light broke in. In judging of the spiritual state of inquirers, I have often been disappointed both ways. Some who came out remarkably clear, and could name the day and hour of their conversion, have not only "lost their first love," but at length given up their hope, and returned like "the sow that was washed to her wallowing in the mire." On the contrary, some who are extremely distrustful of themselves at first, and cannot date their hope, gradually wax "strong in the Lord and in the power of his might." It is delightful to watch their progress, and see how their path, as the shining light, "shineth more and more unto the perfect day." "By their fruits shall ye know them." It is by leading a humble, devoted, and prayerful Christian life, that one gains, and gives, the best evidence that he has been born again.

I. I do not know what to think of myself, and I fear I never shall. If I had not lived so carelessly the greater part of my life, I should sometimes think, that if ever my heart was changed, it must have been in early childhood. I can recollect some of my feelings then, which were as much like love to God and love to Christ as any I have had since, if not more. Is it your opinion that any are *converted so early* that they cannot remember the time when they began to love the Saviour?

P. I think there are some such, and that as the millennium approaches, there will be many more. The testimony of Scripture seems not only to favor this belief, but to require it. The prophet Jeremiah was called and sanctified from the womb. So was John the Baptist. There can be little doubt that Joseph and Moses and Samuel and Daniel and Josiah were all converted in early childhood; and almost every pastor must have found individuals among his flock, giving evidence that they were converted to God in their early days. Whether, if you are a Christian, you was brought in at an earlier or later date, I do not pretend to decide; but I fully believe, not only that all infants need to be born again, but as I have just said, that some who afterwards shine as lights in the world are thus early renewed by the Spirit.

I. Do you think the *first holy exercises* after regeneration are in all cases *alike?*

P. By no means. No two cases probably are exactly alike. I have found a great diversity in the experience of those with whom I have conversed. One first rejoices in the love of Christ. Another is overwhelmed with shame and contrition in view of his base ingratitude. Another breaks out in admiration of the infinite holiness of God, and the reasonableness and purity of his law. One wakes up, as it were, in a new world—the sun shines brighter than it ever did before, the earth looks lovelier, and all nature seems to be praising God. Another has found a new Bible; another feels his heart drawn out in love to the church, and another in compassion for impenitent sinners. For these and other diversities of views and exercises when men are first renewed, we cannot perhaps fully account, but I apprehend they may be partly explained in this way. The thoughts of different persons are directed to different objects and truths at the time of their conversion. One is thinking of the goodness of God, another of the holiness of his law, another of the death of Christ, and so on; and the heart of each is naturally drawn out first towards the object then in view. It is love, or it is repentance, or it is faith; and then other holy exercises follow, one after another, as the appropriate objects are presented to the mind.

I. I thank you for the indulgence you have granted me, and hope I shall profit by your instructions. On some points which were not clear to my mind, I feel relieved. Allow me to ask a continued interest in your prayers, that I may not be deceived but be led into all truth.

P. "Examine yourself whether you are in the faith," not so much *when* or *where* you first embraced Christ, as whether you have truly embraced him. Compare your feelings and exercises with the Bible—with the tests which you will there find, both in the Old Testament and the New, in the law and the prophets, in the teachings of Christ and his inspired apostles. Pray for the teaching of the Holy Spirit, yield your whole heart and soul to God, and he will guide you by his counsel, and afterwards receive you to glory.

The American Tract Society,

ISSUE

THE RELIGIOUS (OR PASTOR'S) LIBRARY,

Of 25 standard evangelical volumes 12mo, at $10.

THE EVANGELICAL FAMILY LIBRARY,

Of 15 volumes, with steel portraits, frontispieces, and other engravings, at $5 50.

ALSO

Twenty-one volumes to match the Family Library, at $7 50.

THE YOUTH'S LIBRARY,

Of 70 volumes, 18mo, comprising Hannah More's CHEAP REPOSITORY, in 8 volumes, and 255 highly finished engravings.

THE FAMILY TESTAMENT AND PSALMS,

With brief Notes and Instructions, and Maps.

A CONCORDANCE TO THE HOLY SCRIPTURES; CRUDEN CONDENSED.

FLAVEL'S REDEMPTION,

Comprising the Fountain of Life, Method of Grace, and Christ Knocking at the Door.

D'AUBIGNÉ'S HISTORY OF THE REFORMATION, 5 vols.

A new translation revised by the author.

STANDARD PRACTICAL WORKS

Of Baxter, Flavel, Bunyan, Alleine, Venn, Edwards, Backus, Romaine, William Jay, John Angell James, and numerous works of kindred characters.

BUNYAN'S PILGRIM'S PROGRESS.

ATONEMENT AND JUSTIFICATION.

By Rev. Andrew Fuller.

MEMOIR OF REV. JUSTIN EDWARDS, D.D.

LIFE OF REV. JEREMIAH AND MOSES HALLOCK,

Laborers in the work of God about the year 1800.

CHALMERS' ASTRONOMICAL DISCOURSES.

www.ingramcontent.com/pod-product-compliance
Lightning Source LLC
LaVergne TN
LVHW020930110826
845150LV00004B/822

9781425552930